Charles Augustus Briggs
and the
Crisis of Historical Criticism

Harvard Dissertations in Religion

Editors

Margaret R. Miles
and
Bernadette J. Brooten

Number 25

Charles Augustus Briggs
and the Crisis of Historical Criticism

Mark Stephen Massa, S.J.

Charles Augustus Briggs
and the
Crisis of Historical Criticism

Mark Stephen Massa, S.J.

Fortress Press   Minneapolis

CHARLES AUGUSTUS BRIGGS
AND THE CRISIS OF HISTORICAL CRITICISM

Copyright © 1990

The President and Fellows of Harvard College

Write to: Permissions, Augsburg Fortress, 426 S. Fifth St., Box 1209, Minneapolis, MN 55440.

Internal design: Chiron, Inc.
Typesetting output: TEXSource, Houston

Library of Congress Cataloging-in-Publication Data

Massa, Mark Stephen.
    Charles Augustus Briggs and the crisis of historical criticism /
Mark Stephen Massa.
        p.   cm. – (Harvard dissertations in religion; no. 25)
    Revision of author's thesis.
    Includes bibliographical references.
    ISBN 0-8006-7079-5
    1. Briggs, Charles A. (Charles Augustus), 1841–1913.   I. Title.
II. Series.
BS501.B75M37   1990
280'.4'092–dc20
    [B]   89-37510
                                                         CIP

Manufactured in the U.S.A.   AF 1-7079

94   93   92   91   90   1   2   3   4   5   6   7   8   9   10

To my parents

Contents

Preface

When I began my graduate studies, I rarely (if ever) read the prefaces to scholarly works, believing that it was far more important to delve right into the text, and leave the encomiums contained in such prefatory essays to be read by those whose names were listed in them. Now that I have graduate students of my own, I know better. For prefaces trace the morphology of ideas, and the people who embody and argue those ideas, and thus are as pertinent to understanding scholarly works as tables of contents.

This study of Charles Briggs, and of the historico-critical world view that he introduced to American evangelical Protestants, was shaped at Harvard University under the direction of Professors William R. Hutchison and C. Conrad Wright. Both of these scholars of the history of American religion, in very different ways, molded my understanding of the critical issues involved in studying the Protestant religious experience. I am privileged to claim them as my mentors, and am quick to confess that much of what is best in the following pages is the result of their insights and criticisms, while all of the errors are, alas, my own.

A community of scholars whom I am proud and lucky to call my friends offered support, criticism, and rounds of beer (not necessarily in that order) while this work was being written. Janice Knight, Patricia Hill, Richard Seager, and Tuck Shattuck — fellow "Americanists" and members of Harvard's New World Colloquium — saw numerous redactions of this work, and offered their valuable insights; each likewise kept me sane after library hours at various Harvard Square haunts. To each I owe a special debt, both personal and academic, which I can but acknowledge here. Cynthia Shattuck, Joe Swierzbinski, Matt Roche, Donna MacKenzie, Reno and Sharon Morgan, Tom Clark, and Ron Mercier (in Rhode Island, New York, New Haven, Washington, Boston, and Cambridge) provided editorial advice, critical distance, and friendly common sense at important junctures in the project: to them, likewise, my debt extends beyond the academic. Ken Jorgenson, Jerry Delamater, Sheryl Kujawa, Ruth Lipper, John Conley, and Jim Keenan (the last two, happily, fellow Jesuits teaching with me at Fordham) have helped in myriad ways in my research, writing, and mental health in New York City: any scholar would be lucky to have such friends in Babylon.

The librarians and staffs of the Andover and Widener Libraries of Harvard University, the Burke Library of the Union Theological Seminary in New York City, the Firestone Library of Princeton University, and the Duane Library of Fordham University have been unfailingly helpful and cheerful in the face of my constant (and often unreasonable) demands upon their time and energies in tracking down books and manuscripts. Craig Pilant, my indefatigable graduate assistant at Fordham, performed yeoman's service in indexing and running down obscure references in the final stages of preparing the text for publication.

Finally, this book is dedicated to my parents, Armand and Dolores Massa, who lived with Charles Briggs as with another child for almost three years, and who uncomplainingly listened to my theories about his historical importance over Christmas dinners and Fourth of July backyard picnics. It is not accidental, I think, that I chose to study and write about modern Christians who faced the challenges of a complex world with unflinching faith and an open mind: my first lessons were begun long ago under their tutelage.

MARK MASSA, S.J.

Fordham University

Introduction

The career of Charles Augustus Briggs reveals in rather dramatic fashion the true nature of the intellectual impulses that produced what scholars have termed the "spiritual crisis of the Gilded Age." During the critical half century following Appomattox, Briggs played a central role in the theological and ecclesiastical battles that led to the fragmentation of the American Protestant "establishment" into modernist and fundamentalist camps. Both religious and cultural historians have long agreed about Briggs's importance for understanding the religious battles of late nineteenth-century America, and have agreed also about the significance of his famous 1893 heresy trial in representing the theological issues behind those battles. But Briggs's engagement with the central problem of his career — the problem of history — has yet to be explained.

As dramatically as any other evangelical figure, Briggs embodied in his own person the confrontation between historicism and an older, Protestant world view. What was at issue in the bitter exchanges during his heresy trial, and what Briggs spent his personal and professional life attempting to reconcile, were the seemingly irreconcilable claims of revivalistic evangelicalism and historical criticism. His was essentially an American story — arguably *the* American story — of the "coming of age" of the evangelical mind

1

in the modern world, a world that defined itself largely in historicist terms.

Briggs had been converted in the great revival of 1858, and he remained committed throughout his turbulent life to the values derived from that experience. But precisely *because* he was so committed an evangelical — educated in the truths of Baconian science and committed to a world entered only through the "new birth" — and because he was the foremost critical scholar of his day dedicated to defending the faith once delivered, his attempt to "baptize" the best scientific thought of the day to support evangelical Christianity was essentially an American form of modernism.[1]

As one of the most famous "modernist martyrs" to the cause of Protestant liberalism, Briggs in fact offers a surprising profile of his cause: he was resolutely evangelical in outlook and piously orthodox in doctrine; he was fearlessly committed to the cause of historical criticism in scholarship and yet abhorred the moral relativism that was implied in much of that criticism. Briggs, as much as any other scholar of his generation, embodied American mainline Protestantism as it moved out of the evangelical nineteenth-century into the historicist twentieth century. He was a transition figure, and his story is that of the culture he reflected so well, a culture that embraced the future while retaining the values and hopes of the past.

Charles Briggs recognized the threat posed by the intellectual heirs of Johann Gottfried Herder to America's evangelical culture, a threat far broader and more disturbing than the questions raised by biblical criticism. His life reflected the efforts of those earnest nineteenth-century evangelicals who sought to retain the older vision even while utilizing radical historicist methods. He remained in many ways a figure of the past while producing the most advanced critical scholarship in America. He was, in short, the embodiment of progressive evangelical Protestantism as it moved towards religious modernism, and his story offers one of the most famous, and one of the most heroic, instances of the venerable evangelical intellectual tradition in America claiming the future for its own before it collapsed into warring camps.

1

The Problem of History

The Organic Unity of History

In the latter half of the nineteenth century a profound crisis occurred in the intellectual life of the West, arguably one of the most dramatic since the emergence of the fundamental value systems of Greece and Palestine two and a half millennia before. The underlying metaphysical assumption of that intellectual tradition — the certainty of the ethical meaningfulness of historical action — seemed in danger of imminent collapse, and the Christian faith that rested on that assumption entered a prolonged (and many of the participants predicted, permanent) identity crisis.[1]

The crisis for Christian believers, as it would turn out, was occasioned less by the new evolutionary theories of Charles Darwin (usually posited as the culprit) than by the less publicized but more epistemologically troubling changes in thinking about history itself. Indeed, it was the fundamental historical preoccupation of the period, with its tendency to explain phenomena in terms of their past development, that created the intellectual climate conducive to the reception of the ideas of Darwin and Spencer. The new theory of evolution might have required no more stringent measure of accommodation on the part of Christian believers than a reinterpretation of the creation story, had not the ancient model of transcendental revelation itself become problematic as a result of the onslaughts of historicism.[2]

Historismus (translated variously as "historicism" or "historism" in Briggs's generation) emerged in Germany in the eighteenth century as a romantic reaction against Enlightenment patterns of thought, especially against the Enlightenment's emphasis on "natural law." While the doctrine of natural law had achieved almost canonical status in the Western intellectual tradition by the eighteenth century, the heralds of the romantic revolt against "formalistic" patterns of thought saw in it an affront to the dignity and unique historical efficacy of human activity within history. Permanent, transcendent categories, outside or "above" the arena of historical activity, appeared purely arbitrary to the new lovers of history and its vagaries, and seemed to be doubtful bases for judging the ethical meaning of contingent, temporal activity. In their place was posited the historicist, developmental approach to the universe, an approach that was espoused by its advocates as a comprehensive philosophy of life and not just an approach to historical problems. This new world view has been termed by one of its most respected chroniclers, Friedrich Meinecke, "the greatest spiritual revolution which Occidental thought has undergone," substituting concepts of development and individuality for a millennia-old faith in the stability of human nature and reason.[3]

As "le sens de la différence des temps," historicism challenged the epistemic constructs that had informed Western thinking from Augustine to Voltaire, constructs that had regarded "time" and "man" as ever the same in their essence. Indeed, this new "sense" became identified with the human-centered world in which post-Enlightenment humanity lived, so that Carl Becker, in one of the most insightful studies of the historicist world view, described the new *Weltanschauung* as itself determinative of the "modern mind":

> What is peculiar to the modern mind is the disposition and the determination to regard ideas and concepts, the truth of things as well as the things themselves, as changing entities... as the points in an endless process.[4]

As first clearly adumbrated in 1774 in Johann Gottfried Herder's *Another Philosophy of History*, a romantic "tract for the times," historicism emerged as a world view that saw all of reality as a historical stream in which social institutions, intellectual constructs, and even logical categories were immersed. The new historicist world view (and the historico-critical methods that its adherents applied) argued that the history of any phenomenon was a sufficient explanation of it, and that all social institutions and belief systems could be understood and evaluated through the discovery of their historical origins and development. Herder, as close to being the "founder" of this new world view as anyone, offered a *Weltanschauung* in which life and reality were synonymous with history and history alone, and all notions of truth and value, even those ostensibly claiming transcendental warranty, were seen as products forged within the historical process.[5]

While the foundation for this new approach to social reality was laid in the eighteenth century by philosophers like Herder and Giambattista Vico, its widespread acceptance within the academy, and the application of the historico-critical methods based on its presuppositions, occurred in the nineteenth century. The intellectual heirs of Vico and Herder, living in "Christianity's greatest century" (as the nineteenth was perhaps too effusively termed), discovered history as an autonomous, self-sufficient domain, a domain where historical consciousness focused on the *immanent* factors that defined "radical historicity."

In Germany especially, the life of the academy was placed on historicist foundations early in the century. Beginning in the 1830s, Ludwig Feuerbach began to use the term "historicism," along with "empiricism" and "positivism," to denote a new understanding of historical relativism and a new critical openness to reality as it presented itself to human perception. In the course of the century, historical study gradually replaced speculative construction among German scholars as the most productive means of studying intellectual and cultural phenomena. The historical school of law (Savigny and K. F. Eichhorn) studied law as the expression of specific cultural configurations, and taught that jurisprudence could not be concerned with the critique of legal concepts apart from the positive law of concrete historical societies. The new science of linguistics (Lachmann and the Grimm brothers) neglected systematic structural analysis to study the evolution of specific languages and language families within discrete cultural groupings. The historical school of economics (Knies and Schmoller) rejected the traditional approach of classical political economy — that abstract, transhistorical laws govern the economies of all societies — and studied economic behavior as part of a wider cultural pattern in which factors such as politics, religious ideology, and military needs deeply influenced economic law.[6]

But it was the historical studies of Leopold von Ranke that established the methodological foundations on which historicism rested. Von Ranke insisted that all study of the human past be based on rigorous examination of primary evidence, in light of which the historian would not judge the past, but merely describe it *wie es eigentlich gewesen* (as it really happened). When history was thus reconstructed as it essentially was, the scholar could rise from the investigation and contemplation of the particular to the general view of reality, recognizing in this view of reality *how* and *why* humankind had arrived at its present pass. Thus history alone, and not some form of abstract philosophy or theology, could provide the most reliable guide to the ultimate questions of human concern.[7]

If von Ranke explored historicism's practical, methodological applications, Georg W. F. Hegel and Karl Marx represented the self-realization of the new *Weltanschauung* in philosophical form. In brilliant essays on epistemology and philosophical methodology (Hegel) and on the nature of history (Marx), both men elucidated the philosophical implications of pure historicity. Neither could countenance an escape from time into a realm of eternal "essences," or into a faith beyond the vagaries of history. Hegel and Marx thus became the most famous precursors of the "modern mood," wherein the historical condition determines the human situation. History, and not any transcendent City of God, became the key to understanding the nature of society and human existence. A radically temporalistic view of culture became the "mark of the modern intellect," and the conviction that all social, institutional, and belief systems were rooted in their historical contexts became the first plank in a modern creed that made the transcendent Creator of the earlier credos an ideational anachronism.[8]

Nineteenth-century German scholars thus tended to emphasize the immanental over the transcendental, the culturally autochthonous over the universal, the developmental over the static. If the epistemological relativism inherent in their studies, derived from historicism, seemed to challenge the stable, transtemporal world view that had supported Western culture for centuries, it appeared to affect most dramatically the belief system of Christianity. For while taking a neutral position on the question of divine revelation itself, the new historical science appeared to threaten the foundation on which Christian belief rested by dismissing the possibility of receiving or understanding any revelation from above or outside of history. Students of historical criticism studied the past by utilizing critical methods predicated on the assumption that all historical phenomena, even the most sacred traditions claiming divine origin, were the products of their cultural milieu and were thus open to critical study and analysis.[9]

Historicists argued that if God were anywhere, God must be radically immanent within the evolving historical process itself. Immanence thus became the trademark of the "modern" theological frame of reference. Any discussion of the divine predicated on a "two-story" universe wherein the Creator reached down from some transhistorical realm to enlighten and redeem humankind became deeply problematic, if not embarrassing, to Christians attempting to frame doctrinal truths in categories that remained meaningful to the wider intellectual world.[10]

The new historicist emphasis on immanence and developmental patterns of thought found practical application in an array of new critical methods that promised to yield vital information about the historical forces that shaped Christianity. But for Western Christians the promise of the new critical methods was more than balanced by the threat of having to recast into startling new categories doctrines and theological frames of reference hallowed by centuries of use. The practice of historical criticism, having produced important insights in other areas of the academy, had been quietly applied by German scholars to the monuments of Western religion for a century, before its presence first became widely recognized and feared among English-speaking Protestants in the middle of the nineteenth century.

The records of the Christian tradition were suddenly subject to the scrutiny of detached and often hostile scientists: exegetes

applied critical methods to Scripture and showed the gradual evolution of biblical stories and doctrines; ecclesiologies that had
claimed *de jure divino* status and divine origin were subjected to
critical scrutiny and were studied as cultural products of a specific
time and place; ancient creedal statements, revered by believers as
faithful monuments to the ancient faith, were analyzed as historical
documents that yielded as much information about the ideational
world of their composers as about the ineffable One they sought
to define.

It is difficult, in fact, to overestimate the impact of historicism
on the religious life of the West in the late nineteenth and early
twentieth centuries: religious liberalism in both Protestant and
Catholic form can be virtually defined by its sympathetic response
to the historicist understanding of culture, positing a revelation
mediated *through* the flow of history. The immanental thrust of
historicist thought, applied to theology, led religious liberals to emphasize God's presence *within* human cultural development. And
because of this immanental divine presence within what had previously been thought to be a "secular" arena, religious liberals called
for the conscious adaptation of religious ideas to modern culture,
an emphasis that earned them the designation "modernists."

Conservatives across the denominational spectrum invariably
claimed that the essential "core" of God's self-revelation escaped
the grip of the historical process, remaining uncontaminated by the
cultural setting of its reception. These opponents of the historicist
world view believed that far from "mediating" God's presence,
modern culture was itself one of the Devil's snares, a stumbling
block to pilgrims on their way. These conservatives believed that
the faith had been delivered *once*, and they held that the meaning
of life and history — the "clues" to life's purpose and the eschatological direction of history — was delivered from *outside* history
and *above* human culture to the elect. The message thus delivered
remained unaffected by history, as one of its prime purposes was
redemption *from* history, from the vagaries of change, accident,
and dissolution.[11]

Historicism thus presented to nineteenth-century Christians an
intellectual challenge made more tangible by a growing array of
critical applications, none more controversial than the new critical
study of the Bible. Indeed, if other forms of historical criticism

would eventually become the focus of debate, the overture to the spiritual crisis of the Gilded Age was played out by the new biblical science known as "higher criticism."

Higher criticism (as distinct from textual or "lower criticism") sought to uncover the process of development by which the present canon of Scripture had evolved historically. If lower criticism sought to establish the integrity of the text itself through critical examination and comparison of manuscripts, higher criticism addressed the theological content, purpose, sources, and editorial intent that had produced the present biblical texts. Scripture was thus seen as itself a product of historical evolution, offering insight into the divine while bearing the thought patterns and presuppositions of the time of its composition. It now became the task of biblical critics to separate the "dross" of the human package from the divine treasure, in the process offering to believers the true divine revelation at the heart of historical evolution.[12]

The initial impulse towards the critical study of the Bible had emerged in part from the desire of eighteenth-century thinkers like Jean Astruc, Johann Eichhorn, and Johann Semler to submit all cultural phenomena to rational analysis. Attempting to win educated folk back to Christianity, "enlightened Christians" like the continental scholars Astruc, Eichhorn, and Semler (themselves deeply influenced by the English deists) sought to illustrate the moral grandeur and practical utility of "revealed belief" by uncovering the reasonable and emotionally satisfying religion buried under the rubbish of biblical fables and miracle stories. But the strength of this critical movement grew immensely in the early nineteenth century, when it came under the influence of historicism's new emphasis on the evolutionary nature and organic unity of history. It was in this intellectual climate that higher criticism developed its characteristic techniques and form. By the end of the century Wilhelm M. L. DeWette, Abraham Keunen, and Julius Wellhausen had brilliantly applied the new critical methods to the records of the Jewish and Christian past, documenting "scientifically" the evolutionary development of revelation.[13]

It was this historico-critical study of the hallowed book, as well as the hermeneutical presupposition behind it (that the Scriptures themselves were the products of historical evolution, containing both historically conditioned data and divine revelation that needed to be separated by sophisticated techniques), that first alarmed Western Christians, and that opened the prolonged and bitter debate over the acceptance of historicism outside the groves of the academy.[14]

Few world religions were more dependent on their sacred books than Christianity, and the evangelical Protestant strain of that faith had pushed dependence on written Scripture to its hermeneutical limit with its doctrine of *sola scriptura*, offering to all believers free access to the record of divine revelation. It is thus hard to imagine an area of Western culture where the potentially corrosive effects of historical criticism would be more passionately contested, or where the intellectual and affective responses to historicism's perceived epistemological threat would be more convoluted, than over the challenge of biblical criticism among Protestant evangelicals.[15]

The threat for English-speaking Christians appeared suddenly in 1860, and thereafter refused to disappear. In February of that year a volume of articles entitled, harmlessly enough, *Essays and Reviews*, appeared in England, and the Victorian wars of religion commenced. The book, a collection of critical essays written by distinguished Anglican scholars, sought to mediate the advances of continental critical scholarship to English-speaking Christians. Benjamin Jowett, Master of Balliol College, Oxford, and the brightest light in the Anglican theological firmament, had penned what became the most famous piece in the collection. Jowett's careful article on the use of reason in the interpretation of Scripture argued that biblical scholars must ascertain what the authors of scriptural narratives actually meant to convey to their readers, as God's revelation was progressive, and what was regarded as "historically true" in one generation could not be so regarded in another. Taking stock of the contemporary situation, Jowett noted that the Christian religion was in a false position when all the tendencies of knowledge were opposed to it; "the time has come when it is no longer possible to ignore the results of criticism."[16]

The response to the *Essays*, and especially to Jowett's learned and restrained article, showed that some fundamental cultural nerve had been struck. As a direct result of the gathering demand, especially from the clergy, that the scholars who had contributed to the abomination be tried for heresy and public scandal, Bishop Hampden of Hereford, who had himself earlier been accused of heresy by the Tractarians, said that the Queen in Convocation should prosecute, and led a three-year battle to accomplish just such an outcome. The appearance of this collection of articles by respected and reputedly "orthodox" Christian scholars convinced evangelicals on both sides of the Atlantic that the time had arrived for addressing the new critical challenge. Indeed, during the last quarter of the nineteenth century the challenge, introduced with the publication of the infamous *Essays*, assumed crisis proportions, and the times seemed to call for heroic measures to deliver the faith *once* delivered to the saints from the onslaughts of historicist "infidelity."[17]

Even more disturbing to the British clergy than the *Essays*, however, were the shocking and impious theories concerning the historical veracity of the Pentateuch advanced by Natal's Anglican bishop John Colenso; these theories sent a tremor of terror through the episcopal ranks of the Victorian church. The bishops now found in one of their own number theories believed to infect only Oxbridge dons and German infidels. And more distressing to the faithful in the pews than these convoluted debates among the learned was the serial publication of the English Revised Version of the authorized Scriptures, beginning in 1881. The new translation, incorporating many of the insights of critical scholarship from the previous half century, offered unfamiliar and often distressing renditions of beloved scriptural passages, in the process raising disturbing questions about the immutability of God's Word, a Word that heretofore had borne the familiar accents of the King James translation.[18]

The anxiety and confusion generated by this application of the new critical methods to the most sacrosanct record of revelation were buttressed by other equally troubling, if less immediately dramatic, applications of historical criticism to the study of the religious past. F. Max Mueller's comparative studies of world religions, published in his *Lectures on the Origin and Growth of Religion* and in his magisterial *Sacred Books of the East*, challenged Christian claims of exclusivity and uniqueness by illustrating the patterns of historical development that all religious traditions, including the Christian, seemed to follow in their evolution towards a mature world view. Charles Darwin's theories of natural selection and uniformitarianism, documented in *The Origin of Species* and even more alarmingly applied to the human animal in *The Descent of Man*, seemed to challenge the Christian tradition regarding the special divine creation of humankind, and made the venerable doctrine of providence appear a cruel irony. Herbert Spencer's boldly optimistic but agnostic philosophy of social evolution, perhaps the most popular form of evolutionary belief, promised an ever brighter day for evolving humanity without the need for a "glimpse behind the curtain."[19]

The works of Darwin, Spencer, and Mueller, no less than the biblical critical theories advanced by Jowett, Pattison, and Powell in the infamous *Essays*, soon generated an acrimonious discussion within the culture at large, a discussion that both religious and secular historians have labeled the "Victorian crisis of faith." This crisis, marked by a peculiar mixture of doubt and confidence, exercised the ever-serious Victorians on both sides of the Atlantic, receiving classic poetic formulation in Tennyson's *In Memoriam*, which voiced the sense of loss of an entire generation.[20]

While these unsettling scholarly applications of historical criticism appeared to threaten the religious foundations of Victorian Protestant culture as a whole, those Christians most distressed by the new intellectual threat were those inclined to the evangelical world view. Accepting literally the words of Scripture as to the purpose, structure, and destiny of the physical universe, evangelicals in both Britain and America perceived the new historicist world view emanating from "infidel Germany" as a direct assault on the veracity and trustworthiness of God's Word. Scripture was clear, they argued, on what God had revealed concerning the human cultural situation: history was the arena wherein humanity discovered its estrangement from the divine purpose, and from which, for those able to discern beyond its temporal horizons, God promised redemption.

Such views constituted the "gospel world" of nineteenth-century evangelicals living in Britain and America, a world which, for all of the social and historical factors that separated the two countries, constituted a cultural and ideological unity. All Anglo-American evangelicals knew that they shared a regenerative experience that marked them off from others, even from fellow church members, and that united them in the fellowship of the invisible church, to which all "vital Christians" belonged. All evangelicals shared "trans-Atlantic revivalists" like Charles Finney, Lorenzo Dow, and James Caughey, who supplied the reborn on both shores with a common language, a shared world view, and a practical commitment to working for God's kingdom in a "united front" whose most famous monument was the Evangelical Alliance. Most American periodicals carried "religious intelligence" from Great Britain, and the *Edinburgh Review*, the *Nineteenth Century*, the *Christian Observer*, and the *Westminster Review*, mainstays of the British evangelical parlor, were all published in American editions. Thus the furor over historical criticism occasioned in Britain by the *Essays*, the works of Darwin, and the studies of Mueller, was soon exercising evangelicals in the New World. For these Protestants who proclaimed *sola fide* and *sola scriptura* as the core of the Christian faith, the new historico-critical scholarship seemed to strike at the very heart of belief itself. And regardless of national allegiance or denominational affiliation, these evangelicals on both sides of the Atlantic united to meet this latest form of infidelity.[21]

The Spiritual Crisis of the Gilded Age

If the applications of historicist principles that generated the Victorian crisis of faith originated in England and on the Continent, those applications quickly found devoted followers in the New World, and generated a cultural crisis that was, if anything, more traumatic than its European parent.

Evangelical Protestants in America had welcomed the separation of church and state, but had stoutly resisted any separation of religion from the public weal. Thus, while most legal establishments of religion had been dismantled in the eighteenth century, an evangelical Protestant moral code, which embodied the values of the "voluntary establishment," had provided the ethical consensus on which American culture rested throughout the nineteenth century, and itself constituted something of a "voluntary establishment." Indeed, the belief that the Christian religion, more particularly the evangelical Protestant strain of it, was absolutely necessary for the social health of civilization remained an axiomatic component of the American ethos. By the middle of the nineteenth century God's people in the New World had effected a complex intertwining of religious and secular values that constituted an "evangelical culture." Thus the "religious" threat of historico-critical methods and theory could not but have profound "cultural" implications.[22]

The overarching vision of a Protestant, Christian America, to be won by voluntary means, became the basis for activity among the "seven sister" evangelical denominations that comprised the religious establishment in America. By stressing the deeply Christian character of their civilization, American evangelicals could identify a unity above their divisions, a unity focused on advancing the realizations of the kingdom of God in this world.[23]

Because of their very success in providing a religion *for* and *of* the culture, however, American evangelicals at the end of the nineteenth century had difficulty in recognizing the true source of the threat to the values on which their culture rested, for the threat of historicism coincided with profound social, economic, and cultural changes that were transforming America, and these socioeconomic changes demanded an immediate response. The rapid pace of industrialization after the Civil War precipitated a crisis of identity for a once agrarian culture. The massive tides of the "new immigration," now from the non-Protestant areas of southern and eastern Europe, introduced widespread fears that the values that had held American culture together were being lost as the unwashed strangers formed an ever-greater percentage of the population. The demographic shift that brought farm and village-born workers to urban centers in ever-increasing numbers transformed the simple, communal patterns of interaction that had defined America in the antebellum period into complex, associational patterns of social interaction, marked by alienation and disorientation.[24]

Most of the new immigrants, a large percentage of whom were Roman Catholics, Jews, and confessional Lutherans, refused to recognize the cultural authority of those evangelical Protestant denominations that had provided the "spiritual glue" for the nation's diverse peoples, while the new, overcrowded urban centers were too large to provide the communal context in which the "pastoral watch and care" of geographical parish models of evangelical ministry had succeeded.[25]

If only because they tried so consciously to be the religious reflections of their culture, the major evangelical bodies in America between the Civil War and World War I found themselves enmeshed in the cultural crises of the Gilded Age. Indeed, because religious discourse had for so long provided the arena and major vehicle for the most basic cultural concerns, it is probable that the new intellectual threat facing American Victorian culture was more dramatically played out in the churches than in the "secular" arena. The ministerial "ordination episode" of James Merriam, as well as the "Andover Controversy" at New England's premier orthodox seminary, exercised Congregationalists for a decade, and laid bare some of the troubling implications of the new developmental approach to reality more vividly than any "scientific" discussion of natural selection. The furor over the episcopal appointment of Phillips Brooks and the demands for "disciplining" occasioned by the preaching of Algernon Crapsey and R. Heber Newton convinced Episcopalians that the disturbing immanental thrust of the "modern mind" would have to be addressed, the comfortingly vague phrases of the Prayer Book notwithstanding. The scandalously "humanistic" biblical interpretations advanced by Ezra Gould and Crawford H. Toy forced Baptists of both North and South to debate the limits within which their traditionally free church could accommodate the new developmental frames of reference.[26]

But the broad epistemological threat posed by historicism as an alternative (indeed opposing) world view to that which had supported American Protestant culture for centuries went largely unperceived: only a vague uneasiness, described tellingly by Washington Gladden as "a going in the tops of the trees," witnessed to the sense that something momentous and irreversible underlay the battles over Genesis and evolution. The denominational and cultural focus on these discrete episodes over the specific forms which the intellectual threat took — Darwin, Wellhausen, Mueller — left the larger and more important threat unexamined, save for one crucial and dramatic instance. It was in the newly reunited northern Presbyterian church that the real battle over American culture, and the religious world view on which it rested, took place.

As the heirs of a Calvinist legacy that balanced emotional fervor with rational inquiry, northern Presbyterians had sought to sophisticate and edify the rough-hewn American evangelical mentality. Presbyterians shared with Congregationalists the first place as founders of colleges and academies in the young nation, and

the Presbyterian tradition of an educated clergy had made Presbyterian ministers a cultured and cultural elite along the frontier,
where they often served as community leaders and spokespersons
for civilized discourse. Their powerful traditions of intellectual
rigor and academic excellence demanded that they confront the
best of modern scientific and religious thought to "baptize" it for
their cultural mission, while the tightly structured hierarchy of doctrinal accountability, organized in ascending church courts, made
theological discussion among Presbyterians more litigious and "official" than in other Protestant bodies. Far out of proportion to
its numbers, the northern Presbyterian church enjoyed a cultural
and intellectual hegemony built on its willingness to act as pre-
ceptor for the American mind, thus making its confrontation with
historicism all but inevitable.[27]

But denominational battles among Presbyterians over historical criticism were also inevitable because their church represented
so broad a spectrum of theological opinion and spirituality. From
the time of its planting in the New World, Presbyterianism had incorporated within itself a theological diversity more analogous to
the American evangelical scene as a whole than to any one denominational group. These diverse and often conflicting religious sensibilities, stemming in large part from the church's dual Scots-Irish
and New England roots, had erupted in denominational division a
number of times in the course of its history. At the time of the First
Great Awakening, these two groups had divided into "Old Side"
and "New Side," representing respectively the Scots-Irish and New
England strains; later, in the 1837 schism, they divided to form the
Old and New School parties. And while the confessionalist Old
School and the more "experimental" and evangelical New School
factions of the northern church had agreed to reunite in 1869, the
merger itself rested on an unspoken agreement to tolerate diverse
theological positions within the denomination.[28]

American Presbyterians, the self-proclaimed missionaries to the
American intellect, were thus more united in 1869 than in several generations; but they were also more divided than almost any
other Protestant group over the spectrum of intellectual issues that
troubled Gilded Age America. It was therefore inevitable that the
challenges of the age should be debated with vigor and oftentimes
brilliance among American Presbyterians; it was also inevitable

that these debates should gain wide public attention. And what sparked the debate in America over the most important intellectual issues of the age was the Scottish trial of William Robertson Smith.

Smith's trials before the General Assembly of the Scottish Free Church in 1880 and 1881 were closely followed throughout the evangelical world, and the American debate over the issues that defined the Smith trial comprised the new world overture to what Paul Carter has labeled "the spiritual crisis of the Gilded Age." More specifically, Smith's trail became the impetus for Charles Augustus Briggs to begin the realization of his plan to make historico-critical methods part of the inheritance of American evangelical Christians.

Perhaps since the theological expertise and political wisdom supplied by the Scottish divines sent to the Westminster Assembly in the seventeenth century, and certainly after the rise of "commonsense philosophy" in the eighteenth century, the Presbyterian Church of Scotland was viewed as the citadel of enlightened religion throughout the Reformed world — critical yet deeply pious, confessional and yet eager for intellectual challenge. And the American branch of that Reformed world looked to its Scottish co-religionists for religious, scientific, and philosophical leadership: the works of Reid, Hutcheson, Stewart, and Beattie supplied the epistemological foundations for intellectual endeavor when the old Lockean world appeared to fall apart. Both Calvinist and Unitarian churchmen, the cream of the ministerial crop, had seized on the "Scottish philosophy" to subdue the threat of "French infidelity," making commonsense realism the single most powerful current in American intellectual and academic circles until well into the nineteenth century. The discussions of the learned — religious and otherwise — in the great universities of Edinburgh, Aberdeen, and Glasgow were therefore reported as a matter of course in American religious, scientific, and literary periodicals, and the furor in the church courts and lecture halls of Scotland over the disturbing new theories being advanced by Robertson Smith was reported and studied with great interest in America, for the fate of the entire enlightened Reformed tradition seemed to hang in the balance.[29]

In 1870 Robertson Smith, at the tender age of twenty-four, had been appointed to the prestigious chair of Old Testament studies at

Aberdeen's Free Church College. In his classroom and in articles carefully read on both sides of the Atlantic, Smith advanced the critical theories of Graf, Kuenen, and Wellhausen as compatible with, and even supportive of, a reverent and wholehearted acceptance of the Westminster Confession. Smith's advocacy of these theories, so new-sounding to Scottish ears, was most cogently and famously argued in his essay on "Bible" for the ninth (1875) edition of the *Encyclopaedia Britannica*. In this lengthy entry Smith introduced Wellhausen's four-fold compositional theory of the Pentateuch to the English-speaking world.[30]

Smith's advocacy of Wellhausen's controversial theory was reinforced by his study of the magisterial Reformers, especially of Calvin, in whose theology he found a forgotten emphasis on the subjective element in receiving God's Word. An appreciation of this subjective emphasis, which Smith maintained had been lost by Calvin's heirs, recognized that the divine *Word* was deeper than the *words* of Scripture; indeed, the written word contained the Word of God, which could be energized and communicated to the reader only through the operation of the Holy Spirit. Thus, as Smith pointed out to his fellow Presbyterians, Calvin himself had claimed infallibility for nothing contained in Scripture that was not illuminated to the reader by the internal witness of the Holy Spirit.[31]

Smith believed that the historico-critical approach to Scripture, which he had advocated in the "Bible" article and numerous other works, freed the Spirit to operate directly on contemporary readers. The latter then could stand in the same position as the biblical characters to hear God's eternal Word spoken to them, a position unencumbered by human editing and the accidental accretions of history.[32]

But Smith also understood that his advocacy of continental critical theories would be met with strong resistance among his church's scholars. Indeed, as early as 1871 he had written to his Scottish publisher:

> I glanced over the standard religious authority — Hodge — a few days ago. He has no conception of the modern form of the problem, and proves nothing. I fear it is so with all our "orthodox" men.[33]

Smith's fears of the "orthodox men" were more than justified, for his 1875 "Bible" article, itself constituting proof positive to many Free Church Presbyterians that he had broken his professorial oath to hold and teach the views set forth in the Westminster Confession, generated an investigation of his orthodoxy. By 1878, the investigation had raised "serious questions in regard to the subject's positions on the sacred Scriptures," questions that were presented before the highest ecclesiastical court of the church.[34]

Smith's response to the accusations against him could easily serve as a classic statement of the emerging liberal agenda. It gave voice to most of the themes that would come to make up the modernist credo: an acceptance of the historical context as normative for understanding all human culture; a belief that modern culture was itself revelatory of God's purposes, serving as the standard to which religious belief must conform; an acceptance of God's historical immanence as the locus of all revelation; and a firm belief that this immanent presence ensured the culmination of cultural evolution in the kingdom of God. This response took the form of a much publicized lecture delivered at the Free Church College at the beginning of the libel action, a lecture wherein Smith brilliantly and concisely presented the historicist cause:

> The Spirit of God works in and through human nature, and so the relation of the redeemed to God becomes a genuine element *in history*, of which historical science is bound to take cognizance, and which is as capable of historical appreciation as any other psychological element in the annals of our race. Accordingly, modern theological science is altogether right when it insists that the Bible must be studied by the same principle of historical continuity which is employed in the examination of other records of the past. The evolution of God's dealings with man cannot be understood, except by looking at the human side of the process. The only idea of moral and spiritual evolution possible to us is that of evolution in accordance with psychological laws.[35]

Robertson Smith's opponents in the General Assembly were not deceived by his subsequent brilliant and witty defense of his "technical orthodoxy" according to a literal interpretation of the *words* of the Westminster Confession. Indeed, his prosecutors recognized early in the trial that the *real* issue was not the fairly abstruse theological question, raised by Wellhausen, of the number of redactors who had edited the Pentateuch; rather, they clearly perceived the real issue was whether the very idea of transcendent, "vertical" revelation, as revelation had been understood among Christians for centuries, must now be abandoned in favor of a resolutely "horizontal" view of reality. This accounted for the ferocity and singlemindedness of their attack upon him. The much-controverted theory advanced in the "Bible" article disturbed them far less than the world view that underlay it. Indeed, in the libel trial they repeatedly returned, not to the "Bible" essay, but to an article published by Smith in 1870 that, for them, exposed the one-dimensional, atheistic universe that he adumbrated:

> The fundamental principle of the higher criticism lies in the conception of the organic unity of all history.... We have no true history where we cannot pierce through the outer shell of tradition into the life of a past age. A tradition that violates the continuity of historical evolution, and stands in no necessary relation to the conditions of the preceding and following age, must be untrue.[36]

Robertson Smith's opponents, with the special strength granted to those who knew that they battled not mere mortals but principalities and powers, pressed their cause with superhuman fervor so that, in 1881, they succeeded at last in inducing the General Assembly formally to remove Smith from his Aberdeen professorship, while issuing a public denunciation, in the name of the whole church, in which Smith's views were described as "so gross and so fitted to pollute the moral sentiments of the community that they cannot be considered except within the closed doors of any court of this church."[37]

Smith's libel trials between 1878 and 1881, fought out within a church famous for bitter denominational battles, were closely followed throughout Britain. The London, Edinburgh, and Aberdeen newspapers offered speech-by-speech accounts of the ongoing drama, and pulpits throughout the British Isles echoed with clerical disquisitions on this latest form of infidelity. But it was outside the Queen's realm that the Smith case would initiate the most bitter battles.

In a manner not unlike that of the "Monkey Trial" of 1925 in

Dayton, Tennessee, the Smith case captured the public imagination of American Protestantism, or at least the evangelical portion of it that comprised the religious establishment. The *Independent*, a religious periodical published in Brooklyn with a wide audience and an even wider reputation, began to report the proceedings of the Scottish church courts on a regular basis, making the issues and personalities of the trial common knowledge among American Protestants. The *New York Times* offered its readers both the texts of speeches delivered in Aberdeen and longer editorial pieces analyzing the "import" of the case. *Bibliotheca Sacra*, published out of Andover Seminary under the editorial hand of Edwards Amasa Park, felt obliged to comment on the Scottish "doings," taking up space usually reserved for New England Congregationalist concerns, while the *Methodist Quarterly Review*, quite unsurprised by this outcropping of heresy among the defenders of irresistible grace, could only hope that Methodism, always more faithful to the Lord's teaching, would escape the influence of such impious and unedifying goings-on.[38]

Charles Briggs and the Crisis of Historicism

Historians of nineteenth-century America have long recognized that the Smith case, or rather the American response to it, constituted the overture to the traumatic cultural upheaval that comprised the "spiritual crisis of the Gilded Age." Historians have likewise perceived that the Smith case adumbrated the very issues that were to become the central theme in "the most notorious event in nineteenth-century American church history" — the Briggs case. Indeed, there has evolved something like a standard narrative line in treating the figures of Smith and Briggs vis-à-vis the larger crisis that they ostensibly symbolized for Victorian culture. After a discussion of the threat of Darwinian theories to the religious world view built on the literal interpretation of the first chapters of Genesis, there generally follows a discussion of biblical criticism as a challenge arising from the application of evolutionary principles to the Scriptures themselves. This threat to the Bible is generally presented as having received most dramatic expression in Briggs's own 1891 inaugural address at Union Seminary (entitled, ironically enough, "The Authority of Holy Scripture"), an address that made the intellectual threat posed by Darwin and Wellhausen to the American evangelical world view too immediate to be ignored. And the house came tumbling down.[39]

What remains most appealing in this explanation of the place of Smith and Briggs in the Victorian crisis of faith is the conciseness and "simplicity of line" that explain both the larger crisis and their roles in it: a "biblical civilization," then Darwin and Wellhausen via Smith and Briggs, then explosion. But the weakest element in the argument lies in the failure of the evidence to prove the centrality of Darwinian, or even higher-critical, challenges as the real issue in the much-studied Briggs case, a case that both announced and precipitated the spiritual crisis that gripped Gilded Age America. Indeed, the "evidence" presented to illustrate Briggs's central role in purveying the threat of higher criticism to America can be read as witnessing to a more profound and disturbing crisis that underlay biblical criticism: that of history itself, and the evangelical Protestant place in it. The assertions of scriptural inerrancy and inspiration, of authority in the church, and even of revelation itself all presupposed a more basic understanding of reality that Briggs recognized as deeply problematic after the onslaught of historicism; that understanding was that the historical arena in which God's dealings with humankind were effected was a stable, circumscribed, and known entity. Briggs recognized the fragility and vulnerability of the evangelical world view in light of historicist claims, and sought to incorporate the new criticism into the arsenal of apologetic methods for the older religious vision. Little did he or his opponents, both committed to the same world view and values, guess that the American Protestant confrontation with history that would be played out in their own lives would leave their world so fragmented and discredited.

Briggs's effort to reconcile the older evangelical world view with the newer, historicist one expressed itself in a number of scholarly forms, witnessed only partially in his biblical studies. Indeed, Briggs himself conceived his work in higher criticism as a minor theme in a much grander symphony; his opponents likewise feared him precisely because his application of historical criticism was so broadly applied. After his studies in Berlin under the great historian of dogma Isaac Dorner, Briggs seemed obsessed with the problem of history. His magisterial biblical works — *Biblical Study* and

General Introduction to the Study of Holy Scripture — remained essentially critical studies of the history of interpretation rather than exegetical or philological works. His mammoth works devoted to church history — *American Presbyterianism: The Fundamental Christian Faith* and his posthumous, two-volume *magnum opus, The History of the Study of Theology* — were among the first large-scale historical works in this country based on a critical reading of primary documents, and brought him widespread popular and critical acclaim. But it was in his works devoted to practical ecclesiastical reform — *Whither?* and *How Shall We Revise the Westminster Confession?* — that Briggs felt that he had achieved his most satisfying and sophisticated application of historical criticism to the records of the past. It is in this last category that his famous inaugural address, "The Authority of Holy Scripture," belongs, its title notwithstanding, and it was precisely because his application of the feared criticism to practical matters of church polity and belief was so masterful and cogent that denominational conservatives felt compelled to challenge him in the courts of the church.[40]

The picture of Briggs that emerges from these works is that of a historian, or more precisely that of a student of historical criticism, obsessed with vindicating the ancient piety through the application of the modern criticism. Likewise, the picture that emerges from the documents of his trial is that of evangelicals locked in mortal combat, not over biblical interpretation, or even over the question of authority in the church, but over the question of how God acts, or perhaps is allowed to act, in history.

Briggs saw himself as a historian of the Christian tradition, biblical, creedal, and ecclesiastical, and his dedication to that self-identity led him to devote himself in the last years of his life to the cause that emerged directly from his historical research — church unity. An appreciation of the broad historical focus of Briggs's professional life might recast the real import of his famous heresy trial. If Briggs's story is essentially that of American evangelical Protestantism as it confronted the historicist demands of the modern world — and it is the contention of this study that such indeed was the case — then our understanding of the spiritual crisis of the Gilded Age will be nuanced by viewing the religious battles of the time through the lens of his career.

2

The Evangelical Basis

The Mantle of the Prophets

The year 1858 was remembered as the *annus mirabilis* by evangelical Protestants, the "miracle year" when an unexpected urban revival in New York and Philadelphia drew lunch-hour crowds of businessmen to pray, without benefit of clergy, for renewed hearts and stock options. Not the least of the year's wonders was the fact that by November the revival had spread far outside the confines of the urban North, so that the good Christians of Charlottesville, Virginia, no less than their Yankee counterparts, found themselves in the grip of a sober but fervent revival. What was even more miraculous, Thomas Jefferson's university — located in the town and long dedicated to exposing the deceptions of religion and its excesses — was likewise caught up in the religious excitement.[1]

At the university, Jefferson's revered tradition of gentlemanly skepticism had, by midcentury, come to be balanced with a newer tradition. This more recent intellectual tradition, moreover, enabled the young sophisticates of Charlottesville — while demanding nothing but "the facts" in good Jeffersonian fashion — to respond to the heart-melting preaching of Dabney Carr Harrison at campus prayer meetings. For like Harvard and Princeton to the north, the University of Virginia had become a bastion of commonsense realism — a "scientific philosophy" attributed to Lord Bacon, the paragon of Protestant enlightenment itself.

The method and epistemology of the Baconian science that formed the philosophical undergirding of most American college curricula can best be understood as a hermeneutical counterthrust directed against the efforts of eighteenth-century deists and *philosophes* who sought to portray the then-emerging scientific movement as innately hostile to traditional religious beliefs. Against these scientific scorners of Christianity the pious followers of Lord Bacon argued that true science must humbly study the "hard facts" of both material and spiritual reality, as the Creator of both had woven them into a subtly interconnected system. Bacon's inductive method ascended from the particular to the general, presupposing that the real work of both theological and secular scientists consisted simply in the observation and summarizing of data that presented themselves to the senses. In America both Calvinist and Unitarian churchmen had seized on the Baconian method to counteract the metaphysical heresies of Hume and Berkeley, in the process constructing an epistemology that stressed a strenuously empirical approach to all knowledge, a greed for objective "fact," and a distrust, bordering on paranoia, of the workings of "hypothesis" and "imagination."[2]

This approach to the study of material and spiritual reality lent a "stolid empirical cast" to the thinking of the Old School Presbyterians, theologically the most vigorous Protestant group outside of New England, and arguably the most devoted practitioners of Baconian science in America. If the Methodists and Baptists (the two largest Protestant bodies in mid–nineteenth-century America) found it necessary to "scathe the head to save the heart," Old School Presbyterians offered a more integrated and rational vision to those cultured and prosperous believers who were the objects of their missionary zeal, a vision of educated and thoroughly modern Christians trusting in the "beefy firmness of the senses" to find empirical validation for the truths of the Westminster Confession.[3]

Students at the bastions of this "doxological science," like the University of Virginia, were taught that the goal of their education was that of educating the evangelical mentality, so that American Protestants would be humiliated out of their acquiescence to Methodist anti-intellectualism. Baconian science offered a vision wherein both heart *and* mind cooperated for the glory of God and of God's righteous empire in the New World, now established on scientific but godly principles. The enduring attraction of this vision of a pious but thoroughly "scientific" Christian republic is witnessed in the fact that, despite the intellectual and social traumas of post–Civil War America, educated evangelicals still operated largely within its comfortable confines well into the last quarter of the century.[4]

Faculty members at Virginia like Francis H. Smith and William H. McGuffey (of *Readers* fame) thus impressed on their students the necessity of applying a scrupulous empiricism both to the natural records of a world brimming with care and to the records of the supernatural world. The gentlemen of Virginia were taught the steps by which thought passed from "rash hypothesis" to ideas founded on cautious observation, in the process reducing to orderly simplicity the welter of data assaulting the senses.

Among the university students most affected both by the Baconian pedagogy and by the religious excitement in Charlottesville was Charlie Briggs, a sophomore from New York, whose letters home reporting the religious fervor on campus were received with joy and mounting expectation by his pious mother. The scion of the Briggs clan was admonished to "inquire about your duty under the guidance of the Holy Spirit," while being reminded in a fashion that would appeal to his newly espoused Baconian principles that "when you are making these inquiries you are seeking for truth just as really as when you are working out a problem in mathematics."[5]

Thus, Charlie's conversion on the last day of November 1858 took the form of a deeply felt but decorous Old School event, resting securely on scientific principles that represented the best thinking of the day. These principles enabled him to defend intelligently the faith that was in him, both when he presented himself for membership before the session of the First Presbyterian Church of Charlottesville, and again shortly thereafter, when he announced new career plans to his family. In this latter announcement, the son of the New York "barrel king" declared that he no longer intended to follow his father, Alanson, into the prosperous family business — the largest barrel-making company in the United States — but rather intended to take up service in the Lord's vineyard.[6]

Alanson Briggs received this announcement with some dismay, and brooded over the new course of events in his comfortable town house on Henry Street in lower Manhattan, where Charlie had been born on January 15, 1841. Alanson had entrusted the running of his expanding household of children, servants, and assorted relatives to his wife, Sarah, and thus a distinctly evangelical atmosphere had pervaded their home. But while the atmosphere was distinctly evangelical, family denominational affiliation was considerably less distinct. Sarah Briggs frequented the Old School preaching of the Rev. John M. Krebs, pastor of the Rutgers Street Presbyterian Church and an important denominational leader. Krebs was a perfect representative of those evangelically inclined but theologically and socially conservative Presbyterians who had commandeered the General Assembly of 1837 to expel their more liberal brethren and proclaim themselves the true "Old School."[7]

Earlier Presbyterian conservatives had both distrusted and denounced the revivalism of the First Great Awakening as a declension from the Calvinist tradition of a pious, sober, and educated spirituality. But these latter religious guardians of the cultured and literate classes heartily approved of revivalistic "new measures" like the anxious bench, the inquiry room, and emotionally powerful preaching, so long as they were not accompanied by the doctrinal heresies so current among their more liberal, New School brethren.[8]

But while Sarah Briggs was a regular attendant at Dr. Krebs's preaching, her husband stayed religiously away. Alanson Briggs never officially joined any church, but he especially found the Presbyterian preference of his wife too formal. Perhaps he desired a spirituality closer to the rough-and-tumble business world he worked in, for when he did attend church he favored the less fashionable, more unrestrained worship of the Norfolk Street Methodist Church. If Alanson was institutionally only semi-attached, however, he was as evangelically inclined as his wife, and rejoiced at his son's conversion. He wrote immediately advising Charlie to "join with the Methodists, as they are the safest group, and are doing more to convert the world than all the other denominations put together." But Alanson's heir had become far too devoted a disciple of Francis Bacon to find the "head scathing" spirituality of the Methodists attractive.[9]

Charlie's uncle, Marvin Briggs, himself a graduate of Princeton Seminary and an important religious influence in his nephew's life, immediately wrote to Charlottesville. Marvin presumed that after graduation Charlie would enter the divinity school at either Princeton or Richmond, since "unless you anticipate a change of heart, you ought to graduate from an Old School seminary. Besides, you will agree that you won't find a superior to Dr. Hodge."[10]

But as things turned out, the neophyte surprised everyone. Increasingly bitter sectional feelings had made return to Charlottesville impossible in the fall of 1860, and so Charlie had thrown himself into an intense course of private studies that would ensure his entrance into seminary the following fall. He spent the year "cramming his theological belly" with Greek, interrupting his intense private studies only to join New York's Seventh Regiment on April 25, 1861, in response to President Lincoln's appeal for volunteers to the Union Army, to help defend the capital from an expected Confederate attack. From the end of April to June 30, Briggs was stationed at Camp Cameron, overlooking Washington and the Potomac, waiting in vain for the expected Southern advance. His "military career" of three months was thus spent uneventfully in the sweltering heat of the Virginia countryside — a career marked only by letters to his sisters Amelia and Sarah, exhorting them to "come to Jesus." Indeed, the letters reveal an earnest young Christian totally uninvolved in either the ethical questions of slavery or the larger course of the war. "Do not let the present excitements distract you from the one thing necessary," he warned his sister Millie, for

> I trust you feel that you are a sinner. I trust that you know that Christ is your Savior, and I want to entreat you to go to him in prayer. I know by experience that Christ is precious, and that I would not give him up for the world.... Do you want to be separated from your brother and sister when they shall be with Jesus? Are you willing to be with the Devil in torment? You can decide the question in a moment.[11]

Exhausted by the heat and his exhortations, Charlie returned to New York City on July 1, taking up his studies where he had left off. In October 1861, he surprised family and friends by enrolling at the Union Theological Seminary, then located on Park

Avenue in New York City. His choice of that irenic New School institution over both Princeton and Richmond constituted both a renewed commitment to the epistemological principles learned at Virginia and a spiritual declaration of independence from the resolutely Old School confessionalism of his family. Falling back on Baconian principles that had undergirded his formal education, Charlie decided that he would pursue the "facts" (whatever they might reveal themselves to be) in the most rigorous seminary program he could find. He thus chose Union Seminary, an institution not quite twenty-five years old that had already gained a reputation for uniting a rigorous academic study of the best thought of the time with a fervently evangelical spirituality. Its charter of 1837 had been purposefully broad and catholic, setting forth an institution wherein "all men of moderate views and feelings, who desire to live free from party strife and from all extremes of doctrinal speculation," might find a prayerful but challenging ministerial preparation. Thus began an institutional affiliation that would become the focus of the battle over historical criticism in America.[12]

Briggs quickly established himself as an outstanding student at Union, ranking at the top of his class by the end of his second year. This was accomplished more by *Sitzfleisch* than by blinding insights, and in the student parodies written by his classmates, Briggs was invariably cast as the "grind," perpetually lost in books. But both classmates and teachers recognized the deeply spiritual motivation that fueled Briggs's sometimes frightening academic energies, and his personal notebooks from his student years reveal the personal piety that informed his studies. In a notebook entitled "Cogitations," he confided a telling meditation on the spiritual bases of his academic pursuits:

> God's love, if truly presented, would call forth all the affections of our heart, mind and soul. Thus, our great duty is to examine into the nature of God and his loving relation to us. Let us cultivate our faculties of mind, as these are the best means for attaining our perfection.[13]

Briggs's search for perfection through the cultivation of "our faculties of mind" would be pursued within an institution whose faculty encouraged perfectionism, especially of the intellectual variety. Two of Union Seminary's faculty members in particular, Edward Robinson and Henry Boynton Smith, had achieved international reputations in the scholarly world, and both, in quite different ways, bequeathed to Briggs a tradition of evangelical scholarship that sought to mediate between the ancient faith and modern critical ways.

Edward Robinson's magisterial *Biblical Researches in Palestine* had been published simultaneously in America, Britain, and Germany, laying the scientific foundation for all subsequent geographical and archaeological studies of Palestine. Although the book had received the gold medal of London's Royal Geographical Society in 1842, it was nonetheless a curious combination of German critical scholarship and New England piety, reflecting its author's idiosyncratic synthesis of German philological training and Westminster orthodoxy.[14]

Robinson had himself been a student of Moses Stuart at Andover Seminary, and he inherited from Stuart the latter's life-long project of reconciling the new critical approaches to Scripture with that redaction of Calvinist orthodoxy that Andover Seminary had been founded to defend. If Stuart stood within the famous Andover Creed, he stretched it as far as it could go to make room for critical methodology. Stuart had maintained that the language of the Bible must be understood according to the linguistic tools applied to all literatures, and impressed on his young student the necessity of a critical mastery of the new hermeneutical methods forged in Europe.

To study the new German methods more closely, Robinson had left Stuart for Germany, where he studied at Halle under the renowned Hebrew grammarian Gesenius, and in Berlin with the two brightest lights in the German theological firmament: Neander and Schleiermacher. But if he developed formidable philological and critical tools under these masters, Robinson remained personally more conservative in piety and theology than they. Indeed, the German scholar whose theological synthesis Robinson introduced to his Union students as most consonant with his own was Ernst Hengstenberg, a pillar of the Lutheran confessionalist movement and the leading evangelical opponent of all forms of historical criticism.[15]

Robinson thus trained his students at Union in the thorough

philological and archaeological methods he had learned in Germany, while endowing them with the firm conviction that their critical studies would, indeed must, lead to the answers contained in the Larger and Shorter Catechisms of the Westminster Confession. It is of critical importance that Briggs, who for a decade was to occupy the Edward Robinson Chair of Biblical Theology at Union, was introduced to biblical study by this scholar who applied careful critical methods in the service of a strict interpretation of Calvinist orthodoxy.

But it was the "hero of Presbyterian reunion" — Henry Boynton Smith — who most influenced Briggs at Union, and whose mantle of progressive, evangelical Calvinism Briggs consistently claimed to have inherited. James Hastings Nichols has placed Smith with Hodge, Bushnell, Park, Nevin, and Schaff as the "first half-dozen theologians of their generation," while George Marsden has stated that Smith was "easily the first among the New School theologians."[16]

From his study under Moses Stuart at Andover Seminary and under Leonard Woods, Jr., at Bangor, Henry Smith had learned of a new movement in Germany, loosely referred to as the "mediating theology," that had developed during the first half of the nineteenth century as a theological response to rationalism and idealism. The movement drew from former students of Schleiermacher, from philosophical idealists with religious concerns, and from academic advocates of evangelical piety. This mediating theology offered a third and intellectually respectable alternative to both orthodox confessionalism and liberal "infidelity" of the Strauss variety. Its advocates sought to mediate between traditional Christian affirmations, trenchantly proclaimed by Hengstenberg and the confessionalists, and scientific inquiry based on emerging historico-critical principles, by combining a supernatural, biblically based faith with the idea of organic historical development. The key doctrinal focus of this developmentalism was the incarnation; it viewed the incarnation as the complete and final divine revelation *within* time, and thus the focal point of world history. The developmental and incarnational theology that resulted taught that the church itself was a living organism, mediating Christ's presence within history, that christology was the key to all systematic theology, and that church history, especially the history of doctrine, was the true method for understanding the church's inner life. It was into this "mediatorial" theological climate, especially strong at the Universities of Halle and Berlin, that Henry Smith arrived in the spring of 1838.[17]

At the University of Halle, then in the midst of a revival, Smith studied under the revival's sponsor, Friedrich August Tholuck, who had been sent to redeem the university from its recent flirtation with rationalism. Smith was captivated by Tholuck, who synthesized Moravian ascetical practices, the christocentric principles of Schleiermacher, and the revivalistic concerns of the evangelicals into a theology both intellectually stimulating and sensitive to religious experience. At the end of his year's study with Tholuck, however, Smith left for Berlin, where he encountered the man who would become his *Doktorvater*, August Neander, professor of church history and the primary formulator of the synthesis of christocentric piety and developmentalism that marked the mediating theology.[18]

But Smith's studies in Berlin provoked a profound religious crisis, brought on by a growing fear that his studies under Neander, unlike those under Tholuck at Halle, endangered his conversion-based evangelical faith. After the crisis had passed, Smith wrote home to assure his family that

> study here has had no other effect than that of making my views more deeply grounded, and of developing them clearly. If I thought that my heart were losing ground, or that I was losing my simple reverence for the Scriptures, and my simple faith in experimental religion, I would not, could not, hesitate to come right home.[19]

Smith was thus one of the first American theologians, with Philip Schaff, to study the new historical science in Germany and emerge with his "simple faith in experimental religion" intact, a feat accomplished largely, Smith claimed, through the mediating, christocentric theology that he had learned under Neander. This "imported" theology was presented in an address that, although delivered at the beginning of his career, remained the most comprehensive statement of his views for his entire life. "The Relations of Faith and Philosophy," delivered at Amherst College in 1849, described the impending intellectual crisis that would challenge the authority of the evangelical Protestant world view, and proposed a "scientific" but orthodox solution to "the great alternative of our times — the choice between Christ and Spinoza."[20]

In the address Smith argued that faith and philosophy were not inherently opposed, but were rather necessary and complementary approaches to a single order of being. The suggestion that faith was possible without philosophy ignored faith's claim to present the most rational account of the origins and order of the universe; likewise, the suggestion that science could operate without faith ignored the limits inherent in the nature of science itself, which could explain only the relations of things, not their origins or ends. Using arguments borrowed in part from Horace Bushnell, Smith declared that faith and science were complementary ways of grasping reality, converging when both accepted the reality of divine revelation. Through revelation we learn the *facts* of redemption, he announced, facts confirmed by the internal testimony of converted hearts, by the evidences of the power of Christianity in history, and by their compelling answers to the question of human destiny.[21]

As George Marsden has observed, it was something of a foregone conclusion that Smith (although himself an Old School man) should immediately attract the attention of the New School Presbyterians, for Smith proposed a creative synthesis of New England and German thought, mediating between the extremes of New Haven and Berlin while proposing a christocentric basis for renewed hope of denominational unity within the divided Presbyterian family. But the address proved to be the turning point in Smith's career in very practical terms. William Adams, a director of Union Seminary, had sat in the Amherst audience, and was directly responsible for Smith's nomination the following year to the church history chair at that New School institution.[22]

Smith was an immediate success at Union, and generations of seminarians found his presentation of theology through its historical development "in itself magnetic." If his pedagogical method came to be characterized as "the teaching of divinity through history," it rested securely on his belief in organic development in both history and revelation and on his christocentric view of world history.[23]

In his classes at Union, Smith bridged the hermeneutical gap between Baconian science and the new science of developmental growth by humbling the latter's spirit of critical independence and taming it to serve a christocentric piety and an orthodox apologetics. Smith captured young Briggs's evangelical loyalties by proclaiming that the greatness of church history lay in its factual character, in the power of historical facts to yield a comprehensive knowledge of human destiny. The very factuality of the incarnation and the manifest historic advance of the church constituted empirical "proof" (magical words to evangelicals of Briggs's generation) of the validity of Christian claims.[24]

Smith thus offered his students, in traditional apologetical language, a thoroughly orthodox understanding of developmentalism, itself linked in his thought to the ongoing witness of the Christian community in history. In his lectures the evolutionary language that would become anathema to religious conservatives serviced a grand vision of Christian history, filled with the power of Christ and leading, step by providential step, to the mission of the Reformed churches in America. The historical unfolding of Christian doctrine showed how divine truth, delivered once for all in the Scriptures, had become progressively clarified to meet the purified understanding of God's people on pilgrimage.[25]

Like his contemporaries Edwards A. Park at Andover and Philip Schaff at Mercersburg, Henry Smith expounded a theology based on the romantic identification of evolution and progress, a theology that mediated between the received doctrine and the emerging evolutionary model of reality. But also like those romantic theologians, Smith believed that the synthesis would be achieved less by a sincere consultation of science than by a benign religious imperialism. As William Hutchison has noted, the cordiality of these "mediating theologians" towards science and modernity was ultimately the cordiality of the spider's invitation to the fly: religion was to make its accommodation with science by enveloping it, by bringing the truths discovered by science within the "total system of God," where all true science belonged.[26]

Smith provided the necessary epistemological continuity whereby students like Briggs, schooled in the Baconian world view, could use the newer evolutionary language without feeling that they had betrayed the older values. Thus long before Henry Smith became "the hero of Presbyterian reunion," he became Charlie Briggs's personal model and guide, the prototypical evangelical scholar committed to experimental religion but unafraid of addressing and incorporating the newest scientific findings in his religious thinking.[27]

In Smith's classes at Union the focus on the evangelical experience of grace and conversion remained constant, and in his courses on natural theology, soteriology, and "Christian evidences," Charlie Briggs read the classic works of Edwards, Bellamy, and Hopkins on that experience, while also being introduced to the new scientific methods (especially of Dorner) that would "prove" this experience to be scientifically verifiable by the most rigorous standards available.[28]

In his course on "Christian Anthropology" Smith introduced Briggs to the wealth of the Christian tradition, as he presented Augustine on imputation, Aquinas on providence, Pascal on original sin, and Edwards on the will; but Briggs was also introduced to the works of Neander, Schleiermacher, and Hagenbach, through whom Smith illustrated the importance of applying the most advanced methodologies in the service of the ancient faith.[29]

In Professor Thomas Skinner's course in "Practical Theology" Briggs and his classmates studied the schism within the Presbyterian church in 1837, and learned of Henry Smith's continuing efforts to reunite the Old and New Schools. Briggs's admiration and respect for the "mediator of Union" can be dated from this time, most concretely in the voluminous correspondence that Briggs and Smith exchanged while the former was a student at both Union and Berlin, and later when Briggs accepted his first pastoral call. From the spring of his first year as a student at Union until the end of his life Briggs referred to Smith as his mentor and guide, that scholar who, more than any other, combined progressive scholarship with an active role in the church for the advancement of God's kingdom in America.[30]

It was thus naturally to Smith that Briggs turned for advice when it became clear that a hiatus would be necessary in his theological education. In the summer of 1863 Alanson Briggs's ill-health dictated that his son withdraw from seminary to manage the family business. The surprising (or perhaps not so surprising) fact that emerged between 1863 and 1866, when Charlie managed the Briggs Barrel Company, was that the younger Briggs (no longer "Charlie" in his correspondence, but "Charles" or "CAB") was a successful and canny businessman. Indeed, so successful was he that when Alanson began to recover his health he attempted to convince his son to jettison his ministerial plans to remain at the head of the barrel company.[31]

But CAB, with support from Henry Smith, had already made other plans. In January 1865, he had met a young lady visiting his sisters, and within a month was sending predictably flowery love letters to Miss Julie Valentine Dobbs of New Jersey. But contained within the love letters were also *Haustaufel* passages wherein Briggs sought to contextualize their personal love within his ministerial plans:

> I thought that it would be well for me, who had resolved to devote myself unreservedly to my Master's service, to make no earthly connection. But now, my Julie, I believe that God has brought us together. But you know the life to which I have been called. My pathway must be one of severe mental and spiritual discipline, and that must be *yours* too, my Julie. It is well that you appreciate this *at once* and prepare yourself for it.[32]

The seemingly heroic Julie pledged her troth to Briggs in October 1865. Immediately thereafter, CAB began studying for his ordination exam with Smith, so that on April 18, 1866, he presented himself before the First (Old School) Presbytery, being rewarded for his efforts with a license to preach. Smith had prepared his young admirer well for the rigors of Presbyterian licensing; but he also taught him that his passion for knowledge could not be fulfilled on the American side of the Atlantic. If he would truly be intellectually perfect, Briggs must travel to the font of modern evangelical study — to Germany, where Smith himself had learned the gift of balancing true piety with academic excellence.[33]

Thus, armed with the license granted by the New York Presbytery and a letter of introduction from Philip Schaff (who had lectured occasionally at Union Seminary) which described Briggs as a "ministerial candidate of good Christian family and of a religious character," Briggs and his wife sailed for Germany in June 1866. By the end of the summer they had settled comfortably in Berlin, where both Briggs and Julie quickly assumed leading roles in the Anglo-American evangelical network of the city. Their rooms became the meeting place for a "Bible circle" that met every Sunday evening, "so that our Sabbaths are ob-

served with an American spirit." Briggs took his turn preaching
in the "American chapel," a British Methodist missionary chapel
that both American and British students in the city used for worship. And Briggs quickly gained a reputation for "heart-warming"
preaching, becoming something of an unofficial guide to evangelical Germany — introducing British and American guests to the
leading figures of the German missionary movement, and guiding admiring evangelicals to such notable endeavors as Wichern's
"Rough House."[34]

But Briggs's evangelical pietism was confirmed and deepened,
not so much by these social experiences in the Berlin evangelical
network, important as they were, as by his study under the brightest
light of the German evangelical firmament.

"A New Divine Light"

When new light dawns from above, most men cling to the old and
can't believe any new light possible. But the world needs new views
of the truth. The old doctrines are good but insufficient.... Let us
seek more light under the guidance of the Holy Spirit. I cannot doubt
but that I have been blessed with a new divine light. I feel a different
man from what I was a few months ago. The Bible is lit up with a
new light.[35]

So Briggs wrote to his uncle Marvin in January 1867, describ-
ing his first six months of study at the University of Berlin. This
remarkable missive was followed a week later by a letter to his
mother, in which Briggs declared that he felt "much nearer to
God, more under divine guidance, than I did this time last year. I
feel more in the way of God, more in his service."[36]

Although Briggs was indeed a Presbyterian evangelical given to
"new light" concerns like personal sanctification (the discussion of
which was the occasion for the letter to his uncle), the language
of both letters is noteworthy, if not extraordinary, for the "new divine light" that he wrote of had been shed by nothing less than
the methods of historical criticism learned from his new German
mentor, Isaac August Dorner. His language in these and other letters witnesses to his painless, indeed celebratory, movement from
the revered nineteenth-century paradigm and methods of Baconian science to the "dangerous" methods of historical criticism,

and that movement had taken place under Dorner's masterful direction.

The fact that Briggs left America before the "paradigm revolution" that historicism sponsored caused widespread epistemological warfare helped him to escape the binary dogmatism that marked so many fellow evangelicals, who could imagine only all-out war between the new historical science and Christian belief. Likewise, the fact that he was introduced systematically to historicist methods in Germany, under the tutelage of "mediating evangelicals," allowed him the freedom to synthesize creatively elements of his evangelical past with the new critical methods, in turn giving a distinctly European cast to his "modernist" thought. For Briggs, the search for "hard facts" that had defined the Baconian scientific enterprise in America was now incarnated in an even more empirical scientific fashion with historical criticism's promise to present reality *wie es eigentlich gewesen ist* — as it really happened. The new critical methods seemed even more serviceable for the older evangelical search for a scientifically informed faith than the methods of the Baconian science that they replaced.

There is little wonder, then, that Briggs should use the language of revelation to describe his historicist studies in Berlin under both Dorner and Emil Roediger, for both seemed to offer precisely the kind of objective certainty for religious belief beloved by American evangelicals schooled in commonsense realism. Roediger imparted to Briggs a lasting appreciation for rigorous training in the biblical languages, and tutored the young American in a cautious linguistic approach to scriptural exegesis that rejected both the "excesses" of Strauss and the retrenchment of Charles Hodge. Indeed, Roediger taught Briggs that *all* theology must proceed from exegesis — from the careful examination of the historical records. Thus Briggs could write home to his old teacher at Union Seminary, Henry Boynton Smith, that

> in America there is a great want of exegesis, but here every great theologian is an exegete. [Germans] are too much influenced by rationalism, as we would say in America, but this perhaps because they have thought more deeply and candidly on subjects, whereas we have overlooked them. But in spite of their coldness in handling

Scripture, it is more satisfying to the student than a devotional spirit without thought.[37]

But if the young American learned the primacy of exegesis in both history and theology from Roediger, the "new divine light" that dawned for him in Berlin resulted from his studies under Dorner. Isaac Dorner was an accomplished and respected master of the new theological discipline of the history of doctrine, having applied the new critical methods in his four-volume *History of the Doctrine of the Person of Christ*. When Briggs arrived in Berlin in 1866, Dorner was editing his magisterial *History of Protestant Theology*, wherein he sought to contextualize the evolution of christology within the larger framework of the history of doctrine.[38]

Isaac Dorner had confirmed the Baconian prejudices of his young American student by insisting that the evangelical experience of grace and regeneration, an experience that had been central in Briggs's own life, could be verified "scientifically," and that the theological questions that arose from this experience could and should be pursued with the same expectation of empirical "proof" as one would expect in studying the natural sciences. Dorner had directed his entire theological effort towards attaining a scientific knowledge of religious truth by using historico-critical methods, and thus promised to provide the hard facts that would legitimate empirically the doctrines of Protestant orthodoxy.[39]

Dorner had worked out his theological system historically, that is, in relation to the entire history of theology. Further, he had recognized that the "christological problem" — or rather the history of discussion over Christ's role and nature — was central to Protestant theology in the nineteenth century even before the publication of David Friedrich Strauss's *Life of Jesus*.

Both Hegel and Schleiermacher figured prominently and explicitly in his theological and philosophical background, and both profoundly influenced his methodology. Hegel's influence was evident in Dorner's concern for objectivity and "cognition," but even more clearly in his dialectical pattern of historical-theological interpretation. For Dorner, the true understanding of faith emerged from the synthesis of the antithetically inadequate notions of merely "historical" faith (intellectual knowledge of the creeds, etc.) and of the purely "ideal." The true synthesis emerged out of the "moments" of history: the "inner course of history" determined and defined true faith because only within the flow of time had the "ideal" been incarnated in the radically historical and specific. For Hegel, and thus for Dorner, the spectacle of history itself offered the clearest example of correct theological method.[40]

Equally decisive in shaping Dorner's theological method was Schleiermacher's approach. Like Schleiermacher, Dorner continually identified the "religious" and the *wissenschaftliche* (scientific) interests as the twin authorities of legitimate theological development. Indeed, these two interests were finally convergent, for *wissenschaftlich* designated not merely "science" in the narrow sense, but rather that which was coercive and universally valid for thought itself. Schleiermacher, in Dorner's view, had recovered the act of faith as the *scientific* starting point for Protestant theology. But the former's restriction of religious knowledge to assertions about the subjective consciousness had to be replaced by a new understanding of religious knowledge, one that allowed for the "actual cognition of the objects of religious awareness" — by truly objective, scientific knowledge of religious truth. And the attainment of this objective knowledge rested, above all, on "the facticity of historical experience." Thus, in a radically new way, Dorner made the historical enterprise basic to Protestant theology: in a real sense, without the methods of historical criticism there could be no theological discussion.[41]

Briggs wrote excitedly to Henry Smith of Dorner's "magisterial methodology," which he described as ascending in a dialectical spirit:

> he gives us 1) the scriptural ground, or biblical theology, and 2) ascends to the historical or confessional ground in the doctrinal development of the church, especially in the comparison of the confessions or symbols, and on these bases he gives us 3) his systematic statement.[42]

Given Briggs's later efforts in confessional reform, church history, and ecumenism, as well as biblical study, it is instructive to note his description of Dorner's method, a method that, in his letters to Henry Smith, he announced that he would utilize in his own scholarship. Biblical criticism was important precisely because it allowed the scholar to move on to larger historical questions of how the Christian community had utilized the biblical doctrines. The second "moment" of this dialectic — the historical — was as crucial for arriving at the synthesis as the first, and it was the entire methodological dialectic that captured Briggs's loyalties. He confided to his journal that at last he had found a "thorough scholar and a man of the spirit," and he dutifully reported to Henry Smith that

> whilst using all his efforts for the pure faith of the Reformation, Dorner is at the same time in favor of modern means. I take great pleasure in attending his lectures, not only on account of his exhaustive examination of the subject, but also on account of the piety that pervades them and which at times manifests itself in a striking manner.[43]

Briggs's search for the best means for preserving the vision of a thoroughly scientific but pious America had led him to a point at which he needed an "evangelical bridge" from the Baconian method to historicism, and it was Dorner's piety — which manifested itself "in a striking manner" in his application of historical criticism to the biblical and Christian past — that provided that bridge. Briggs's "conversion" from the nineteenth-century Baconian world view to the newer critical one was accomplished without trauma, or even the sense of loss, because it was not a conversion at all. Briggs simply switched methodological allegiance to the new critical ways, while retaining the older evangelical world view largely unchanged. He believed that he had found the key for mediating the older evangelical vision by utilizing the new historicist methods "doxologically" — for the purpose of glorifying God — just as evangelicals had previously used Baconianism to provide the "hard facts" on which pious but scientifically informed believers could rely.

Briggs's studies in Berlin with Roediger and his courses with Dorner confirmed and deepened the "evangelical liberalism" that he had learned under Henry Smith, and in his regular correspondence with Smith, then engaged in political efforts to reunite the

Old and New School parties, Briggs clearly enunciated his allegiances:

> I feel very thankful for your efforts on behalf of union. I am connected with the Old School and would prefer that side to the other, but I feel more sympathy with the mediating theology which it seems to me you advocate.[44]

It was, then, Henry Smith's practical efforts in implementing his mediating theology (most recently evinced in his central role in reuniting the Old and New School Presbyterians) as much as his scholarly achievements that elicited Briggs's praise. But Briggs's model of an "active theologian" was derived equally from his German mentor. Looking to Schleiermacher's ideal of the theologian as "prince of the church" — as the Christian who combined the highest attainments in scholarship with the fullest leadership in the Christian community — Isaac Dorner had combined his scholarly activities with an active role in the "Inner Mission" movement for social reform.[45]

Briggs's personal appropriation of this model of theologian as active member of the Christian community, impressed on him by both Smith and Dorner, would become evident in his denominational crusades for creedal reform and ecumenical relations with non-evangelical Christians. More immediately, it found concrete form in his preaching. In the pulpit Briggs revealed the practical ends which he believed his academic endeavors served, and he focused especially (and surprisingly for one so resolutely "intellectual") upon perfectionism and holiness teaching. Early in his Berlin sojourn he had written that

> here is the center of my studies and my thought: to study the human nature of Jesus, to strive to become like Jesus and to teach others so to do.... What I want to preach then is Christian perfection and holiness — Christ our law, our obligation and the necessity for us to follow after him.[46]

Perfectionism — the belief that converted sinners could achieve sinless lives through cooperating with the power of the Holy Spirit — had long been a staple of the evangelical message in America. "Methodists" of all varieties, reformed theologians like

Nathaniel W. Taylor, revivalists like Charles Finney, sectarians like those at Oneida, and even "heretics" as different as the transcendentalists and the followers of Joseph Smith had all preached perfectionism as the *right* of American Christians. Such a right constituted the personal analogue to the millennial vision towards which all evangelicals worked, and on which they built their goal of an educated, prosperous, and redeemed America. Charles Briggs now rested the gospel of perfectionism on the most impeccable scientific foundations: the ancient call to perfection seemed to enjoy the *imprimatur* of modern science itself, having been recovered and repristinated through the efforts of biblical exegetes and critical theologians employing historico-critical methods. Briggs believed that the critical methods employed by historicist scholars had uncovered irrefutable evidence that Jesus' own call to perfection had been a basic part of the kerygma, and the records of the ancient church witnessed to the importance that perfectionist arguments had played in the initial success of Christianity.[47]

This perfectionist emphasis emerged clearly in Briggs's preaching in the Berlin chapel, but it received fullest expression and rhetorical maturity after June 1869, when Alanson Briggs's ill-health again required his son's presence in New York. Briggs returned to America reluctantly, having planned to spend more time in study under Dorner; but he now withstood his father's pleas to resume the managerial position in the family business, accepting instead the call of the First Presbyterian Church of Roselle, New Jersey, to become its first pastor. To this recently formed but affluent offshoot of an Old School congregation in Elizabeth, Briggs announced that he intended to preach the "strong meat" of an evangelical Calvinism, one that utilized the most advanced theological tools towards the conversion of sinners:

What the Church needs today is the strong meat of Calvinist, Augustinian, and Pauline doctrines, reiterated in all their sublimity and power. It is a mark of the degeneracy of our times that the grand doctrines of the Reformation, expressed in our Catechism, are not brought out in as much prominence as heretofore.... I fear that the world is gaining on us, and Christians ought to be as different from the world as light is from darkness.[48]

This strong meat, delivered in fifty-eight sermons throughout 1871, seems to have worked, for during his first year at Roselle he gained nineteen converts and paid off the sizeable ($6000) church debt. Briggs lamented that the very critical methods he utilized for conversion preaching were also being applied in the cause of what he (scornfully) labeled "liberal Christianity":

> It is not a good sign of the times that men boast of having thrown off the restraint of our pious ancestors in praise of a "liberal Christianity" — one that will allow people to believe whatever they choose.[49]

But Calvinism's "strong meat" had to be offered in both the pulpit and in the academy. Indeed, the call to preach and the call to teach did not constitute two separate, much less antithetical, tasks, but rather made up two aspects of a larger, more inclusive call: the call to witness to the gospel. It is important in understanding Briggs's own sense of mission to see his "ministerial" and his "academic" efforts related in this intimate way. Throughout his career, each of the two activities informed the other, and as early as 1870, while he was just beginning to exhort his Roselle congregation to "attain the full-grown stature of the perfect man in Christ," he was likewise supplying articles for Henry Smith's *American Presbyterian Review*, including thirty pages on the history of biblical theology since Astruc, and a column entitled "Recent German Works," which appeared in the January, April, and July numbers.

The critical perception, combined with the evangelical tone, of these articles quickly came to the attention of Philip Schaff, who had arrived at Union Seminary two years earlier and who was then American editor for the Lange series of biblical commentaries. Schaff approached Briggs in 1872 to translate and edit Karl Moll's *Commentary on the Psalms* for the series. Published in America in 1872, Briggs's extended introduction to Moll's commentary brought him scholarly acclaim and the attention of his former teachers at Union, who noted with approval both his sophisticated use of critical methods and his staunchly orthodox interpretation of the text. Thus, in 1874, when Henry Smith's ill-health forced him into retirement, both Smith and Schaff pushed for Briggs's appointment to the faculty. As a result of their efforts Briggs was named "Provisional Professor of Hebrew and Cognate Languages" for the 1874–75 academic year.[50]

To view Briggs's appointment at Union as a "replacement" for Henry Smith is, in a technical sense, incorrect, for Smith had lectured in historical and systematic theology, and Philip Schaff now took over the teaching of those areas. But Briggs viewed his appointment as something like the passing of Smith's mantle: he saw himself as a replacement for the "hero of reunion," a replacement who would expound a theology both orthodox and progressive, pastoral yet deeply committed to the intellectual apostolate, scriptural yet conversant with the most advanced critical methods. Further, Briggs's academic interests and projects, like those of Smith and Dorner, were broad-ranging and interdisciplinary, difficult to categorize as "biblical," "historical," or "practical."

Like his mentors Smith and Dorner, Briggs would apply sophisticated methodological techniques to a broad range of theological issues; also like them, he would remain firmly evangelical in temper and commitment, pursuing his scholarship within a world view largely formed in the revival of 1858. Thus, as in the case of Smith and Dorner, it would be difficult to categorize Briggs as a theologian.

Shortly after Briggs's professional career at Union commenced in 1874, the first faint rumblings of the collapse of the united evangelical Protestant establishment began. Briggs set himself, both personally and professionally, against the divisive tendencies of the time, utilizing, ironically enough, precisely those methods of historical criticism that frightened so large a part of the evangelical establishment. And therein lies the irony of the story: both Smith and Dorner had built better than they knew.

The Wounds of Protestantism

The Evangelical Alliance is accomplishing a mighty work, and will heal the wounds of Protestantism.... If Protestantism could be purged of its unevangelical Christians and were united in one compact body on some general principle, the heathen and the corrupt churches would soon yield to them. *That* is the great problem before the churches in the latter half of this century.[51]

The evangelical quest for a "Christian America" seemed, in 1874, both closer and further from realization than ever before. Denominational mergers, like that of the culturally important Presbyterians, and transdenominational efforts, symbolized by the Evangelical Alliance, promised to provide firmer support for the task of "baptizing" American culture into the evangelical Protestant fold. But at the same time, the first stirrings of a culturewide trauma were beginning to be felt by American Protestants, stirrings aroused by the "new immigration," the demographic changes within urban areas, the rapid pace of industrialization, and, intellectually, the first reflections on the implications of historical criticism.[52]

In the fall of 1873 Isaac Dorner arrived in America amid these first faint rustlings in the evangelical treetops, and ventured to the village of Roselle, New Jersey, to visit his former student before both journeyed into New York City as delegates to the Sixth General Conference of the Evangelical Alliance. At that meeting of evangelical Protestants from both sides of the Atlantic the standard rhetorical fare consisted of speeches that reflected the belief, like that voiced by Briggs in the citation above, that the evangelical Protestantism which was sponsoring the meeting could provide a firm foundation both for the reunification of Protestantism and for the converting of those cultures that Protestantism was called to evangelize. And while many who were present at the conference discerned unmistakably ominous portents of an impending crisis for the Christian mission to North Atlantic culture, few, if any, publicly voiced their doubts that the religious progress that had been made in the nineteenth-century for evangelical Protestantism, for American and northern European culture, and thus for the kingdom of God, would continue indefinitely.[53]

But the expressions of unity, confidence, and strength voiced at the conference betrayed a discernible uneasiness just below the surface of most of the addresses delivered, an uneasiness reflected in almost shrill assurances that, indeed, all remained well. These assurances take on an irony that is difficult not to overplay, as the unified evangelical tradition they lauded was about to collapse and splinter, if not with the visual drama of Oliver Wendell Holmes's "One Hoss Shay," then at least with unseemly haste. The "new theology" and the various conservative lines of thought that opposed it (the latter being unified somewhat later and eventually labeled "fundamentalism") spread so rapidly during the 1880s and 1890s that the demise of the "old style orthodoxy," symbolized by the Evangelical Alliance and so strong in appearance as late as the 1873 alliance meeting, had clearly been underway for some time.[54]

Well before 1878 Briggs had seen the threat to the evangelical tradition posed by those who had once been safely within the mainstream but who now sought certainty in very "un-Protestant" kinds of infallibility against the new intellectual and social challenges facing America. But in the fall of that year the threat took very concrete form when a group of eight premillennialists, drawn largely from the leadership of the Niagara Bible Conference, published a call for a public conference in New York City to "listen to a series of carefully prepared papers on the pre-Millennial advent of the Lord Jesus Christ and connected truths." The proposed conference would be the first such American nondenominational meeting, but it was also emblematic of a much broader movement that was taking place during the 1870s, when American evangelicals of all types debated with unusual fervor the question of the return of Christ.[55]

This debate over the timetable and manner of the "last times" was intimately related to the crisis over basic assumptions that was rending the evangelical heritage; these basic assumptions, moreover, appeared to be deeply undermined by the historicist methods utilized by Briggs in his introduction to the Moll biblical commentary. The new premillennialism was a defensive and pessimistic response to those same challenges that were eliciting the response on the theological left, but it attempted to shore up those places in the foundation of Christian belief that appeared most in danger of erosion. In those areas where liberalism was unsatisfyingly vague and "hypothetical," premillennialism was comfortingly explicit and certain, thus supplying precisely the kind of concrete "scientific" data beloved by believers raised in the older, Baconian world view. The Bible was absolutely precise and literal in all matters of fact, and its meaning was plain and evident to reason; Christ's kingdom, which all American evangelicals until recently had assumed to be tied in some way to the fortunes of the American republic, was wholly supernatural in origin and discontinuous with events in history. Indeed, so corrupt were the "redeemer nations" of the Puritan reformations that "already in the counsels of God, 'Mene, Mene Tekel, Upharsin' is written concerning the modern democracies no less than concerning Babylon of old." It was in this chastened spirit that what the New York *Tribune* called a "novel religious conference" was opened on the morning of October 30, 1878, in New York's Holy Trinity Episcopal Church.[56]

If publicity for the growing millenarian cause was one of their aims, the conveners of the 1878 conference succeeded far beyond anything they could have imagined, for denominational newspapers and theological journals well into the next year discussed the meeting and the creedal statement it adopted. Briggs had come to believe that the dispensational millenarianism behind the New York meeting was something radically new and deeply alien to the Protestant and Reformed traditions, betraying the evangelical cause precisely by making unsubstantiated claims of infallibility for it. Thus, in 1878, Briggs undertook a careful historical analysis, using the very critical methods that most premillennialists perceived to be the causes of the crisis, of the writings of patristic, Reformation, and Westminster theologians to "show where the heresy lies." The result was a series of eleven articles, published in the New York *Evangelist* throughout the fall and winter of 1878–79.[57]

The articles were widely read and commented on, for Briggs was already widely recognized as a conservative but competent scholar, careful in his examination and evaluation of scriptural and historical materials. From the first, Briggs made no secret of his disdain for the millenarian cause, attacking its claim to the "true orthodoxy" by exposing its sin against the Holy Spirit:

> It shows a weakness of judgment and a historic pessimism to leap over 16 centuries to find in the three earliest a purer life and a sounder doctrine. The Church of Christ has *not* gone from bad to worse through 19 centuries, but with the Holy Spirit it has advanced in life and doctrine all through the centuries.[58]

This faith in the Holy Spirit's ongoing guidance of the church was centered on both the written Word and the witness of Christian history itself, and the evidence of both convicted the premillenarians of schism and heresy. Millenarians from the time of the Montanists had mistakenly advanced one part of the Christian tradition as the "true core" of belief — an unbalanced position that had always fostered divisiveness and controversy. But Briggs noted that the witness of both Scripture and history illustrated that the catholic tradition, a tradition that Reformed Christians had consistently claimed as their own, had always been marked by unitive, not divisive, impulses, impulses that found expression in their own day in the work of the Evangelical Alliance.

If Briggs viewed with alarm the splintering of his religious heritage between the "ultra-evangelicalism" of the millenarians and the dangerous novelties that, since the retirement of Edwards Park, were being advanced at Andover Seminary, he looked to the alliance to maintain evangelical Protestantism's united character, and to work towards the reunification of all evangelical Christians. Since its founding in August 1846, at London's Freemason's Hall, the alliance had sought to unite "true believers" from all parts of the world — the true believers being those who held "the same essentials of Faith and [were] desirous of bearing visible witness to the true unity of Christ's church" — into a force that would realize the postmillennial dream of converting this world into the kingdom of God and of Christ.[59]

Briggs had been impressed and encouraged at the 1873 alliance meeting in New York, and in August 1879, as a delegate to the Seventh General Conference in Basel, he wrote to his Union colleague and fellow-delegate, Philip Schaff, that the need for the unified and certain voice of the alliance had never been more urgent than at that moment, when evangelicals seemed in imminent danger, not of the Lord's return, but of betraying the unified tradition that they had inherited.[60]

To Briggs the dream of a "Christian America" was too precious a heritage to leave in the hands of "unscientific heretics." If Christians could unite and utilize the scientific advances of the day in the service of the gospel, the realization of Christ's kingdom on earth might be accomplished within their generation; if the divisive tendencies, represented by groups like the millenarians, won the day, the dream might be lost forever, and their generation would be held accountable at the dreadful judgment. Briggs believed that the promise could be realized, and the threat averted, through the application of historical methods in the evangelical cause. But Briggs's personal diaries from this period are marked by an urgent tone, as if he were reminding himself of the stakes involved in his scholarship:

> These are the critical times. Beware of postponement, of committing the unpardonable sin of refusing to perform known duty. The blindness may be healed now that Jesus is passing by, but if you neglect the opportunity it may no more return forever.[61]

Briggs's sense of the urgency of the times, expressed both in his diaries and in his articles against the millenarians, arose directly out of his evangelical temperament: the decision, personally and as a culture, for or against the Lord could not be avoided or postponed. The challenges of the times demanded, as it had always been demanded of Christians, that believers utilize the best tools at hand to preach the gospel. For Briggs, there could be little doubt that the Lord, working through servants like Henry Smith and Isaac Dorner, had delivered the necessary tools to defeat infidelity and schism. But the urgency of the times also required ecumenical cooperation among all Christians if those tools were to be effective. Briggs recognized that before the transnational union of evangelical Protestants envisioned by the alliance could be effective in combating the splintering tendencies of the time, incremental steps towards cooperation, on both the denominational and national levels, were necessary:

> You cannot sufficiently estimate the importance of the reunion of the Presbyterian Church. We ought to be grateful to God for the reunion of the two great branches of the church, not only as Presbyterians, in that it is the beginning of an organic union of all the Reformed Churches, but as Protestants, as it is the sweet foretaste of a more intimate union of all churches.[62]

Briggs thus saw the reunion of the Old and New School as a prototype of the coming reunification of all evangelical Protestants into Christ's catholic church on earth. Such a union would not only effectively answer schismatics like the premillennialists, but would also end the waste of ministerial labor and money in home and foreign missions:

> When one billion heathen are unconverted and more than half the Christian world is unevangelical, it is a sin and a shame to waste

men and money merely to swell the number of churches. If these were transplanted to foreign lands, they would soon make the world ring with the triumph of the Cross.[63]

If the American Presbyterian church, now recently united, could show fellow evangelical bodies how good and pleasant it *really* was for brethren to dwell together in unity, the movement towards a "Christian alliance that would combine all Christians against idolatry and infidelity" (in the words of the alliance's charter) would be greatly accelerated. Further, it was of the greatest moment that a forum be established wherein the growing debate over the methods of historical criticism could be freely aired and judged. Briggs was convinced that a journal shared, less by "Old" and "New School" men (for Briggs himself belonged to the Old School), than by those who differed in their judgment over the merits of historical criticism, would provide just such an arena. The appearance of their recently reunited church freely debating the greatest intellectual challenge of the day would provide a needed example to fellow evangelicals of the best means for defending the ancient faith from perceived threats. And as a firm devotee of doxological science, Briggs had no doubt that such a free discussion would eventuate in the vindication of the new critical methods.

It was thus at Briggs's urging that President William Adams of Union wrote to "brother" Archibald A. Hodge at Princeton Seminary suggesting the need of a theological journal for the now united church. Such a journal was needed, Adams suggested, to represent the true Presbyterian view against a growing number of Presbyterians, located mostly in the Midwest, who were resentful of eastern "elitist" hegemony and who since the 1878 Prophetic Conference had sought to identify the true Reformed tradition with Darbyite dispensationalism; and, more importantly, the journal was needed to demonstrate to fellow American evangelicals the strength and vitality of their "catholic" church.[64]

To Briggs, it seemed like a blessing of God on his vision of a stronger and more unified evangelicalism, and not the beginning of one of the greatest religious dramas of the Gilded Age, when Hodge replied less than a week later that it seems to me very plain that it is both the right and the interest of the Presbyterian Church to be represented by a theological review, and that it is best that Union and Princeton, representing the two great halves of the past, should cooperate in the management of such a review.[65]

3

The Politics of Truth

A Political Journal

On the afternoon of January 11, 1880, the first number of the *Presbyterian Review* — a "new series" in a revered line of Princeton journals — was sent out by a New York publishing company to several hundred advance subscribers. If the mailing was not accompanied by any of the dramatic portents usually assigned to cultural turning points, it nonetheless marked an important moment when the spiritual crisis of the Gilded Age entered the public (and published) arena. For the new quarterly that made its appearance on that afternoon both abetted and documented the initial stages of the fragmentation of that unified world view that had held together the American evangelical mainstream.

The *Review*'s importance in expressing the tensions of the 1869 reunion of "sides" in the northern Presbyterian church has long been recognized by religious historians. What has been generally underplayed, however, is the fact that the *Review* also adumbrated — with an almost eerie accuracy — the issues that would preoccupy the evangelical mainstream in the early decades of the twentieth century as it dealt with a civil war within its own ranks. That civil war — embodied most famously in the "Fundamentalist Controversy" — did not arise suddenly in the early years of the new century. Rather, it had been well rehearsed a number of times; it had, in fact, been played out quite realistically for a decade in the pages of the *Presbyterian Review*.

From the initial planning stages of a shared denominational quarterly, Presbyterian conservatives had recognized — with a battle-scarred conservative instinct for potential conflict — the danger that such a joint venture with New School liberals might pose as a vehicle for importing the "fearsome battles of the Scotch church" onto peaceful American shores. Princeton professor Charles Aiken, voicing Old School fears in 1879, had written to Briggs that

> Allegheny and Princeton are both divided and hesitating on the project. It would be hard to make some of our friends [if not some of ourselves] feel that we were not compromised by the Scotch issues.[1]

Nor were these idle fears. There was a certain probability, if not inevitability, that a journal representing the ideologically diverse and fractious constituency of the recently reunited Presbyterian church would emerge as the arena for debating the intellectual "challenges of the age" to the American evangelical conscience. The *Christian Register* (Unitarian) and the *Andover Review* (Congregationalist) presented an almost uniformly liberal, "accommodationalist" view of the relation of religion to the demands of the age, while Southern Baptist journals like the *American Baptist Reflector* — arguing from the other side of the theological fence — displayed a consistent hostility to any and all forms of theological adaptation to modern culture. Methodist publications like the *Methodist Review* tended to reflect the traditional Wesleyan disdain for intellectual wrangling, while the tripartite division of the American Episcopal church into high, low, and broad church resulted in a careful avoidance of journalistic jousting on disputed theological points in publications like the *American Church Review*.[2]

Only Northern Baptist publications like the *Baptist Quarterly Review* were as theologically diverse and as "politically" partisan as Presbyterian periodicals. But the loose Baptist ecclesiology made doctrinal accountability difficult, while the old denominational tradition of "soul liberty" made heresy charges profoundly unpopular.

Both of these factors helped to postpone Northern Baptist battles over the intellectual challenges of the age until well into the twentieth century.[3]

Thus, just as the Presbyterian conservatives had predicted, it fell to the new ecumenical publication of their church to provide the journalistic arena in which American evangelicalism would "officially" meet the challenges of historical criticism. The new journal represented a denomination claiming a proud intellectual tradition of scholarly debate and engagement with secular learning; it represented a denomination beset by profound ideological differences — differences that reflected the theological spectrum of American evangelical culture at large; and it represented a denomination equipped with the ecclesiastical machinery that made doctrinal uniformity both possible and expected. Thus would the new *Presbyterian Review* serve as a primer for the pitched battles that would preoccupy American evangelical culture in the years to come.

The first number of the new quarterly opened with a "Statement of Idea and Aims," an announcement written in its entirety by the moving force behind the founding of the *Review*, Charles Briggs, but signed as well by his Princeton co-editor, Archibald A. Hodge. The statement declared that the new publication sought

> to combine all the varied interests and sections of our church. It
> will be the aim of the Review to treat all subjects in a broad and
> catholic spirit, comprehending those historical phases of Calvinism
> which combined in the Presbyterian Church at the reunion.[4]

The *Presbyterian Review*'s effort to incorporate the "varied interests and sections" of the church was clearly witnessed in the *Review*'s first issue, an issue that revealed as well the highly unstable ideological powder keg on which the new journal rested. Princeton Seminary's Benjamin B. Warfield, a pillar of confessionalist orthodoxy, offered an analysis of the recently discovered "Testament of the Twelve Patriarchs" that read like (and was) a paradigmatic exercise in commonsense realism, while William G. T. Shedd, a conservative Union colleague of Briggs's, offered a classic Baconian exercise entitled "Hume, Huxley and Miracles." And Charles Briggs himself contributed an article that, its innocuous title notwithstanding, rang all the changes on the historicist carillon, tolling a warning of the conflict to come.[5]

"The Documentary History of the Westminster Assembly," Briggs's first offering in the *Review*, represented the fruit of his previous summer's research in libraries throughout Britain — research that Briggs claimed made him the "first authority on the Westminster Standards in our country." The article attempted to illustrate, by a careful critical study of the diaries, letters, and debate records of the seventeenth-century divines who had composed the Westminster Confession, that a decided American declension from the "pure faith of the Reformation" had indeed occurred. But the decline was not due to confessional laxity or to creedal infidelity, as the Old School confessionalists asserted, but rather to very un-Protestant claims being made for the authority of humanly constructed creedal statements themselves. Using previously ignored or unknown primary sources, Briggs offered a classic historicist interpretation of how the Westminster divines had conceived of their confession-making project — as a contingent, committee-produced affair full of compromises. None of those revered divines had ever claimed the kind of "normative orthodoxy" for the resulting symbols later ascribed to them by Protestant scholastics.[6]

But while thus cheerfully laying historicist dynamite in the foundation cracks of Old School confessionalism, Briggs was spared the wrath of the conservatives by the mass of erudite and arcane detail that constituted the body of the article. Few confessionalists bothered to reflect on the radical implications that his decidedly abstruse study of seventeenth-century texts held for the highly charged questions of denominational politics. Briggs's Princeton co-editor approved the piece without comment.[7]

The swift approval granted by the Princeton editor to Briggs's first article in the *Review* would prove to be the last such effortless editorial exchange, however, for unpleasant events being reported from Aberdeen soon changed the honeymoon atmosphere pervading the early editorial meetings of the journal. The publicity surrounding the Scottish libel trial of Robertson Smith in the summer of 1880 made some notice of it in the new "catholic" Presbyterian journal mandatory, a fact that all the *Review* editors anticipated with some dread. But dread turned to outright fear when Charles Briggs volunteered to write a "historical account" of the case for the

October number of 1880. Despite grave reservations from others on the editorial board, Briggs was assigned the notice; but Briggs was likewise cautioned from both sides of the editorial counter as to the "wisdom of great reserve on our part in reporting the case." The result was everything that the conservatives had feared and predicted.[8]

Briggs's notice did, in fact, confine itself in large part to a straightforward narrative of the Robertson Smith case, making only occasional editorial lapses, such as his comment that Smith had been "providentially called" to write the much-controverted encyclopedia articles. But the blood pressures of at least half of the editorial board must have soared when the last paragraph of the notice was reached. For in that final section Briggs noted that any reasonable evaluation of Smith's theories must take place

> free from the complications and technicalities of ecclesiastical proceedings, by competent scholars on both sides, seeking earnestly and prayerfully for the truth. It seems to us that both parties desire to vindicate the divine authority and inspiration of the Word of God. If therefore the discussion should be conducted still further, in the proper spirit, with Christian charity and mutual toleration of legitimate differences, the result will be that many troublesome difficulties will be removed.[9]

With breathtaking alacrity Briggs thus appeared to dismiss, in an aside utilizing the editorial "us," the competency of church courts to judge the veracity of the complicated new critical theories. Likewise, he had more than intimated that the "technicalities" of ecclesiastical trials hindered more than helped the honest search for theological truth, a search that only competent scholars, and not good-willed but ignorant church officers, could evaluate. But most unconscionable by far was Briggs's description of Robertson Smith's theological positions as "legitimate differences" that might be accepted within a broadly evangelical Presbyterian church, a description that itself constituted the theological position against which conservatives in both Scotland and America had fought for some time.

Briggs was informed from Princeton, in a note that was itself a model of studied understatement, that what he had appended to the historical recital "seems to go beyond our understanding." The

Smith case, Hodge declared, involved "many delicate and vexed questions on which we have all along known that we are divided." For that very reason Briggs had been commissioned to write a *historical* notice. Only those portions of his notice that the entire editorial board could agree were historical should be printed. But Briggs, somewhat disingenuously, professed innocence to Princeton's charges of editorial heavy-handedness. He declared that he had remained well within the constraints imposed on him by the *Review*'s board. Indeed, he refused to revise or withdraw the notice, revealing in the process a personality in which truculence and a genuine passion to serve the evangelical cause were mixed in about equal proportion.[10]

The long-dreaded specter of evangelical civil war over the new criticism, like that lately witnessed in Scotland, now appeared to be imminent on American soil. This was the more bitter for Old School supporters of the *Review* because it appeared to be precipitated by the trial of a notorious Scottish heretic (public discussion of whom the *Review* had assiduously avoided), and in a denominational publication that they had helped to found in order to stave off precisely such internecine warfare.

Archibald A. Hodge, with his wonted good sense, recognized at once that quibbling with Briggs over the notice would be fruitless. Briggs's notice would be printed in the October 1880 issue, as planned. But it would not stand alone. The entire editorial board — as stipulated in the journal's constitution — was responsible for all editorials published in the *Review;* for Briggs's notice to appear without a rejoinder would be read as acquiescence in the opinions stated therein. A "full, free and frank" discussion of the issues that had splintered the Scottish church now appeared to be necessary, Hodge declared, if only to vindicate the *Review*'s claim of representing *all* the viewpoints of the reunited American church.[11]

Such a full, free, and frank interchange — agreed upon by Hodge and Briggs in the early months of the new year — would prove to be the first, and in many respects the most decisive, discussion about historical criticism to take place among American evangelicals in the Gilded Age. The "debate" conducted in the pages of the *Review* outlined the positions that, in the next generation, would come to be known as "modernism" and "fundamentalism." But it also revealed more clearly than any other such exchange the true epistemological bases from which those respective positions battled.

The plan agreed upon was that the *Review* would publish a series of eight articles, to begin in April 1881, after the Scottish church had decided the fate of Robertson Smith. Both "sides" on the Smith affair would present their cases calmly and reasonably. Dr. Hodge was to open and close the series, although both Briggs and Hodge were to choose two other scholars to take part in the discussion.[12]

The Roots of Fundamentalism

"Inspiration," coauthored by Hodge and Benjamin Warfield, appeared as the opening article in the series, and represented, in the comparatively brief space of thirty-five pages, the culmination of a half-century of Princeton theology. But the article was much more than a simple defense of the conservative understanding of biblical inspiration. It represented as well the classic exposition of that "certainty" provided by commonsense realism over against the threats of historicist relativity. Indeed, the article joined such epistemological certainty so closely to the cause of an inerrant Bible that it largely defined the public debate for the next generation.[13]

For most of the nineteenth century Princeton theologians had merely shared the universal but vaguely defined evangelical belief in a "high" view of biblical authority and inerrancy, a view usually expressed in the categories of commonsense realism: the trustworthiness of the plain meaning of Scripture; the perspicacious nature of biblical doctrine; the divine warranty for ecclesiastical structures and creeds based on biblical authority. The Presbyterians at Princeton, like the orthodox Congregationalists at Yale and the Unitarians at Harvard, had relied on the "commonsense" approach to truth, with its attendant assumptions as to the value-free character of scientific investigation and the ahistorical nature of truth. But what emerged as distinctively Princetonian with the "Inspiration" article was a militant perpetuation of the older, ubiquitous evangelical view with a new mathematical specificity and concreteness — a militancy and a concreteness foreign to the older world view. Against all quibbling about the historically conditioned character of cultural constructs, the "Inspiration" article announced the Princeton belief in theology as a static entity unaffected to any appreciable degree by historical development. Further, Princeton contended that the Westminster Confession had elucidated, once for all, the orthodox interpretation of scriptural authority. The task of modern theologians was simply to restate, as succinctly and cogently as possible, the clear doctrine of the confession.[14]

The article thus offered a "commonsense" explication of what the Confession of Faith had always taught (and would always teach):

> The scriptures are a *record* of divine revelations, and as such consist of words; as far as the record is inspired at all, and as far as it is in any element infallible, its inspiration must reach to its words. Infallible thought must be definite thought, and definite thought implies words.[15]

In response to the epistemological threat posed by historicism, Hodge and Warfield offered to Christian believers the firm ground of a literally (indeed, verbally) exact Bible — a Bible read through the lenses of commonsense realism. Hodge and Warfield thus offered a rallying-cry that conservatives in succeeding generations would cling to as itself encapsulating the essence of the faith once delivered:

> The historical faith of the Church has *always* been that all the affirmations of scripture of all kinds, whether of spiritual doctrine or duty, or of physical or historical fact, or of psychological or philosophical principle, are without any error.[16]

The "Inspiration" article thus constituted the first clear intellectual statement of an emerging conservative position that would achieve full stature among "fundamentalist" Christians in the next generation. This statement grounded the conservative, antihistoricist spirit — which was then emerging as an antimodernist stance — on the firm rock of Scottish commonsense certainty. Far from evincing any anti-intellectual or unscientific sentiments, Hodge and Warfield's article outlined a resolutely *rational*, scientific position that claimed the ancient and respected Baconian title.[17]

But the very stridency of Hodge and Warfield's arguments betrayed the novelty of their position, their claims to its antiquity notwithstanding. The calm reasonableness of Baconian science had been constructed to answer other, equally calm and reasonable challenges to the Christian view of the universe — challenges that spoke a similar language of transcendence and transhistorical certainty and permanence. The immanental, relativistic claims of historicism, as represented in the Robertson Smith affair, constituted something radically new and far more disturbing than the challenges offered by seventeenth-century German infidels or British deists, and the tone of crisis that pervaded the "Inspiration" article witnessed to this. The sudden need to spell out exactly *how* scriptural affirmations were inerrant witnessed to the disturbing if unspecified sense that the very groundwork of reasonable argument itself — the trustworthiness of the senses, the ubiquity of scientific truth, and the "givenness" of history — was giving way.

With almost mathematical precision Hodge and Warfield's article elucidated, in Baconian language known to all evangelical Protestants, the unchanged and unchangeable Christian truth that was contained in static, timeless categories. The article constituted, in fact, an important "cultural moment" at which the Princeton theology declared its independence from an American evangelical mainstream that had begun a quiet but widespread exodus from the fortress of Christian Baconianism.

But even the militant specification of scriptural inerrancy "of all kinds" did not constitute the most alarming "ancient" doctrine now affirmed through the application of Baconian realism. Benjamin Warfield, assigned the second half of the article by Hodge, raised the theological ante of the debate exponentially by drawing this ancient position regarding inerrancy to its logical conclusion. While hedging his bets somewhat by appealing to the hypothetical "original autographs" (the actual manuscripts written by the inspired biblical authors) over the present, defectively transcribed versions, he nonetheless declared that "a proved error in Scripture contradicts not only our doctrine but the Scripture claims and, therefore, its inspiration in making those claims."[18]

Princeton had thus rejected the historicist hermeneutics of Robertson Smith and, by implication, of the entire historico-critical method, on the grounds that such hermeneutics were profoundly un-Christian, demonstrably unhistorical, and decidedly unscientific. Since truth remained unchanged from age to age, what the church had taught as true in one age *must* remain true in all other ages. If the highest expressions of truth were those which most closely followed the commonsense canons of the Baconian inductive method (and Princeton, with nearly all educated American Protestants, believed precisely that), then the "speculative" and "hypothetical" constructions of the new critics were unconscionable flights from the most basic canons of reality itself. The church had *always* taught that the Scriptures were without error. Paul at the Areopagus had applied the methods of commonsense realism to the Scriptures as faithfully as Lord Bacon himself, demonstrating for first-century Greeks and for nineteenth-century Americans the unchanged and unchangeable nature of divine truth. If some "modern" scholars now offered other supposed scientific methods to show that the Scriptures contained errors of fact, those scholars should have the courage of their convictions and — on both religious and scientific grounds — simply leave the church.

Briggs responded in the April 1881 issue of the *Review*, in an article entitled "The Critical Theories of the Sacred Scriptures." Like the "Inspiration" article to which it formed the counterpoint, Briggs's article represented far more than an explication of one approach to scriptural interpretation: it constituted rather an apologia for an entire world view.

From the very outset Briggs took the high ground of historical precedent and "scientific demonstration" (music to Baconian ears), utilizing a *lingua franca* understood and accepted by all Presbyterian debaters. And therein lay the key to both his brilliant rhetorical strategy and to the resulting confusion among his conservative opponents. It was precisely his Baconian-sounding appeal to the "hard facts" of the real world that masked the profound intellectual dichotomies that had called forth the debate in the first place, and that left the Princetonians genuinely confused as to how he could profess such orthodox, scientific principles and yet arrive at such heterodox, unscientific conclusions.[19]

Briggs's article offered, in fine, both a summary of his concerns as a biblical critic, and a clearly enunciated apologia for the methods and values of the new critical world view. The body of the article consisted of a close historical examination of the place of "critical principles" in theological systems deriving from the Reformation — itself a "great critical revival." Indeed, the Reformation revolt against the identification of historically conditioned theological systems with divine revelation should have illustrated to all Protestant scholars the constant need for a critical examination of new theories claiming divine warranty. And among such new theories Briggs placed the Princeton doctrines of verbal inspiration and the original autographs:

> The course of religious history has clearly established the principle that there is a constant tendency in all religions, and especially in the Christian religion, to constrain the Symbol as well as the Scriptures into the requirements of a particular formative principle and the needs of a particular epoch. Not infrequently the constructed system becomes an idol of the theologian and his pupils, as if it were the Divine Truth.[20]

Briggs thus argued, on the basis of the "hard facts" of the Reformed past, that the Princeton doctrine of inspiration (and by implication the larger part of the Princeton theology itself) was just such an idol. It was precisely on the ancient Reformation principles of *sola scriptura* and *sola fide*, over against the "Roman Catholic principle of the supremacy of tradition," that modern evangelical criticism rejected the unhistorical and unscriptural doctrines being advanced out of Princeton:

> It simply will not do to antagonize the critical theories of the Bible with traditional theories, for the critic appeals to history *against* tradition, to an array of facts *against* so-called inferences. History, facts and truth are all Divine products, and must prevail.[21]

Briggs allowed that the theory of *plenary* inspiration, which he had learned from his own mentor, Henry Boynton Smith, and had taught since his own seminary days, was far less exact and concrete than Princeton's theory. But the plenary theory — interpreting inspiration and divine infallibility to extend only to the inward, *spiritual* sense of Scripture, and not to its external words and meanings — represented a far more faithful witness to the true catholic doctrine. The plenary theory, moreover, offered a better tool for dealing with the results of modern science, which *had*, in fact, found numerous errors in Scripture.[22]

But implicit in this appeal to the Reformed and Puritan past, as well as in the appeal to "modern science," was a historicist understanding of reality inaccessible to those against whom those charges were directed. Briggs offered an understanding of reality in which all human institutions and ideals, including the church's formulations of divine truth, changed *of necessity*, precisely because they took form in history. But the lack of genuine communication underlying Briggs's charges was compounded by his firm belief that his own relativistic approach to the monuments of the religious past, whatever its scientific worth, was an intrinsic part of the Reformed tradition itself.

Briggs claimed for his own decidedly historicist approach to the question of biblical authority and inspiration no less an authority than the clerk of the Westminster Assembly himself, John Wallis. The Scriptures, Wallis had written, were "lamps, vessels of a most holy character," but vessels that had come into contact with "human weakness, ignorance, prejudice and folly." Briggs thus contended that to identify the external, *written* word of Scripture with the *immanent*, saving Word contained therein, and to rest scriptural authority on the puerile denial of "one proven error" in the written records, was a denial of the Confession of Faith. The revival of true evangelical religion, towards which all Protestant scholars worked, would come not from the acceptance of the unscientific and unscriptural theories of Hodge and Warfield. Such a revival rather depended on "a revival of the evangelical life and unfettered thought of the Reformation and of the Puritans of the first half of the 17th century," a revival that only the new critical methods could effect.[23]

Briggs's article thus represented a skillful and politically astute attempt to baptize historical criticism into the evangelical cause by claiming that criticism as an intrinsic part of the evangelical Calvinist tradition. But Briggs's article had likewise revealed, in its very oversights, the deep fissures that now appeared in the foundations of the American evangelical establishment. It had failed to address the fact that Hodge and Warfield had presented the literal understanding of biblical infallibility held by most English-speaking evangelicals. His article had likewise failed to admit that, even if Hodge and Warfield labored under the "fallacy of misplaced concreteness" in their biblical theory (as some recent historians have charged), they had nonetheless faithfully argued for Scripture's authority on sound and widely shared, if now problematic, *scientific* principles.

Briggs's article thus offered documentary proof of the yawning intellectual chasm between the commonsense presuppositions of Hodge and Warfield, and the historicist model of reality presupposed by Briggs, where truth manifested itself in constantly changing historical forms. As noteworthy, then, as the force and brilliance of the arguments presented by the two "sides" in the exchange, was the lack of any real engagement between them. Two self-contained universes of discourse collided in the pages of the *Presbyterian Review*, a collision whose larger implications for American evangelical culture were yet to appear.

The exchange of the first two articles in the *Review* debate had been closely watched by evangelicals of all denominations, and following his rebuttal to Hodge and Warfield, Briggs received the accolades of the modernist pantheon. Robertson Smith himself wrote to Briggs, noting that his American supporter's brilliant arguments had "made the extreme conservative position now visibly untenable." Crawford Toy, Southern Baptist martyr to the cause of higher criticism, sent Briggs hearty congratulations on having "struck a strong blow for liberty," and promised to "render any assistance" that he could. And Newman Smyth, the early standard-bearer of the progressive cause, congratulated Briggs for providing "a good historical lever under a mass of dogmatism." But Smyth also advised Briggs that his "historical argument might be followed up to advantage by an article setting forth the *true* Protestant principle."[24]

Smyth's advice seems to have been decisive for Briggs, for after the publication of four more, rather unremarkable, articles in this debate, Briggs decided to supplement his "good historical lever" with a second article, published in January 1883. "A Critical Study of the History of the Higher Criticism," like his earlier essay in the exchange, was a sophisticated fusion of church history, biblical exegesis, and denominational polemics.[25]

But Briggs's second article also marked a crucial moment in the debate, and a decisive turning point in Briggs's own career, for in it he clearly and decisively stated that which he had only adumbrated in previous works: that the new "paradigm" of historical criticism clearly offered to American evangelicals a better understanding of how God worked in history than the older Baconian model. Because Briggs believed that historical criticism merely represented in more detailed scientific form the working out of the "critical spirit" of the Reformation itself, he set forth a detailed historical reconstruction of Pentateuchal criticism from Calvin to Crawford Toy and Robertson Smith.[26]

Briggs contended that his detailed account of the development of Pentateuchal criticism among evangelical scholars underscored the "providential emergence" of historical criticism within Protestant culture. And this emergence offered concrete support for the ancient Christian hope of that day when the Word of God, freed from the corruptions of dead traditions, would shine with such power and strength that it would effect the coming of "the Kingdom of our Lord, and hasten the realization of our blessed hope, the coming of the Messiah in glory."[27]

"The History of the Higher Criticism" was followed in the next issue by the eighth and last article for the series, written by Princeton's warhorse in matters disputative, Francis L. Patton. Patton, himself the veteran of numerous bloody denominational battles (most famously, the David Swing heresy trial in Chicago a decade before), was clearly equal to Briggs on the debate floor and his "summation article" for the exchange witnessed to this. "The Dogmatic Aspect of Pentateuchal Criticism" noted with approval that all the contributors from both "sides" had rejected Wellhausen's purely naturalistic theory of biblical composition; moreover, all contributors had likewise sought verification for their views in the Westminster standards, as all good Calvinists were bidden to do. Further, Patton allowed that *probably* all the contributors advanced their protestations of orthodoxy and denominational loyalty in good faith, sincerely believing that they were working for the same evangelical goals.[28]

But protestations of loyalty, and even good faith underlying such protestations, did not orthodox Presbyterians make. Subscription to the Westminster standards imposed very clear limitations on the hermeneutical explorations of Reformed scholars, limitations that were violated by "any opinion inconsistent with the inerrancy of Scripture, or belief in the non-Mosaic authorship of the Pentateuch." Patton thus joined Hodge and Warfield in offering a "commonsense" explication of the Westminster standards. To continue to appeal to those standards while advocating theories that they were erected to demolish was, at best, an insidious confusion of the meaning of language, and, at worst, a cabal to undermine the unchangeable truths to which those standards witnessed.[29]

There was little doubt in either Princeton or New York who Patton had in mind as the unnamed object of his journalistic wrath. Briggs's disingenuous claims of upholding the tradition of the Westminster divines while denying what most conservatives thought of as basic parts of that tradition — like the Mosaic authorship of the Pentateuch and the verbal inerrancy of Scripture — seemed to Patton an unconscionable overturning of the canons of common sense. And indeed, by Patton's standard of common sense, Briggs was doing just that. The true, underlying issue of the debate — an issue on which an entire intellectual culture rested — was hence left unaddressed by either Briggs or his opponents at Princeton.

Thus had the *Presbyterian Review*, with the close of the "Robertson Smith debate" in the spring of 1883, both announced and abetted a conflict that would mark the history of American evangelicalism for the next half century. It had revealed the profound epistemological differences that had developed within the evangelical camp itself, differences that underlay and informed the host of discrete doctrinal and political issues over which "fundamentalists" and "modernists" would divide in the next generation. The debate had revealed with special poignancy the lack of engagement that would characterize future discussions between liberals and conservatives — a breakdown of shared feelings and values that itself would lead to further charges of ill-will and conspiracy. Most importantly, the *Review* debate had revealed, in the very lack of intellectual engagement that characterized its exchanges, the real issue that underlay all the spiritual battles of the Gilded Age, informing all the confrontations over Bible, creed, and doctrine. Beneath those conflicts lay an ineffable but pervasive sense that the very possibility of divine communication with humankind was now deeply problematic, problematic in a way that had no precedent in the Christian tradition. That tradition now seemed in imminent danger of collapse, and both "sides" rushed to place it on firmer, if no longer shared, high ground.

Whither?

If the debate in the pages of the *Review* had constituted both an announcement and an overview of the crises to come, it also revealed something of the confusion among evangelical Protestants generally as to how, and where, to meet the challenges of the new critical methods and world view. Briggs himself initially believed that the passions generated in the *Review* debate marked biblical criticism as the arena where the contest would be most closely fought, and thus turned his attention to explicating (and defending) the higher criticism in more extended, detailed form. *Biblical Study*, the first published product of his new resolve, was the result of a summer's efforts at collating and synthesizing previously written articles and addresses into a comprehensive monograph. And although almost the entire work had already appeared in various published forms, the book represented a landmark in American biblical scholarship in its comprehension, critical sophistication, and popular accessibility. It likewise witnessed to a synthesis of biblical and historical exegesis that would inform Briggs's scholarship for four decades:

> True progress in theology is to be found in the working out of the principles of the Reformation and of Puritanism, in carrying them on to higher and grander results. It has been a constant aim of this book to call attention to these principles, and to the methods of Biblical Study based upon them, and to explain the doctrine of the Bible in the chief Puritan symbol, the Westminster Confession.[30]

The working out of those Puritan principles for the modern age, Briggs announced, depended on the method of knowledge known as "criticism," a method implicit in the Protestant world view itself, but recently buried beneath a false scientific method and a defective epistemology. The foolhardy Baconian trust in the unaided processes of human reasoning and in the "plain evidence of the senses" was, in fact, a deeply un-Protestant approach to knowledge. Basic to the entire Reformed world view was the firm belief in the fallen nature of both humankind itself and of its perceptions.[31]

Briggs assured his readers that the daunting critical approach to Scripture outlined in the book's first chapter simply enabled modern evangelical Christians to appropriate and experience *immediately* what all the Reformers had likewise experienced, without the accretions of the intervening centuries: the voice of God speaking directly to believers in the Word. The elaborate linguistic and hermeneutical methods applied by biblical criticism simply sought to recover the "formal principle of the Reformation," *sola scriptura* — the witness of God's Spirit in the written Word, freed from human invention and human error. It was this *internal* witness of God's Spirit, uncovered for modern believers through the methods of historical criticism, and not the *external* witness of the church, of tradition, or of creedal formulation, that assured to Christians the authority, inerrancy, and authenticity of Scripture.[32]

Biblical Study represented Briggs's first, and most successful, apologia for the evangelical use of higher criticism in interpreting the Bible. George Foote Moore's review of the work in the *Andover Review* was typical of the warm if unexceptional reception accorded the book by progressives. Moore applauded Briggs's "manly and strong defense of the right of criticism," and noted that the latter's defense of that right had "the more weight because his views on most critical questions are so conservative." But the response from the other side of the theological fence was likewise "warm" and unexceptional. The book provoked widespread notice and even some sharp criticism from conservatives, but it sparked no general controversy. T. W. Chambers expressed the critical but somewhat bemused conservative sentiments well in his hostile notice of the book in the *Presbyterian Review*. Briggs was, he derisively remarked, "full of cheerful hope that much was still to be learned from the Scriptures by patient study." There would doubtless be new utterances, Chambers confessed, "but it will only be because they are not true."[33]

Thus, despite *Biblical Study*'s "advanced" positions on biblical inspiration, inerrancy, and composition — positions that Briggs would replicate almost verbatim eight years later in his famous inaugural address at Union Seminary — the explosion that such a frontal attack on America's "biblical civilization" should have evoked simply failed to materialize. After several (expected) critical notices, denominational conservatives turned to other, far more immediate and dangerous, critical efforts as the targets for their wrath, while progressive evangelicals lauded the book and then quickly forgot about it.

Indeed, the lack of controversy following the book's publication would have profoundly upset Briggs's political campaign for the historico-critical cause had he not already turned his efforts to other more politically volatile issues that would bring that cause more publicity than he dared dream. Briggs himself would later dismiss the theory of the "higher critical basis" of the theological conflagration that would soon grip American evangelical culture generally, and the northern Presbyterian church specifically, with the observation that

> in fact, the Presbyterian Church was deliberately thrown into a panic about the Bible in order to defeat the revision movement. I was only an incident in this warfare. Circumstances made me the convenient target on which to concentrate the attack. In all respects this conspiracy was successful: the revision movement was defeated.[34]

As recent historians have labored to document, trans-Atlantic theological trends played a critical role in the intellectual life of Gilded Age America, and the Free Church of Scotland contributed more than its share of issues to the debates that troubled the previously serene waters of American evangelical thought during that time. Indeed, some years before the Robertson Smith affair claimed their attention, American evangelicals began to hear of fierce debates over creedal revision exercising the Scottish Kirk, debates the more startling because of the notoriously conservative, confessionalist spirit of that communion. But the intellectual heritage of the Scottish Enlightenment — a heritage of vigorous critical inquiry — no less than the emergence of modern cultural sensibilities offended at many of the "harsh" doctrines expounded by the Westminster Confession, had raised serious questions in the Free Kirk about the ability of the Westminster symbols to meet the moral demands of a new age.[35]

More specifically, many Free Kirk Presbyterians felt the Westminster standards to be woefully deficient (if not altogether silent) on central Christian doctrines, especially on God's love for all humankind. It was while engaged in debating if and how these overlooked doctrines were to find creedal expression that the Free Church's General Assembly affirmed, in 1866, that no creedal statement (even its own beloved Westminster Confession) "can ever be regarded by the Church as final or permanent," for all churches must "lie open always to the teaching of the Divine Spirit."[36]

The Free Kirk's sudden interest in remedying the oversights of the Westminster Confession might have remained a purely Scottish concern had it not been for the energetic American Presbyterian involvement in the meetings of the "Alliance of Reformed Churches throughout the World Holding the Presbyterian System." This new international council of Reformed churches sought a more realistic (and orthodox) basis on which to found the growing ecumenical impulse among Protestants than the older and more inclusive Evangelical Alliance, just then entering a prolonged identity crisis.[37]

The first General Council of the new Reformed Alliance, meeting in Edinburgh under Free Church auspices in 1877, gave the questions of revision and creedal subscription a new immediacy when the representatives of the fifty-odd Presbyterian churches began discussions on the "distinctively Reformed" doctrinal system that underlay their various confessions. The Babel that ensued on the floor of the assembly led to the startling realization that most of the European Presbyterian churches belonging to the alliance had already revised either the confession itself or their terms of subscription to it.[38]

American Presbyterians, having thus encountered the revision question firsthand in the meetings of the alliance, soon began discussing the possibility of revising their own standards. No less a watchdog of Calvinist orthodoxy than Archibald Hodge himself included a detailed discussion of the "import" of the British revision movements for American Presbyterianism in his *Commentary on the Confession of Faith*. Likewise, even non-Presbyterian publications like the notoriously liberal *Andover Review* (usually bemused by Scottish confessional goings-on) reported with keen interest the impact of the British revision controversies on American Reformed bodies.[39]

But it was the *Presbyterian Review* that gave the Scottish revision issue currency among American evangelicals. Its regular coverage of the progress of the "ecumenical presbyterianism" of the alliance, and its detailed reports on the revision debates preoccupying almost all British Reformed bodies, offered American readers a steady stream of information on the progress of the issue.

Briggs himself wrote the *Review* notice of the second alliance meeting in Philadelphia in 1881, a notice that was largely descriptive and unexceptional. But if Briggs's reflections on the 1881 alliance meeting went largely unnoticed, his report on the third meeting of the alliance in 1884 caused considerably more disquiet in the denomination. His notice of that Belfast meeting, in fact, alerted denominational conservatives to his new political (and scholarly) strategy for incorporating historical criticism into the American evangelical cause.[40]

Briggs observed in the 1884 notice that the "consensus" issue remained the most pressing question before the Belfast council, as in many ways it remained the most pressing theological issue before all Presbyterian churches. How could this *not* be the case, he asked, as it involved the central question of what the church believed? Further, the resolution of this politically volatile issue remained dependent on evangelical scholars who alone could provide the "critical expertise" necessary for the project:

> There are few who have the patience to study the Confessions [of member churches] in their historical circumstances, and to interpret them by the legitimate methods of historical interpretation. There are not a dozen divines in the Presbyterian world at present who have such a knowledge of the Westminster divines, and the historical forces that generated and produced the Standards, that can speak with the necessary authority on these mooted questions.[41]

These ostensibly neutral editorial reflections, in fact, appeared positively ominous to the Old School faction in light of Briggs's own recent scholarly publications. For in the first months of 1884 Briggs had revealed a new focus for his critical studies in a series of eight articles published in the New York *Evangelist*. These articles, devoted entirely to the history of colonial Puritanism, were widely perceived as a conscious political move by Briggs to document and publicize his earlier claim of being the "first authority" in America on the Reformed past. Even more ominous in the eyes of the conservatives, however, were Briggs's "reflections" on his summer's research in the Puritan library collections of Britain, published as "The Principles of Puritanism." These reflections evinced the kind of magisterial tone and apodictic style that clearly announced Briggs's arrival on the Presbyterian political scene as the preeminent American authority on Reformed confessional history.[42]

Briggs's obvious bid for political power within the denomination with these scholarly works on Reformed creedal history, however, did not go either unnoticed or unopposed. Archibald A. Hodge himself had been monitoring for some time Briggs's extended "scientific" forays into Presbyterianism's confessional and constitutional history. As an accomplished master of both Presbyterian constitutional history and of the Baconian method, Hodge offered his own, very different, reading of both the church's confessional history and the modern revision question. "The Consensus of the Reformed Confessions" presented Hodge's own interpretation of this sudden interest in, and appeal to, the development of the Reformed creeds. Such appeals, he announced — "ostensibly for the sake of Presbyterian unity and evangelical truth" — actually masked heterodox impulses desiring to be "relieved from the pressure of the old creeds," and evinced a cowardly "restlessness under the obligation of subscription." These restless impulses, Hodge declared, could have no better refutation than a truly scientific study of the confessional history of the church, and he offered in the article a short course therein.[43]

But as the earlier *Review* debate had already manifested, both science and the past constituted something quite different for Hodge than for Charles Briggs. Hodge's scientific study of the Reformed past, in fact, uncovered not an evolving, developmental pattern of confessional truth, but an almost mathematically exact identity of creedal witness, in churches of widely differing cultural and intellectual backgrounds, to the same doctrinal system that he had already drawn in his own *Commentary on the Confession*. A consensus could indeed be constructed from the resulting system, a consensus with a scientifically "verifiable character, which may be discerned with certainty and defined with precision," but it would be indistinguishable from the confession to which the American church already subscribed.[44]

Francis Patton likewise joined forces with Hodge in marking off the conservatives' position on creedal "development" and revision, if on a less abstract and more political level. Patton enunciated a clear warning on behalf of the conservatives in the *Review's*

annual notice of the northern church's General Assembly. Overture number thirteen, from the Washington City Presbytery, had
in fact requested from the assembly a constitutional revision of
the confession's twenty-fourth chapter, a "pastoral" chapter forbid-
ding remarriage after the desertion of one's spouse. Allowing that
the overture undoubtedly proceeded from the highest of pastoral
motives, Patton nonetheless warned that

> as the mode of effecting the slightest amount of the Confession in-
> volves the mode of effecting an entire revision of the Confession,
> the Assembly acted very wisely in declining to take initiative in a
> matter which would be very apt to involve troublesome debate, and
> might possibly end in litigation.[45]

Warfield and Patton had thus signaled the conservatives' resolve
to stand by an unrevised Confession of Faith, at the very least to
the extent of preventing "troublesome" debate and litigation. But
they had also signaled the fact that the issue of creedal revision, at
least as much as that of biblical criticism, touched a conservative
nerve very close to the bone. Indeed, many of the best minds of the
Presbyterian church were coming to recognize in the revision issue,
more clearly than in any other, the potential arena for the dreaded
conflict between seventeenth-century orthodoxy and nineteenth-
century science and criticism, a conflict that appeared to be seeking
a "cause" to set off full-scale denominational warfare.

The fearsome intellectual challenges once neatly contained in
theological exchanges between academics, on a gentlemanly and restrained level, now threatened to erupt into the broad plain of worship. The prize at issue was no longer some disembodied "right" of
biblical scholars to incorporate varying amounts of criticism into
their interpretations of Scripture, interpretations generally con-
fined to seminary classrooms. Rather, the focus of debate now
centered on a doctrinal statement, to be used catechetically and
liturgically, of what and how the American Presbyterian church
received divine truth.[46]

The suspicions of Hodge and Patton as to Briggs's political
strategy proved to be well founded, for in January 1885, Briggs's
essay on the "Principles of Puritanism" appeared as the preface to
American Presbyterianism. The monograph following that preface

revealed the scope and brilliance of Briggs's critical expertise, and brought Briggs the political influence within the counsels of the church that he sought. But it also established Briggs, at least in the eyes of certain elements in the church, as an extremely dangerous man who would have to be carefully watched.

American Presbyterianism constituted a watershed in American denominational historiography in its use of primary sources, in its sophisticated critical apparatus, and in its insight into the impulses that created distinctively "American" redactions of European churches. It likewise offered a brilliant reconstruction of American Presbyterianism's past, outlining a historiographic pattern of the church's origins that would be followed by all subsequent studies of the denomination. Briggs argued that the American Presbyterian tradition emerged out of the institutional synthesis of two major streams of Calvinist spirituality — the revivalistic, evangelical piety of New England–based "Presbygationalists," and the staunchly orthodox confessionalism of Scotch-Irish immigrants.[47]

But underlying the book's painstaking scholarship and often brilliant interpretative analysis was a quite specific *political* agenda, an agenda that announced Briggs's emergence as a major player on the field of denominational politics. Basic to Briggs's historiographic purposes in the book, in fact, was an almost transparent political move to win American Presbyterians to the cause of creedal revision. Such a victory would be brought about by using the historico-critical methodology to elucidate the Adopting Act of 1729, the centerpiece of the entire five-hundred-page monograph. That act had effected the historic compromise over subscription to the Westminster Confession that had enabled the New England and the Scotch-Irish factions of the colonial church to unite into one body.[48]

The 1729 act had rejected *both* loose and strict subscription to the confession in favor of a formula that demanded only that ministerial candidates accept the Westminster standards as containing "in all essential and necessary articles the system of doctrine contained in the Scriptures." What constituted the "essential and necessary articles" had varied, of course, from period to period and from presbytery to presbytery; such was precisely the point. The founders of the American church had recognized from the very beginning that all creedal symbols *more* or *less* approximated scriptural truth, and that thus no creed could command absolute conformity. Indeed, the founders of the American church had allowed sufficient room within the terms of ministerial subscription to allow consciences to disagree with specific points of the confession, until such time as that confession could be revised.[49]

Implicit in the Adopting Act's distinction between the standards and the "essential doctrines" which they contained, Briggs observed, was a healthy Calvinist distrust of identifying any creed, even one as excellent as the Westminster Confession, with biblical truth:

> Would that that agreement in the *essential* and *necessary* articles of the Westminster Standards had ever prevented strife and disunion on account of differences with respect to unessential and unnecessary articles! *This* act is the pivot of the history of the American Presbyterian Church.[50]

More than *Biblical Study* or his articles for the *Review* debate, *American Presbyterianism* genuinely alarmed denominational conservatives, for it offered a far more politically volatile application of critical methods to the religious past. The "true American party" that had carried the day in 1729 and since — the party of Francis Mackemie, of the Tennents, and of Jonathan Dickinson — had resolutely (and largely successfully) opposed the type of confessionalist "strict subscriptionism" to the external *form* of the Westminster Confession that antirevisionists seemed to favor.[51]

In the spring of 1888, the Presbytery of Nassau (Long Island) quite unconsciously initiated the theological trauma that had been well rehearsed in the pages of the *Presbyterian Review*. That April the Nassau Presbytery overtured the General Assembly for revision of the third chapter of the Confession of Faith. Unlike the overture initiated four years previously by the Washington City Presbytery, however, the offending chapter did not address pastoral, bureaucratic, or constitutional issues, but rather the central Calvinist doctrines of the predestination and effectual calling of God's elect. Like the Scottish Free Church two decades before, the Nassau Presbytery announced that the doctrines contained in that chapter overemphasized God's sovereignty and power at the expense of God's love, and that as constituted, it "assaulted the sensibilities of good Christians."[52]

Overture number forty-five from the Nassau Presbytery, quite predictably, stunned everyone on the assembly's Committee on Bills and Overtures, to whom it was remanded for consideration and action. The committee was composed of seasoned church officers — denominational politicians adept at recognizing potential problem issues — who immediately recognized in the overture the makings of an issue that could conceivably destroy the fragile confessional bonds that held together the reunited church. After a series of hurried (and harried) conferences, the committee recommended to the assembly that "it be deemed inexpedient to take any action upon this request," a recommendation that was overwhelmingly (and gratefully) accepted by the assembly. The assembly, moreover, quickly referred it to the next General Assembly, by which time they sincerely hoped that the Nassau Presbytery could be reasoned with.[53]

The sigh of denominational relief, however, was short-lived. The Nassau Presbytery, heretofore a quiet and moderate church court, circulated letters throughout the following year to all the presbyteries in the church, urging support for confessional revision. By the meeting of the next General Assembly, fifteen other presbyteries had likewise taken up the revision cause, overturing the assembly for revision of other "doctrinal chapters" of the confession as well. The assembly's Committee on Bills and Overtures now realized that any possibility of burying or re-referring the question was impossible, and recommended to the assembly that it officially overture all the presbyteries of the church, asking them if they desired a revision of the Confession of Faith, and, "if so, in what respects and to what extent?"[54]

The overture of the General Assembly of 1889 to the two hundred and nine presbyteries of the northern church set off a paper war that, in both volume and ferocity, was unrivaled in American Presbyterian (and perhaps evangelical) history. General religious periodicals like the New York *Evangelist*, the *Independent*, and the *Interior*, as well as distinctively denominational journals like the *Presbyterian Banner* and the *Herald and Presbyter*, were substantially transformed into debate arenas for the revision controversy, making Warfield, Briggs, Patton, and Henry Van Dyke household names across the nation.[55]

Charles Briggs, in contrast to most of the delegates at the 1889 General Assembly, was jubilant over Nassau Presbytery's overture. For Briggs saw in the creedal revision issue the most immediate, practical opportunity to present the needed scientific theology in a form accessible to church-going Christians, while reconstructing the entire Reformed doctrinal system along more critical, modern lines.[56]

The Politics of Truth

In September 1889, Charles Briggs published what may well represent his most famous (and most widely feared) scholarly work. *Whither?*, both in tone and content, read like a tract for the times, a tract that firmly wed the relativism and evolutionary values of the historicist world view to the cause of Reformed orthodoxy itself. The book identified the confessionalist "betrayers" of that orthodoxy by name. Indeed, the most powerful sections of the book were those that portrayed antirevisionists (like the Hodges) as unwittingly caught in the meshes of the historical process and its attendant relativities while making embarrassingly unscientific claims for "immutable truths." Their alarming departures from orthodoxy in theories like verbal inspiration, in fact, constituted a doctrinal betrayal of that core insight of Reformed theology that recognized "how greatly the truth of God transcends human knowledge." Orthodoxy was rather "variable and progressive, partial and incomplete." Thus, "for all practical purposes, Orthodoxy and Progressive Orthodoxy are convertible terms."[57]

The stance of the confessionalists was not that of orthodoxy at all, Briggs announced, despite all of their heated claims; it was rather a position profoundly opposed to orthodoxy, a position Briggs labeled "orthodoxism":

> Orthodoxism is unwilling to learn; it is haughty and arrogant, assuming the divine prerogatives of infallibility and inerrancy; it hates all truth that is unfamiliar to it, and persecutes it to the uttermost.... [Orthodoxism] refuses to accept the discoveries of science or the facts of history on the pretense that [these] conflict with the ortho-

doxy of the standards, preferring the traditions of man to the truth of God.[58]

But what made the book the most influential, and the most feared, of Briggs's career was not his application of highly memorable epithets like "orthodoxism" to the positions of leading denominational figures like the Hodges (although such epithets, peppered throughout the work, undoubtedly contributed to the book's almost immediate popular success). Rather, Presbyterians of all parties, and evangelicals generally, purchased the book faster than Scribners could reprint it because Briggs had provided an engaging and lucid exposition, accessible to the educated but nonspecialized lay person, of critical theological issues that preoccupied the evangelical conscience.

Whither? promised to explain, in language that a passionately interested but technically untutored reading public could understand, why creedal revision on the basis of the new historico-critical methods was the only course that could preserve the Reformed evangelical tradition in a new age. Borrowing heavily from his history of American Presbyterianism, Briggs documented how the revision of all creedal standards in America had been "so thoroughgoing that it was revolutionary." Using Princeton's standard of an unchanged confessional tradition as normative for Reformed orthodoxy, Briggs proceeded to show how the fathers of the American Presbyterian tradition had "betrayed" the intentions of the Westminster divines in radically revising all the standards to meet the new conditions found in America. But such a betrayal, Briggs argued, proceeded from a profoundly scriptural impulse: to jettison all tools, even excellent ones like the Directory for Worship, that stood in the way of an effective gospel ministry. The true "orthodox" Presbyterian position — illustrated in the lives of Mackemie, the Tennents, Edwards, and Dickinson — had thus been pragmatic and progressive throughout its history of preaching the gospel.[59]

Briggs presented his own position on creedal revision, moreover, as a model of these pragmatic and progressive virtues that had always defined true Presbyterian spirituality. A revision of the creed in both form and content, he announced, could only aid the cause of Reformed orthodoxy, while likewise facilitating what

Briggs now considered the "great burning question of the day" — Christian unity:

> The Westminster Standards are the banners of Protestantism, but they did not claim infallibility, inerrancy, or completion. They did not propose to speak the final word in theology. The only hope of a reconciliation of differences and a removal of errors is by advance into the whole truth of religion, doctrine, and morals. Theological progress is not in the direction of simplicity, but of variety and complexity.[60]

The review of the book in the Princeton-based *Presbyterian Quarterly* gave classic expression to the fears that *Whither?* aroused among conservatives. The reviewer acknowledged that Briggs's book undoubtedly was the most widely read evangelical work to appear in America for some time, having been "reviewed by more periodicals of all denominations than any other publication in years." Further, it was a work that "hundreds of intelligent people who had not the requisite scholarship to appreciate his previous studies will read with avidity." But these observations were not offered as positive points. Rather, it was precisely these points that constituted the chief reason why the work was so dangerous. The book "contained enough truth to make its errors dangerous" among the masses who read it. Indeed, Briggs's entire book witnessed in vivid and frightening fashion to the result of applying the "scientific" methods being advocated by Briggs and his supporters to the most cherished symbols and records of the religious past. What was evident in the exercise, in fact, was that the *real* intention of Dr. Briggs and his cohorts was not the revision of the standards at all; rather, "Dr. Briggs has undertaken to write the Presbyterian Church out of existence."[61]

But *Whither?* represented a challenge that threatened not only the fragile bonds that united the faction-ridden northern Presbyterian church, but those even more fragile bonds that united the editorial board of the *Presbyterian Review*. Relations between the two managing editors had been deteriorating for some time before the tensions generated by the revision controversy and especially by *Whither?* found expression in an editorial difference of opinion that resulted in the demise of the *Review*.

By 1889 the Princeton managing editorship had devolved upon

Benjamin B. Warfield, Hodge having resigned the position for reasons of health, and Hodge's successor in the position, Francis Patton, having resigned to take over the presidency of Princeton College. But Warfield manifested in his new editorial position neither Hodge's irenic temperament nor Patton's dynamic energy; what he did manifest was a growing apprehension over his Union co-editor's political campaigns in the denomination. At least since the *Review* debate six years before, Warfield had viewed with mounting alarm Briggs's ever more militant attempts to win the denomination for the new critical methods.[62]

There had already been a brief published debate between Briggs and Warfield on the revision issue, a debate that had reached a dangerous level of unpleasantness for two seminary professors within the same communion. But a new level of acrimony between the two men was reached in May of 1889, when Briggs delivered to his Princeton co-editor the draft of his notice of the recent General Assembly. Briggs was immediately informed by Warfield that the editorial arrangement by which the *Review*'s notice of the assembly had always been exchanged would simply have to be discontinued. The revision issue that had occupied the central place in the General Assembly's proceedings was simply too important to both sides, and "we in Princeton are touched very closely by the agitation on the subject, and we wish to be fairly, fully and equally represented on it in the Review."[63]

Princeton was touched far more closely on the subject than Warfield admitted in his missive to Briggs, a fact borne out in the fate of the *Review* itself. The October 1889 number of the *Presbyterian Review* did indeed carry only one editorial notice of the recent General Assembly, penned as planned by Briggs. That notice observed that the revision question constituted the most important issue to come before the church since the reunion of 1870; he went on to say that, in relation to the revisionist movement,

> opposition is so slight, and support so hearty, that it would appear that the movement has already assumed great dimensions, especially among the younger and more silent members of the Presbyteries.[64]

But if Briggs appeared to be the victor in the editorial battle over the *Review*'s official notice of the assembly, who was the victor

of the larger editorial war over the revision issue in general was by
no means as clear. For the entire October number was given over
to consideration of that thorny issue. All parties were heard on the
issue, an ironic and poignant fact, as the October 1889 number of
the *Review* proved to be the last. On October 4, Briggs tendered
his resignation as managing editor to the Union Seminary faculty,
citing irreconcilable differences with his managing co-editor over
editorial policy; the Union faculty in turn voted unanimously to
withdraw from the journal's publication, an action repeated a few
days later in Princeton.[65]

On the issue of creedal revision, communication between
Union and Princeton had thus broken down entirely, and it was
after that breakdown that the events leading directly to the Briggs
trial gathered momentum. The sedate Presbyterian Social Union
of New York — more gentlemen's club than debating society —
decided near the close of 1889 that the revision issues exercising
the church should be presented to them by the leading figures in
the debate. Both Charles Briggs and Francis Patton (substituting
for an ailing Warfield) were invited by the union to present their
views before it on the evening of December 2. On that historic
evening, Briggs and Patton offered cogent and impassioned statements of their respective positions. But Briggs, by common agreement among those present, seemed to carry the evening with what
amounted to a call to arms:

> We are in the beginnings of a theological reformation that can no
> more be resisted than the flood of a great river. It is one of those
> movements that are long in preparing, but suddenly burst forth with
> irresistible might.[66]

More important than the actual exchange on the evening of December 2, however, was the political use to which that exchange
was applied on the next evening. The *Mail and Express*, a non-
denominational secular paper under the firm editorial hand of a
deeply conservative Presbyterian layman, published a bitter editorial attack on both Union Seminary and Briggs as violators of
their ordination oaths to hold and teach true Presbyterian doctrine. Further, the paper sent copies of its editorial to leading
Presbyterian clergy and laity throughout the church, calling for

united action against Briggs and his institution at the next General Assembly.[67]

The rising polemical tide was aided in no small fashion by the unseemly spectacle of Presbyterian seminary professors rushing into publication to join in the fray. W. G. T. Shedd's *Proposed Revision of the Westminster Standards*, published early in the year, assailed both Briggs personally and the revisionist cause in general, while Princeton's James McCosh produced a sophisticated and masterfully argued satire on Briggs's work entitled *Whither? O Whither? Tell Me Where*. Briggs responded in kind with *How Shall We Revise the Westminster Confession?*, a collection of articles by various hands, the centerpiece of which was a revised form of Briggs's much-controverted Social Union address, now entitled "The Advance Towards Revision."[68]

As dangerous as his heightened polemical tone in the published form of the December address, moreover, was Briggs's presentation of a revised, and more politically feasible, plan for creedal revision. In view of the numerous difficulties in revising so synthetic a work as the confession, he now advocated a new, shorter creed. Such a "simple, devotional statement of our faith" would serve, not to displace the confession, but to stand beside it to express "the faith, life, and devotion of the present time, born of our experience and needs." Briggs thus outlined a proposal that sought to emulate the structure of the famed Adoption Act, formulating terms of subscription that embodied only those "essential and necessary doctrines" that all Presbyterians confessed as the core of their tradition.[69]

"The Advance Towards Revision," while lacking the scholarly breadth and rhetorical power of *Whither?*, nonetheless proved to be the most practically successful of all of Briggs's political efforts. Its concrete plan for a "simple, devotional statement of faith" gained almost immediate and widespread support within the church, support evinced at the General Assembly in May of that year. At that Saratoga, New York, meeting, one hundred and thirty-four presbyteries called for a revision of the Confession of Faith, and twenty-five presbyteries advanced models of a new and simpler "consensus creed" to stand beside the larger confession, models drawn directly from Briggs's article.[70]

The meteoric advance of the revision issue at Saratoga thus

appeared to most of the Old School faction to be a direct result of Briggs's critical efforts; indeed, those evangelical conservatives who had always proudly worn the sobriquet of "confessionalists" viewed the revision campaign under his direction as the last theological straw. It was now time for them to mount a massive campaign against Briggs and his "cause" before the next meeting of the General Assembly. Little did they dream, as they left Saratoga, that their campaign against Briggs and his critical methods would be most successfully pressed by Briggs himself. For on the evening of November 11, 1890, the Board of Directors of Union Seminary formally accepted the large donation offered by their chairman, Charles Butler, to establish a new chair at the seminary, to be named after Union's first scripture professor, Edward Robinson. The Board of Directors likewise accepted Butler's request that Charles Briggs, himself a student of Robinson's, be named the chair's first incumbent, and voted (in what they thought would be a routine administrative action) to transfer Briggs from the Davenport to the newly created Robinson Chair. Thus did the Board of Directors of the resolutely progressive Union Seminary create the means for defeating the most successful (and most feared) campaign for the cause of historical criticism in America.[71]

4

The Theological Crisis

The Authority of Holy Scripture

On the evening of January 20, 1891, Charles Augustus Briggs delivered one of the most famous inaugural addresses in American religious history, an address that has spawned a venerable historiographic tradition in its own right. And while the address indeed constituted a cultural and ecclesiastical "moment" of singular importance (thus justifying the historiographic attention bestowed on it), it is likewise important to note that the address represented both considerably more *and* less than the most famous manifesto for biblical criticism delivered in America.[1]

As in the "Robertson Smith debate" a decade earlier, biblical theology and exegesis formed the framework both for the address itself and for the subsequent disquiet in the northern Presbyterian church. But Briggs had delivered himself of far more radical (and offensive) opinions on biblical and exegetical questions both in the pages of the *Presbyterian Review* and in his exhaustive monograph on the subject, *Biblical Study*. Both the *Review* and that earlier monograph had presented Briggs's higher critical positions in great (indeed, voluminous) detail, and the conservative response to both had been deeply critical and disapproving. But that had been the response of more conservative, but nonetheless fellow, evangelicals. The ferocious and immediate response to Briggs's address, however, was radically different from the earlier conservative reaction.

In January 1891, the various factions of the evangelical mainstream, soon to divide into "modernists" and "fundamentalists," still generally claimed the unrent mantle of a culturally established evangelical Protestantism for all of their increasingly disparate redactions of the ancient faith. The northern Presbyterian church, itself representative of the embattled mainstream, shared this self-perception. For while the Old School and the New School factions could, and did, battle like theological cats and dogs the rest of the year, they nonetheless concluded their annual General Assembly by singing together, often tearfully, "Blest Be the Tie That Binds."[2]

This perduring sense of unity and cohesion within both the mainstream and the Presbyterian church, despite mounting evidence of an ever broader range of issues that divided them, was based on the widespread (indeed, almost universal) assumption that a common world view underlay and united all evangelicals. This world view informed and shaped even that most basic of evangelical principles voiced by Chillingworth two centuries before — that "the Bible, and the Bible alone, is the religion of Protestants." In fact, the cracks in this shared cultural and religious world view had already widened into fairly deep fissures by the last decade of the nineteenth century, a fact that had been revealed in grand fashion in the debate over biblical inspiration and authority a decade before in the *Presbyterian Review*. But that debate had also announced the fact that the continued sense of unity and cohesion — indeed, the very concept of an evangelical mainstream itself — depended on a perceptual lag between the sheer fact of division and the widespread recognition of it.

The events of the evening of January 20, 1891, went a long way towards demolishing that perceptual lag. As dramatically as any other event of the time — because of both the representative character of the Presbyterian church and the strategic position of Union Seminary itself — Briggs's inaugural address announced to the culture at large that the shared religious world view upon which a continued united identity among evangelicals depended had indeed collapsed, and that the civil war was well in progress. The impact of the address was further heightened because its subject — biblical authority — was of intense interest to all American Protestants.

On the evening of January 20, after solemnly declaring his acceptance of the Scriptures as the "only infallible rule of faith and practice," and of the Westminster Confession as containing "the system of doctrine taught in Holy Scripture," Charles Briggs delivered an address that lasted one hour and forty-five minutes, an address entitled "The Authority of Holy Scripture."[3]

Despite the title and ostensible subject matter of the address, however, actual consideration of biblical authority was broached only after an extended foray into other, more basic, concerns. Briggs opened his inaugural with the broad observation that the present age, more than any previous period, was

> in quest of certainty. Divine authority is the only authority to which man can yield implicit obedience. [But] the progress of criticism in our day has so undermined and destroyed the pillars of authority upon which former generations were wont to rest, that agnosticism seems to many the inevitable result of scientific investigation.[4]

Briggs asserted that the progress of criticism had rendered the "pillars of authority" of previous generations deeply problematic as a basis for religious knowledge and cultural authority. But that very same criticism offered to evangelicals firmer *scientific* ground for claims to theological certainty and to cultural and moral authority. Indeed, a theological world view based on the new historical criticism rested on the firmest evidence of all, the "testimony of human experience." The critical appropriation of the human past provided unassailable evidence that

> it is the testimony of human experience in all ages that God manifests Himself to men, and gives certainty of His presence and authority. There are historically three great fountains of divine authority — the Bible, the Church and the Reason.[5]

The hard facts of "scientific evidence," to which all good evangelicals had always appealed, were now being used by a fellow evangelical to make distinctly unevangelical-sounding claims for the "evidence of history" rather than for the evidence of Scripture itself. But Briggs further declared that "the majority of Christians from the apostolic age have found God through the Church." The church was a seat of divine authority, and "multitudes of pious souls in the present and the past have not been mistaken in their experience when they found God in the Church."[6]

But Briggs proceeded onto even thinner evangelical ice in his reflections on "The Authority of the Reason." Conceiving of reason in a broad sense to include the "metaphysical categories, the conscience, and the religious feeling," Briggs asserted that "here, in the Holy of Holies of human nature, God presents himself to those who seek him." There were those, Briggs knew, who would refuse rationalists a place in the company of the faithful; but those who did so forgot that the essential thing was "to find God and divine certainty." The church and even the Bible itself were "means and not ends; they are avenues to God, but not God."[7]

It was in the third section of his address, however, a section entitled "The Authority of Holy Scripture," that Briggs clearly and definitively revealed the historicist presuppositions of his distinctly environmentalist approach to salvation. The historical record, Briggs asserted, clearly showed that

> men are influenced by their temperaments and environments which of the three ways of access to God they may pursue. There are obstructions thrown up by the folly of men in each one of these avenues, and it is our duty as servants of the living God, to remove the stumbling-block out of the way of all earnest seekers after God, in the avenues most familiar to us.[8]

No one of the historical avenues to God, Briggs announced, had been "so obstructed as the Holy Bible, upon which Protestant Christianity builds its faith and life." Modern Christians could no longer approach the living Word except "through the breastworks of traditional dogmatism and the barriers of ecclesiasticism" — barriers that had been erected to protect the Word, when in fact they had betrayed it. Thus, as Scripture was the avenue to the divine most familiar to his listeners, and the one to whose study he would be committed in his new chair, Briggs announced that the remainder of his address would consider "The Barriers of Divine Authority in Holy Scripture." What became immediately obvious, however, was that the larger pattern of these barriers, as it began to emerge in the address, bore a striking resemblance to the Princeton theology.[9]

The "doctrines" of verbal inspiration, literal inerrancy, and "prophecy as minute prediction" — lately presented by Princeton Seminary as fundamental Christian truths — actually represented barriers to the divine Word. Against all such timid defenses, Briggs issued a clarion call, a call for a new critical vision of Christianity itself:

> Criticism is at work with knife and fire. Let us cut down everything that is dead and harmful, every kind of dead orthodoxy, every species of effete ecclesiasticism, all those dry and brittle fences that constitute denominationalism and are the barriers of Church Unity. Let us remove every encumbrance out of the way for a new life; the life of God is moving throughout Christendom, and the springtime of a new age is about to come upon us.[10]

Briggs adumbrated a gospel wherein the divine call to conform to the example of Christ reached humankind through various media, "depending on men's temperaments." This call, moreover, extended beyond history itself into a "Middle State" between death and the general resurrection. He likewise presented an "inspired and inerrant" Bible that nonetheless bore the marks of its composition within the historical process, making the critical efforts of evangelical scholars like himself absolutely necessary. And he outlined a system of "biblical ethics" in which the "Incarnation is the structural principle, [a system] built firmly upon the Bible and the Creeds, the History of Doctrine and the highest attainments of human reason."[11]

Briggs's address, in fact, represented a frontal assault on the older, two-story, religious world view, a world view that Briggs believed could no longer provide a viable intellectual framework for the evangelical cause. In its place Briggs offered a thoroughly scientific but deeply pious model of how God worked with humankind, a model set within the framework of "biblical theology" but outlining a far broader vision. The address outlined a historicist evangelical faith, wherein evolutionary, immanentist, and perfectionist concerns mixed in about equal proportions.

But for confessionalists in the audience and for other conservative evangelicals who would shortly read about it in journals across America, the address represented a shocking misuse of language and of the truths that language communicated. The ostensible "facts" presented by Briggs to demonstrate the authority of Holy Scripture bore little or no relation to the hard realities that Baconian science had offered to demonstrate a far more "unchastened" biblical authority. The address, then, was both shocking and nonsensical in about equal measure to educated and pious evangelicals who had been schooled in the inductive method.

But if many were disquieted by the address, a sizeable number of confessionalists were likewise overjoyed. Here was a way to defeat the "critical campaign" that appeared most likely to succeed — the seemingly irreversible campaign to revise the Confession of Faith. The address appeared as the perfect propaganda tool against the confessionalists' *bête noire*, Briggs himself — an uncomplicated tool for the folks in the pews that was easily disseminated and easily understood. Briggs, and the critical methods that he championed, they averred, had launched a frontal assault on the foundation of Protestant culture — the Bible itself.[12]

The Theological Crisis

The religious and the secular press immediately featured the address in a way that implied some "official" status for it, beginning on the morning after the inaugural. The morning edition of the New York *Tribune* for January 21 included both a long article on the "import" of Briggs's manifesto for evangelical religion in America, and two extended "letters of regret" over the episode from Princeton's William Henry Green and James McCosh. But the journalistic fever unleashed soon spread to other papers as well. The New York *Evangelist* announced that "no abstract can do any justice to its learning, comprehensiveness and eloquence" in setting forth the various avenues by which divine authority has *actually* manifested itself in history. The New York *Sun*, somewhat more interested in selling copy, rang out the alarm about "heresies (if they are heresies) spreading, and the laity being infected." The *Christian Intelligencer* predicted that the inaugural would "gladden the hearts of errorists of all sorts," while the *Independent* bemoaned its polemical tone, observing that it seemed "calculated to spread more darkness than light."[13]

Amidst the welter of conflicting journalistic coverage, it was generally overlooked at the time by the press that Briggs himself published an article that purported to explain the real import of his address, as well as the furor it set off. Briggs argued in "The Theological Crisis" that he had sought to elucidate a religious and cultural crisis that was essentially neither biblical nor creedal, but far more troubling. This crisis involved the recognition that traditional religious ways of conceiving the universe were no longer viable, and that an entirely new theological world view was called for:

> We stand on the heights of the last of the great movements of Christendom.... It must be evident to every thinking man that the traditional dogma has been battling against philosophy and science, history and every form of human learning.... There can be little doubt but that the traditional dogma is doomed. Shall it be allowed to drag down into perdition with it the Bible and the Creeds?[14]

Briggs asserted that the most important theological questions of the day were "beyond the range of orthodoxy itself," a state of intellectual affairs brought about by a new understanding of historical evolution and relativity. "Progress in doctrine and life is a necessary experience of a living church," and such progress never ceased until the church had attained its goal in the "knowledge of all the truth, in a holiness reflecting the purity and excellence of Jesus."[15]

Their age was a "period of transition" because modern evangelical scholars offered, over against "American dogmatic systems," a critical new *historical* theology, or rather a theology both critical and historical in a new way. The modern basis for proceeding in theology, Briggs announced, was no longer "dogmatic speculation" based on any of the older sources — Scripture, creed, or theological system. Rather, modern theology must proceed on the basis of that "given" upon which all modern scholarship proceeded, the facts of the historical process itself:

> The historian recognizes that men have found God in the Bible, the Church and the Reason. If this is so, it is evident that those who use the three media of communication with God, and use them to the

utmost, will be the most likely to attain the highest degree of union and communication with God.[16]

Battling against these scientific historians were those "blind guides" and irrational scientists who opposed the new critical methods, and proffered instead

> American dogmatic systems that depreciate the reason and then go to extremes in dogmatic speculation; that ignore Biblical theology and then search the Bible with a lantern for props for their dogma; that turn their backs on the historical church and then chase after every shadow of tradition — such systems are but castles in the air, schoolboys' bubbles, the delight of a body of ministers in a period of transition.[17]

Higher criticism, Briggs asserted, provided a dramatic example of how modern critical science could document, with incontrovertible scientific proof, God's ongoing revelation within history. Against this progressive critical program, especially in its higher critical form, "there is a rally of dogmaticians and traditionalists against those biblical and historical scholars who are aiming to dethrone *tradition* and put Holy Scripture and the creeds in their *proper* position of authority in the church." But the inevitable processes of theological evolution, Briggs announced, would relegate those opponents of the new theology to the past, where they seemed more at home. Indeed, the theological crisis was moving steadily onward to the next great phase of Christian history, thus promising the evangelical cause an even brighter future:

> The evolutions of Christian theology which have brought on the theological crisis are preparing the way for a new Reformation, in which it is probable that all the Christian churches will share; each one making its own important contribution to the worldwide movement whose goal is the unity of the church and the redemption of the world.[18]

It is noteworthy that Briggs himself contextualized the threat of higher criticism within a larger theological framework, the latter constituting the true "theological crisis." It is likewise revealing that Briggs identified ecumenism as one of the most important goals of the new critical theology, a goal that would eventually claim most of his scholarly energies. But most noteworthy by far was the fact that Briggs's own understanding of the "present crisis" was, almost literally, incomprehensible to those for whom he had written it. Briggs's careful exposition of the theological crisis set off by his inaugural went unanswered; indeed, given his new definitions of words like "evidence" and "authority," it was almost literally incomprehensible to evangelicals schooled in the ways of commonsense realism.

But the time for calm philosophical discussions of the issues involved in his address had already passed by the time Briggs offered his explanation. On April 13, 1891, in response to lobbying from the Reverend George Birch of Manhattan's Bethany Church (a staunch confessionalist who had sparred, early and often, over the revision question with Briggs), the Presbytery of New York had appointed an investigatory committee "to consider the Inaugural Address and its relation to the Confession of Faith." As ominous as the very existence of such an investigatory committee, however, was its leadership, for the clerk of the presbytery had appointed Birch himself as chairman of the investigating committee.[19]

The investigatory committee appointed by the New York Presbytery met throughout the spring of 1891, unaware that their "secret" deliberations were being faithfully reported to Briggs by J. H. McIlvaine, a committee member who strongly if secretly supported both Briggs and Briggs's critical enterprise. McIlvaine's information to Briggs offers an important glimpse into the "collective psyche" of the anti-Briggs faction, as well as critical information about the plan of attack that would be followed by the prosecution throughout the subsequent series of trials.[20]

McIlvaine reported that nearly everyone on the committee appointed by the presbytery had agreed that basic evangelical values had been assaulted by Briggs's inaugural address, assaulted so violently that the word "heresy" seemed the only one strong enough to designate the views that caused such disquiet. McIlvaine likewise reported that it was Briggs's statements about Scripture and its authority that were particularly offensive to everyone on the committee. But McIlvaine further announced that great uncertainty had gripped the committee, both as to precisely how the address was *formally* heretical — that is, heretical according to the statements of the Westminster Confession — and as to the best means of successfully prosecuting any tendered heresy charges in a church court. McIlvaine thus informed Briggs that it appeared almost certain that formal charges of heresy would be brought against him. But McIlvaine also predicted that, as the investigatory committee was more certain and united in its outraged sensibility than in its understanding of the exact nature of Briggs's heresies, scriptural and otherwise, the prosecution would consciously "cast a wide net" in the charges presented against him. Such a net, they hoped, would snag at least one of Briggs's positions as formally heterodox.[21]

McIlvaine's information and evaluation, in the event, proved to be infallibly correct. On May 11, 1891, the investigatory committee formally recommended to the New York Presbytery that it enter at once into judicial proceedings against Briggs for holding three positions in conflict with the Westminster Confession: that reason was a source of divine authority that "savingly enlightened men"; that the process of sanctification was not complete at death, but extended into the "Middle State"; and that there were proven errors in the original text of the Scriptures. The "wide net," thus cast, evinced both a profound disquiet over the "gist" of Briggs's theology, as well as an equally profound uncertainty as to the exact nature of the heterodoxy that had aroused such disquiet.[22]

The report and recommendation thus delivered to the New York Presbytery on May 11 launched a debate on the floor of the church court that lasted for three days, a debate of unprecedented length in the New York Presbytery. It was only on the third day, after Briggs had announced that he *welcomed* a public trial to vindicate both his piety and his methods, that the presbytery voted to accept the report and its recommendations. The presbytery therewith appointed a prosecuting committee, again under the chairmanship of George Birch (but without the presence of McIlvaine), to prepare the case against Briggs.[23]

Five days after the close of these dramatic events in the New York Presbytery, the one hundred and fourth General Assembly of the northern church opened in Detroit, an assembly which, as the New York *Sun* observed, would "serve Professor Briggs as Calvin served Servetus" if the conservatives had their way. And the likelihood of the assembly's following Calvin's sobering lead in rendering such service appeared almost certain after its opening session, in which the Old School faction engineered the election of Princeton Seminary's William Henry Green as moderator.[24]

The careful marshaling of conservative support quickly paid off. Green buried the creedal revision question remaining from the previous assembly (considered the most volatile issue on the agenda) by remanding it to a special committee for further consideration. This was an especially masterful political feat, given the fact that it was on the docket for general discussion on the floor of the assembly. But Green then went directly after the revisionists' avowed standard-bearer by turning the floor over to the Committee on Theological Seminaries, a committee chaired by Princeton's Francis L. Patton.[25]

Patton reported to the assembly that his committee had received overtures from sixty-three presbyteries requesting that some action be taken in regard to Briggs's inaugural address. Further, Patton announced that his own committee, experiencing the same disquiet that had motivated the presbyteries, recommended that the assembly formally veto Briggs's election to the Robinson Chair in light of such widespread disapproval of the inaugural address. Patton then explained that such a veto was well within the provisions of the 1870 reunion agreement, whereby the appointments of all professors in the church's theological seminaries, both Old and New School, were to be approved by vote in the General Assembly. What Patton failed to include in his report before the assembly was that Union Seminary's Board of Directors had already communicated its formal response on this issue to his committee. The Union board had stated its belief that Briggs's election was not an "appointment" at all, but rather only a transfer of duties from one chair to another, and thus entirely beyond the veto right outlined in the 1870 compact.[26]

Both Patton's recommendations and the subsequent debate on the floor of the assembly, like Green's election as moderator, had been carefully choreographed by the confessionalists well ahead of time. Thus, on May 28, Patton's resolutions were formally accepted by the assembly, therewith "constitutionally" vetoing Briggs's transfer to the Robinson Chair. The assembly likewise accepted the recommendation of Patton's committee that a representation from it confer with the Directors of Union Seminary as to the relations of that richest seminary in the church with the General Assembly.[27]

The "Union faction," generally a powerful political force in meetings of the assembly, recognized immediately that it had been resolutely out-maneuvered by confessionalist politicians at the assembly. Union's president, Thomas Hastings, lamented shortly after the assembly that

> the facts make the action at Detroit seem very clearly to be the fruit of what a distinguished friend calls a "Princeton conspiracy." *Whither?* rankled the minds of some. But was it a capital offense, that its author should be so murderously assailed not by arguments but by votes? But *Whither?*, at least in their minds, must be revenged.[28]

But the Union faction viewed the war as far from over, even if the confessionalists had won that particular battle. Less than a week after the assembly's meeting, Union's Board of Directors issued a public statement that announced its intention to abide by its decision to transfer Briggs to the new chair. The assembly's veto of Briggs's transfer, Union's Board declared, constituted a flagrant intrusion of partisan politics into the running of a legally autonomous, constitutionally governed institution.[29]

On June 7, 1891, the *New York Times* editorialized on the actions of the late General Assembly as well as on the more recent stand taken by Union's Board of Directors. The editorial, entitled "The Presbyterian Schism," observed that the entire "Briggs Case" (thus christening and unifying the trials that would follow) really involved "the source of a new type of religion, if not of a new type of church." And that source went far deeper than the discrete questions over the redemptive possibilities of reason, the middle state, and biblical authority that appeared to consume the attention of the General Assembly of the northern church. Further, the article intimated that the debates in both the New York Presbytery and the recent General Assembly had failed to bring either side closer to an understanding of the *real* source of conflict.[30]

It was perhaps indicative of the broad cultural issues involved in the Briggs Case that it was the *Times*, and not a religious or denominational periodical, that offered the most sophisticated and perceptive commentary on the Briggs Case, even if it failed to elucidate the exact nature of the real source of conflict between Briggs and his prosecutors. But the *Times*'s prediction of imminent denominational civil war appeared close to realization on the morning of October 5, 1891, when Birch's prosecuting committee — now supported by the veto of Briggs's transfer, a veto issued by the church's highest court — presented its "charges and specifications" to the New York Presbytery.

The charges presented by the committee accused Briggs with teaching "various doctrines in conflict with the Scriptures and the Standards": that history showed that there were *multiple* fountains of divine authority; that the "environments of men determine which way of access to God they pursue"; that Moses and Isaiah were not the authors of the biblical books traditionally ascribed to them; that "predictive prophecy" had been reversed by history; and that "the process of redemption continued after death."[31]

The charges actually constituted an impeachment of evangelical theology refracted through the lens of historicism. But such an impeachment was too vast and too unfocused to be actually debated on the floor of a church court, presuming even that most of the officers of the court could have understood the issue. Further, the Book of Discipline provided no rubric whatsoever for prosecuting "world views." Thus, the battle was juridically joined on another, more accessible, level, a level where all Presbyterians actually spoke the same language: that of church discipline.

On November 4, 1891, Briggs responded to the prosecuting committee's charges by reaffirming his "complete and unqualified assent" to the oath he had taken on the evening of the inaugural — to the Scriptures as the "only infallible rule of faith and practice" and to the Westminster standards as containing the true system of scriptural doctrine. But the very fact that the prosecuting committee was not pacified by Briggs's sworn affirmations revealed fears far more profound than could be answered by theological propositions.[32]

Briggs declared that it was a "simple question of *fact*," easily decided by a recourse to the historical record, whether God "may work directly on souls *apart from* the Bible, the church and the sacraments." The prosecution, he allowed, might find it difficult to believe that God would act in such a manner, "but they cannot adduce from sacred Scripture or the Confession any evidence to show that God *may not* so act."[33]

But quite apart from such rather abstruse theological considerations, Briggs informed the court, on a level that all could understand, that the charges tendered against him were invalid according to the Book of Discipline. Presbyterian discipline demanded that heresy charges be framed in as specific a form as possible, with the Articles of Faith "violated" specifically listed. The charges against him had failed to specify *what* doctrines in the standards his address had ostensibly violated, and without specific charges to respond to, any plea on his part would be both unreasonable and unconstitutional. Further, Briggs appealed to the famous Craighead Case of 1824, which established that in all heresy cases no verdict of guilt could be based on declarations or expressions that could be interpreted in a nonheretical manner. Such an appeal by Briggs, in fact, was decisive, as he had already solemnly sworn his acceptance of the standards' understanding of biblical authority.[34]

Even more infuriating to the prosecution than this flawless defense based squarely on the Presbyterian Book of Discipline, however, was the "lecture" that Briggs then proceeded to deliver to Birch's committee on the correct juridical procedures in these matters. *Implied* heterodoxy, Briggs loftily informed them, had no place in Presbyterian discipline. *Facts*, and facts alone, were what the Book of Discipline considered relevant in such cases. The prosecution, Briggs declared, had offered no such facts — had in fact deliberately ignored his repeated sworn allegiance to those standards, the denial of which alone constituted guilt.[35]

The prosecuting committee then sat in helpless (and enraged) silence as Dr. Henry Van Dyke rose to move, to widespread murmurs of assent, that in light of the irreproachable legal argument offered by Briggs, the presbytery had to dismiss the case "in the name of the peace and unity of the church." Such a dismissal, Van Dyke declared, was mandated by the fact that the prosecution had failed to present any proof for its charges save for "implied meanings," and that Briggs himself had solemnly affirmed, under oath, his acceptance of both Scripture and the standards. Van Dyke's motion was carried by an overwhelming majority of the presbytery, which declared that, "without approving of the positions stated in his inaugural address," their church court nonetheless was convinced by Briggs's sworn affirmations "touching his loyalty to Holy Scripture and the Standards, and [by] his disclaimers of the interpretations put on his words," and deemed it best "to dismiss the case, and hereby so dismiss it."[36]

The Peace and Unity of Christ's Church

A large section of the evangelical world had focused its attention on the rather unprepossessing structure of Manhattan's Old Scotch Church on November 4, where the New York Presbytery had constituted itself a "court of Jesus Christ," so that the dismissal of the case appeared like a major victory for the entire progressive cause. Washington Gladden, Arthur Cushman McGiffert, William Robertson Smith, Crawford Toy, Frances Willard, William Rainey Harper and Newman Smyth — among the brightest lights in the liberal firmament — sent "victory notices" to Briggs's Park Avenue residence.[37]

But the peace and unity of Christ's church had been anything but well served in the eyes of George Birch and his committee. Everyone in the presbytery, Birch knew, had recognized that Briggs held theological positions at variance with the accepted doctrines of the church, a fact that had been circumvented only by a disgraceful, casuistic appeal to the *letter* of church discipline. Thus, on November 13, Birch and his committee filed a formal appeal from the decision of the presbytery, *not* to the Synod of New York, the immediately superior court to which any appeal would normally have proceeded, but rather to the General Assembly itself. Such an appeal was (literally) "extraordinary" both because of its bypassing of the synod and because the New York Presbytery had formally "dismissed" the prosecuting committee, thus juridically removing it as an "original party" in the case. But Birch offered as reason for his extraordinary appeal the fact that Briggs's case was "one of the most important in the history of the church, by reason of its great and dangerous errors."

W. G. T. Shedd, a fellow faculty member of Briggs's at Union Seminary soon to emerge as an important figure in the trials against Briggs, joined with Birch in publishing a public apologia for an appeal bypassing the synod, arguing that such an appeal involved a question more serious and important in results than any that has ever been presented to the Assembly, the question, namely, whether a type of theology utterly antagonistic to the traditional theology of the denomination shall be solemnly condemned by its highest tribunal, or whether it shall be indorsed by it.[38]

The "legal casuistry" utilized by Briggs to get his obviously heterodox positions dismissed by the presbytery had convinced both Birch and Shedd that a vast conspiracy to subvert the life and belief of their church was being waged under the crafty hands of Briggs himself. Thus, at the presbytery's mid-April election of delegates to the upcoming General Assembly, the members of the presbytery were supplied with printed ballots by the two, with an anti-Briggs delegation already marked. The result was that four of the five members of the prosecuting committee won seats in the delegation.[39]

Throughout the spring of 1892 Briggs collected addresses that he had already delivered to various church groups in New York, addresses in which he had sought to "set forth more fully the views expressed in the inaugural address," hoping that the published explication of those views would form a *theological* (as opposed to juridical) apologia for what was emerging as a nasty fight at the upcoming assembly. The resulting collection of essays, published in April 1892 as *The Bible, The Church and the Reason*, claimed to address "matters which lie at the root of Christianity, which force themselves upon us in this generation of our race." Indeed, these "root matters," Briggs announced in his preface, went far beyond theoretical abstractions, addressing rather "questions of truth and fact to be determined by the weight of evidence and by the witness of realities." And as would have been expected, the "weight of evidence" documented the fact that "the divine Spirit, ever at work guiding the Church in its training in quest of all truth, uses the Bible and the Church, and interprets them in the forms of the Reason."[40]

Large sections of the essays in the collection, dealing with biblical inspiration and inerrancy, the authority of creedal symbols and religious authority generally, were lifted entire from *Biblical Study, American Presbyterianism*, and the inaugural address, thus lending the resulting collection a "patched together" feeling. But the impression of the book's incoherent structure, at least among the conservatives, was further strengthened by the fact that the central essays in the collection offered reflections on the "truths of history" in language that appeared to be *deliberately* opaque. Phrases like "inerrant Bible" and "Divine superintendence" — offered by Briggs to illustrate his orthodoxy — only alarmed confessionalists the more because they seemed to witness so clearly to Briggs's bad faith. Briggs seemed to deny the essence of central Christian doctrines in the process of "explaining" them.

The review of the book in the staunchly Old School *Presbyterian Journal* thus declared that Briggs's entire theological effort, evinced most recently in his collection of addresses, constituted "an immense fog bank." But through the fog the reviewer nonetheless recognized that Briggs's book "undermined the foundations of Christianity itself." The New York *Evening Post*, however, found no such fog bank surrounding either the author's intentions or the political target at which the published collection was aimed:

> The case of Dr. Briggs is intimately connected with the revision movement, and the conservatives have lately made the attack on Dr. Briggs in order to frighten the timid and obstruct the revision movement. . . . Long before the delivery of the now-famous inaugural address certain Presbyterian papers had been carrying on a vigorous campaign against Dr. Briggs, a campaign that will be decided at the General Assembly.[41]

An immense fog indeed seemed to have settled over the 1892 General Assembly in Portland, Oregon, when it began its consideration of whether to entertain the appeal of the New York prosecuting committee. Briggs informed the gathered church officers that it was without precedent in Presbyterian constitutional law for the prosecution to appeal over a synod to the General Assembly. The Book of Discipline forbade exceptions to the general rule in the interests of the prosecution. But there were, Briggs argued, more substantial grounds for dismissal as well. Briggs had repeatedly and without reservation declared his sincere subscription to all of the doctrines deemed essential by the prosecuting committee. Indeed, Briggs declared that it was unclear *what* he could do or say to convince his prosecutors of his orthodoxy.[42]

Briggs's unqualified expressions of subscription to evangelical doctrine left the majority of delegates in the assembly unmoved. His writings represented an unparalleled assault on their understanding of the Presbyterian faith — of this they were quite certain. Thus, on the afternoon of May 28, 1892, the assembly voted 431 to 87 to entertain the appeal of Birch's prosecuting committee, and appointed a committee to decide on the best way of proceeding in the case.[43]

The committee appointed by the assembly lacked immediate or clear evidence for heresy proceedings. Briggs had sworn his unqualified acceptance of all doctrines deemed essential by the prosecution; further, Briggs's appeals to Presbyterian precedent and constitutional law had been (infuriatingly) flawless legal arguments. But just as clearly, the majority of the committee (and of the assembly) felt sympathetic with, and shared the fears of, the New York prosecuting committee respecting Briggs's theological aberrations, even if those aberrations remained beyond formal constitutional reach as such. The committee appointed by the assembly thus recommended a course of action that might circumvent the constitutional constraints by demanding that the New York Presbytery render judgment on Briggs's address. It offered as its considered judgment, overwhelmingly accepted by the General Assembly, that

the judgment of the Presbytery of New York of November 4, 1891, dismissing the case against Charles A. Briggs be, and the same hereby is, reversed. The case is remanded to the Presbytery of New York for a new trial, with directions to the said Presbytery to proceed to pass on and determine the sufficiency of the charges.[44]

The assembly's action in remanding the case to the New York Presbytery represented, like Briggs's inaugural address itself, a cultural and ecclesiastical "moment" of some importance quite apart from its immediate juridical implications. Conservative evangelicals thereby announced that even if the threats posed by the new critical methods were, on some basic level, "beyond" the constitutional reach of church courts, those threats would nonetheless be met and defeated — either by greater efforts within those courts or, if need be, by any efforts that worked. And part of the "if need be" was worked out the next morning, in the assembly's last official act before adjournment. The strong confessionalist faction, under Birch's lead, pushed through the half-empty assembly hall a pronouncement that would come to be known as the "Portland Deliverance." The deliverance asserted that the assembly

> would remind all under its care that it is a fundamental doctrine of this church that the Old and New Testaments are the inspired and infallible Word of God. Our church holds that the inspired Word, as it comes from God, is without error, and the assertion to the contrary cannot but shake the confidence of the people.[45]

The Portland Deliverance represented a multileveled response to the real and imagined theological threats of the age. It witnessed to the widespread belief that Briggs's critical methods represented a direct challenge to biblical authority and thus to all of evangelical culture; it likewise witnessed to a poignant if misplaced desire for stability and certainty amidst what appeared to be the collapse of all certainty. But most practically, the Portland Deliverance represented a politically astute move in the effort to contain Briggs's technically unimpeachable heresies by changing the rules of the game.[46]

The theories of "verbal inerrancy" and the "original autographs," offered by Hodge and Warfield a decade before, were now raised from the level of adiaphora (the level at which theologians could honestly differ about theories) to the canon of orthodoxy. The ancient Christian belief in the divine authority of Scripture had been elucidated for a specific political purpose. The *genius* of the plan was that while it presented a fairly narrow field of battle on which to meet the far broader challenges of historicism, it would at the same time serve to defeat the most concrete and immediate threat of the new criticism, temporarily "buried" in a subcommittee of the General Assembly — creedal reform. By discrediting Briggs as an heresiarch who undermined the very source of evangelical truth, the confessionalists hoped to discredit the entire revision movement.[47]

But if the long-term strategic plans of evangelical conservatives had been thus announced in the Portland Deliverance, more immediate institutional consequences flowed from the assembly's pronouncement. On October 13, 1892, the Board of Directors of Union Seminary issued a public statement announcing that, in light of the recent enactments of the northern General Assembly that threatened the institutional and academic integrity of the seminary, "the agreement (of 1870) between the Union Theological Seminary and the General Assembly of the Presbyterian Church should be, and hereby is, terminated."[48]

The Evidence That Pervades History

Dr. Pentecost's Hindoo philosopher in central India, who replied to the evangelist's greeting with the query, "What is the latest phase of the Briggs case?" might have listened to a new chapter in the Scotch Presbyterian Church yesterday afternoon.

New York Tribune
November 10, 1892

Whether the "Hindoo" philosopher utilized by revivalist Hugh Pentecost to demonstrate his favorite missiological points actually inquired after the Briggs Case or not, the *Tribune*'s point was well taken. Most of the North Atlantic evangelical world (and many missionary points beyond) followed the various trials of the Briggs Case with that same mixture of circus excitement and reverential awe usually reserved for the annual revival conducted by popular preachers like Pentecost himself. And the latest phase of the Briggs Case would provide the drama and pathos that popular revivalists seldom achieved.[49]

On November 9, 1892, the prosecuting committee, in compliance with the directions of the recent General Assembly, presented its list of amended charges to the New York Presbytery. Following the tactical lead lately set at the General Assembly, the new charges emphasized how far short Briggs's theological positions fell of the biblical doctrines of the Presbyterian church lately enunciated at Portland. But the "amended" charges represented a change of approach so dramatic and obvious that Briggs himself opened his response on November 28 by noting that

it is not in the interest of justice that I should be required to prepare a defense against another set of charges. This is the third time that I have appeared before this presbytery with a long and carefully prepared defense.... Life is too short to justify me in constantly readjusting my work to suit the intellectual and rhetorical processes of such unstable prosecutors.[50]

Briggs thus refused to readjust his defense to suit the new tactics of his "unstable prosecutors." He alleged that the prosecution's inclusion of "verbal inspiration" and "inerrancy" under the rubric of Westminster doctrine, clearly taking its lead from the recent deliverance, was so obviously an anticonfessional use of that symbol as to constitute itself serious grounds for judicial proceedings. The late assembly, he declared, had overstepped constitutional limits in defining doctrine outside of an official heresy trial. The confession clearly affirmed that "by God's singular care and providence, the Scriptures have been kept pure in all ages"; thus, adherence to those standards "no less than to common sense" demanded that Presbyterians affirm that the *present* text of Scripture was as pure (and as corrupted) as the original text. Jerome, Augustine, Luther, and Calvin had freely admitted to errors in Scripture; this admission in no way constituted a compromise of biblical authority. But all the "deliverances" in the world, Briggs announced, could not change

> historical facts which cannot be gainsaid without closing our eyes to the evidence that pervades history. Convict me of heresy and you challenge the Christian centuries. All the ages will be against you, and in a multitude of voices like the roar of many waters, will denounce you as knowing neither the truth nor the power of God.... The prosecution are as blind as owls and bats to the truth of history and the facts of the world of reality.[51]

The "dogmatic" faith through which his prosecutors saw the world, Briggs declared, made it all but certain that they would never rest until they had succeeded in branding him a heretic, and with his exasperated appeal to the "truth of history and the facts of the world of reality," the presbytery adjourned for Christmas. But whatever the effect of his arguments on the prosecuting committee, when the proceedings commenced again on December 29, it became evident that Briggs's dramatic appeal had made a deep impression on the largely sympathetic presbytery. When the final vote was taken on December 31, Briggs was acquitted on all counts charged against him. On January 9, the committee appointed by the presbytery to formulate a public statement of the judgment of their court delivered its draft, overwhelmingly adopted by the presbytery, stating that, "without expressing approval of the critical or theological views embodied in the Inaugural Address, or of the manner in which they have been expressed," their court nonetheless pronounced Briggs acquitted of all charges against him. Further, the presbytery exhorted "all subject to its authority to regard the many and great things in which we agree rather than the few and minor in which we differ."[52]

On January 18, 1893, the prosecuting committee, furious over the refusal of the presbytery to pronounce on the orthodoxy of Briggs's views, filed yet another official appeal to the General Assembly regarding the decision of the presbytery. It formally requested that the highest court in the church render an official pronouncement on Briggs's theological positions, the New York Presbytery having demonstrated its unwillingness to do so despite the clear pronouncements of the 1892 assembly. And the General Assembly to which they appealed, by agreement in both the religious and the secular press, would prove to be the most conservative such gathering within recent memory. The 1893 assembly of the northern church, meeting in Washington, D.C., was taken over by a confessionalist, midwestern faction, moderated by a no-nonsense professor from McCormick Seminary. This faction, moreover, had come to distrust the "gentlemanly" eastern tactics of Princeton Seminary in containing the theological poison of the "progressives" operating out of Union Seminary.[53]

For the five days during which the assembly considered the Briggs Case, every available seat on the floor of the sanctuary was occupied, with many standing in the aisles, while the gallery which extended around three sides of the church was filled with spectators, mostly women. George Birch presented the prosecuting committee's appeal, arguing that the New York Presbytery had committed an act of open disobedience to the General Assembly in refusing to follow an explicit directive to render a judgment as to the orthodoxy of the positions enunciated in Briggs's address. Indeed, the final form of that presbytery's judgment gave the impression that Briggs's theology was in itself unimportant, when in fact "the errors charged against it are fundamental."[54]

The presentations of Birch, Joseph Lampe, and John McCook

for the prosecution rehearsed the now-familiar list of charges already presented to previous church courts, only now argued with a new passion with the prospect that the assembly might actually offer an official pronouncement on Briggs's theological positions. But the press reported that most commissioners in the hall paid little attention to the prosecution's presentation. There was, in fact, little reason for close attention, as most of those present already knew by rote the arguments of the prosecution and of the defense, and awaited only the completion of both sets of arguments to deliver their own opinions on the floor of the assembly.[55]

Briggs's response to the charges occupied two days of the sessions; it was a response that, if less brilliant than his performance before the presbytery six months before, was nonetheless both masterful and poignant. Briggs argued that, at its present pass, his case was important *not* because of the doctrinal issue at stake — there were, strictly speaking, no doctrinal issues at stake, as he continually reaffirmed his ordination and professorial oaths — but because of the flagrant violations of constitutional procedure and precedent that were being used against him. He announced to the assembly hall that even if his teachings were condemned by that body ("God knoweth how"), it would have been accomplished by such unconstitutional maneuverings that neither he nor the church at large would recognize the judgment.[56]

By the evening of May 25, when both the prosecution and the defense had finished, it was generally agreed that Briggs had had the better of the argument. John Crosby Brown, vice-president of Union Seminary's Board of Directors, wrote a note to Briggs the next morning, thanking him for his "glorious" presentation, and assuring him that "whatever happens, you have put yourself in the right, and have done a great service to all loyal Presbyterians."[57]

But the next morning Briggs was disabused of his naive confidence in the persuasiveness of the "evidence" he had offered in his defense. Each of the commissioners to the assembly was allowed ten minutes to address the case, and that forum revealed how little the arguments of either Briggs or of the prosecution had been really understood by the assembly at large. It thus came as no surprise at the end of the four hours that the assembly voted, 405 to 145, to entertain the appeal of the prosecuting committee.[58]

Briggs had sat with head bowed throughout the entire proceedings, and the next morning he announced to friends that he
intended to withdraw from the Presbyterian communion, a communion that clearly wished to avoid engagement with the modern world. But Briggs's announcement provoked an immediate
response from the entire Board of Directors of the seminary. John
Crosby Brown wrote to him that

> of course the verdict will be against you, but I am clear that you
> must not retire from the church. *You* are not on trial so much as the
> Presbyterian Church. You can afford to be beaten. It cannot.[59]

But most of the commissioners to the assembly clearly felt that
the Presbyterian church could indeed afford to "lose" him. The
sheer physical exhaustion of the encounter in the assembly hall had
taken its toll; at the close of his remarks the next morning Briggs
began to stumble verbally, and the press reported that a glance
around the chamber revealed that a number of the commissioners
were sound asleep.[60]

The judgment of the assembly on the case was rendered by
a roll-call vote, each commissioner in delivering his vote being
allowed three minutes to speak on the case. Over one hundred
commissioners took advantage of the opportunity to give their
reasons, a number being interrupted in midsentence by the moderator. During the four hours that it took to thus render a decision,
"an almost painful stillness prevailed throughout the Assembly
Hall."[61]

The decision of the assembly was against Briggs, 295 voting to
sustain the appeal of the prosecutors as a whole, 84 to sustain the
appeal in part, and 116 against the appeal. The moderator therewith appointed a "committee of judgment" to formulate an official
statement. The next afternoon, the chair of this committee delivered its judgment, which was accepted, *viva voce*, by the assembly.
Immediately thereafter, the press received copies of this judgment,
which declared that

> this General Assembly finds that Charles A. Briggs has uttered,
> taught and propagated views, doctrines and teachings as set forth
> in the said charges contrary to the essential doctrine of Holy
> Scripture and the Standards, and in violation of his ordination

vow.... Wherefore this General Assembly does hereby suspend Charles A. Briggs, the said appellee, from the office of minister in the Presbyterian Church in the United States of America, until such time as he shall give satisfactory evidence of repentance to the General Assembly of the violation by him of the said ordination vow.[62]

5

The Advance towards Church Unity

Historicism and Ecumenism

The singular importance of the ecumenical impulse in defining the realignment of modern American Presbyterianism hardly constitutes news to scholars dedicated to reconstructing the recent religious past. Indeed, as the most important (and divisive) institutional movement to emerge in American religion in the twentieth century, ecumenism has spawned a vast scholarly literature in its own right. The "news," rather, lies in the intimate relationship between this decisive institutional impulse and historical criticism — the most important (and divisive) intellectual challenge facing the evangelical mainstream during the same period.

These two progressive impulses intersected in the career of Charles Briggs, himself both critical scholar and ecumenical theorist. Briggs's ecumenical career provides a compelling human story elucidating how the new critical scholarship offered ready support for the growing unitive impulse within the American evangelical mainstream. But Briggs's story likewise offers a revealing portrait of the fears that divided advocates of Christian unity into "federationist" and "organicist" camps in the early years of the twentieth century, camps that witnessed to a house divided even as they worked towards a united church.

Winthrop Hudson has noted that by the middle of the twentieth century the traditional classification of Protestant groups according to their polity or church government (such as "Congregationalists" or "Presbyterians," etc.) really served to obscure a more important shift taking place. This shift — dividing American Protestantism into three loosely defined camps — was "theologically and sociologically grounded in a way that bypassed the older (denominational) distinctions." The new religious realignment, in fact, was defined in large part by the acceptance or rejection of the ecumenical vision as determinative of modern Christianity itself.[1]

The ecclesiastical configuration resulting from the shift described by Hudson centered on "cooperative Protestantism" as the inheritor of the establishment status of the previous century's united front. This twentieth-century Protestant establishment was composed of those mildly liberal or progressive denominations that favored continued denominational identity but opposed sectarianism and creedal rigidity for the sake of working together in interdenominational ventures, ventures that after 1908 were coordinated by the Federal Council of Churches.

The second grouping in Hudson's configuration was the conservative "non-cooperative Protestants" who saw in the Federal Council and its brand of social progressivism the engine of modernist heresies, and the institutional betrayer of the revivalistic and individualistic values of the older evangelicalism. These foes of ecumenical consolidation fought against the crusades of progressive "cooperationism," in the process becoming marginalized as religious spokespersons for the broader culture. Opposed to both of these groups were those "disaffected Protestants" — Adventists, members of Holiness churches, and Pentecostal Christians — who disclaimed establishment status altogether, and who offered an alternative understanding of the relationship of religion and culture.[2]

The modern cooperative mainstream, in its bid for establishment status, could claim as its heritage earlier ventures in Protestant interdenominational cooperation like the united front of the antebellum period, the trans-Atlantic Evangelical Alliance, and the interdenominational missionary ventures at the turn of the century.

Indeed, it was missionary groups like the Student Volunteer Movement, the Interseminary Missionary Alliance, and, most directly, the Ecumenical Missionary Conference (which introduced the term "ecumenical" into twentieth-century Protestant usage) that provided the working models for the modern Protestant cooperative establishment.[3]

It was this practical, federationist model of denominational interaction, incarnated in the Federal Council of Churches, that came to define the most popular and institutionally realized form of Protestant ecumenical thinking in the twentieth century. But while this federationist model of church unity — a model that envisioned a congeries of distinct bodies united for good works and fellowship — undoubtedly constituted the most widespread form of Protestant ecumenical thinking in the early twentieth century, a few prophetic figures offered a far more challenging vision of church unity.[4]

Drawing on antebellum prophets of "evangelical catholicism" like the Lutheran Samuel S. Schmucker, the Episcopalian William A. Muhlenberg, and most importantly Philip Schaff, ecumenical theorists at the end of the nineteenth century sought the institutional incorporation (as opposed to federation) of all English-speaking Protestants into one church. This organically united national church, in turn, would be itself the Anglo-American component of the Church Catholic.[5]

The two most important theoreticians of this organic approach to church union in the early twentieth century — Newman Smyth and Charles Briggs — were the direct heirs of this earlier (largely Anglican) strain of Protestant ecumenism. Both Smyth and Briggs viewed "federation for service" (the watchwords of the cooperative ecumenical vision embodied in the Federal Council) as a sop offered to provide unearned comfort to the justly troubled consciences of Christ's divided followers. For both Smyth and Briggs, moreover, the claims of the past (represented by continued denominational divisions) were indeed far more relative and plastic than most Christians thought, just as Schmucker, Muhlenberg, and Schaff had argued. But the relativity and plasticity in which Smyth and Briggs framed their arguments for Christian unity represented an important elucidation of earlier theories. Indeed, an elucidation of the historicist presuppositions on which they rested their organicist campaign reveals important factors influencing the early history of the ecumenical cause in America.[6]

Briggs's personal odyssey from avid supporter of the missionary ventures of the Evangelical Alliance, to early advocate of the federationist movements of *fin-de-siècle* Protestantism, to chief academic theoretician and spokesman for organic reunion, offers, in fine, the story of the development of an entire strain of Protestant ecumenical thinking. But Briggs's odyssey reveals as well the fears that divided evangelical progressives in America in their efforts to reunite Christ's followers into the *oekumene ekklesia.*

Briggs's conversion as an undergraduate at the University of Virginia in the great urban revival of 1858 baptized him, like many other midcentury evangelicals, into the practical interdenominational spirit of the united front. In this practical federation of committed individuals, the personal regenerative experience of the new birth bound Christians from many denominations into a non-denominational army battling for the American incarnation of God's kingdom. Also like most evangelicals desiring to incarnate their *metanoia* in works of charity, Briggs turned to the practical cooperative ventures of a voluntary society for a focus, in his case to the newly founded Y.M.C.A. of Charlottesville. Further, Briggs's baptism into the cooperative irenicism of the united front was expressed in his initial indecision as to denominational affiliation in Charlottesville. Since all Bible-based denominations represented "various phalanxes of one great host," Briggs hesitated and considered several before joining that one that he knew best.[7]

But if Briggs's initial experience of interdenominational cooperation faithfully mirrored the widespread midcentury evangelical experience, his later commitment to the ecumenical cause was far more decisively shaped by his studies in Germany. In Berlin, Briggs's exposure to the successful program of ecclesiastical reunification sponsored by the Evangelical Union Party (among whose creators was his *Doktorvater*, Isaac Dorner) convinced him that "the period of disintegration has passed, and the period of integration in church and state is in progress."[8]

But most decisive in shaping Briggs's mature ecumenical thinking was his introduction in Berlin to the historico-critical world view. His critical assays into both the biblical and historical past convinced Briggs that there were far more compelling reasons for

Christian unity than the efficient management of human and material resources. For an age impressed by the witness of science, Briggs believed that he had discovered incontrovertible scientific proof for the spiritual ideal of one holy church. Since all historical phenomena — including mutually exclusive claims of biblical interpretation or ecclesiastical polity — had been thoroughly conditioned by their cultural environments, their claims were far more relative, and far less immutable, than their ardent advocates claimed.[9]

These historicist seeds, planted in Germany, flowered during Briggs's early years of teaching at Union Seminary, during which he sought to show how biblical theology "has an important influence on the union tendencies of our time," for

> in exhibiting the diversities of view in the apostolic church, it will enable churches representing different phases of human nature, corresponding more or less with the scripture differences, to come closer together in the spirit of Christian charity, according to the example given in biblical theology.[10]

But it was Briggs's research into church history — largely for his creedal revision campaign within the northern Presbyterian church —that first revealed the full ecumenical implications of his critical principles. Briggs in fact offered his seminal denominational study of American Presbyterianism with the express hope that his own denomination might prove to be the "stepping stone to a higher form of Christianity which will transcend the Protestant Reformation by its omnipotent energy and world-wide sweep."[11]

In the years after the publication of *American Presbyterianism*, moreover, Briggs began to focus his historical studies quite consciously around the question of Christian unity, a focus evinced in articles on irenic Reformed figures like Rupertus Meldenius and John Durie. Thus, by 1888, Briggs could issue his first public call for organic church reunion in a *Presbyterian Review* editorial entitled "A Plea for an American Alliance of the Reformed Churches."[12]

Briggs had long been a fervent supporter of, and active participant in, the Alliance of Reformed Churches throughout the World, warmly encouraging the northern Presbyterian church's support for it in the pages of the *Review*. But Briggs's "Plea" constituted something new and radically different from his earlier editorial notices of the alliance's meetings. Briggs announced that he supported the organic union of all the churches of Protestantism "so soon as such a union could be accomplished in an honorable manner on the basis of historical achievements." But it was also clear that the unions being formed by good-hearted but powerless individuals would do nothing towards realizing the goal of a united church.[13]

The Reformed group of churches in America occupied a position of special cultural power and status, Briggs declared, a position that exerted considerable influence among other Christians. "It is the more important," he therefore announced, "that we should set our faces towards something that is easier of accomplishment" than the complete reunion of Christendom. Briggs proposed that the various Presbyterian and Reformed groups combine into an alliance modeled after the Alliance of Reformed Churches. Such an alliance, whose triennial meetings would constitute the highest court in their respective churches, would more effectively coordinate their considerable human and material resources.[14]

So passionate was Briggs's description of the benefits accruing from such an alliance for evangelizing the world, and so evident was Briggs's desire to become himself the house philosopher for such a reunited body, that many presumed that his "Plea" represented a manifesto announcing the new focus for Briggs's emerging political interests. But in fact both Briggs's call for such an alliance, and his own interest in pressing his plan, all but disappeared a few months later, when the bishops of the Anglican communion, meeting at Lambeth Palace, issued the "quadrilateral platform" of American Episcopalian William Reed Huntington as the basis for future discussions of church reunion.

In 1870, Huntington had published his "essay toward unity," *The Church Idea*, in which he had asserted that most of the debates over theological formulae and polity that had preoccupied Christians, and that kept them in different bodies, were in fact adiaphora — things indifferent. The core truths of Christianity were few and easily stated, Huntington declared, thus making the continued division among Christians scandalous. Huntington then set out a four-point platform for the organic union of all Protestant churches based on what he argued were the essentials of the Christian tradition: the acceptance of the Old and New Testaments as containing all things necessary to salvation; Baptism and the Lord's Supper as the two great scriptural ordinances defining the church's liturgical life; the Apostles' and Nicene Creeds as the sufficient statement of the Christian faith; and the historic episcopate as a universal polity "locally adapted in the methods of its administration to the varying needs of nations and peoples."[15]

Huntington's call for a return to organic Christian unity around the "Mother Church of all English-speaking Protestants," and his practical four-point platform, stirred up a wide and surprisingly receptive response among American Protestants. Indeed, in 1886, the Episcopal House of Bishops adopted Huntington's quadrilateral as their church's official basis for all future discussions of Christian unity. The call of the American bishops found ready ears: the bishops of the Anglican communion, meeting at Lambeth in 1888, called for the reunification of Christ's church on earth on the basis of Huntington's platform.[16]

In the October 1888 issue of the *Presbyterian Review* Briggs offered his considered opinion on the proposed four-point platform now known as the Lambeth Quadrilateral: Briggs pronounced it "entirely satisfactory" as the basis for organic Christian reunion. Indeed, Briggs proceeded to build his entire satisfaction with the Anglican plan on the firmest foundation of all, that of historical criticism:

> Recent historical research is very damaging to all *jure divino* theories of church government. The question [of church government] is to be determined by historical research, and not by dogmatic statements or ecclesiastical decisions. The Episcopate has in its favor the historical usage of the Christian Church from the second century to the sixteenth. History is a powerful argument for the Episcopate: this, added to its practical usefulness, makes its future sure unless the old blunders be renewed.[17]

Briggs's pronouncement, built securely on the work of his Union colleague Philip Schaff, represented the wedding of the cause of organic church union to historical criticism in dramatic (and as usual, provocative) form. And the marriage prospects for the union appeared promising when Briggs took his new cause to the lecture circuit, where he soon became one of the most sought-after speakers on Christian unity.

The secular and religious press, moreover, began to balance their portrait of the bellicose denominational politician with regular reports of Briggs's irenic efforts on the lecture platform. Thus, the *New York Times* published the entire text of Briggs's keynote address before the annual convention of the Church Unity Society in 1890, noting with astonishment Briggs's remark that "the unity of the Christian Church is vastly more important than questions of theology." Briggs's observation was especially remarkable, the *Times* noted, in light of Briggs's acknowledged leadership of the progressive theological party then causing considerable disquiet within the northern Presbyterian church.[18]

Briggs's bald statement of ecclesiastical priorities before the Church Unity Society, in fact, was reiterated during January 1891, when most of the secular and religious press focused public attention on his famous inaugural address. During that month Briggs published an article that cast a distinctly irenic light on the fractious intellectual disputes that followed his inaugural address.

"The Advance towards Church Unity" adumbrated with disarming accuracy the realignment of twentieth-century American Protestantism described by Winthrop Hudson. This realignment, Briggs noted, was built on the recognition that the doctrinal controversies that had given rise to denominations in the first place

are dead and buried; it is impossible to revive them. The questions of the times force men to range themselves into new parties, for times indicate that Christians are rapidly approaching a crisis that will destroy "denominationalism," and make the Church of Christ one.[19]

But such signs pointing towards the dissolution of denominationalism were, Briggs averred, hopeful rather than distressing, for it was now possible for a reunited Christian church to preach the gospel to every creature. And such a possibility had emerged — for the first time in the history of the church — primarily because of a radical re-formation of ecclesiastical parties, not along doctrinal lines, but rather according to the reception or rejection of the new critical world view. The victory of the new world view results in the decay of denominationalism; for in most, if not all, of the denominations, there are those who break over the lines to the right and the left and clasp hands with kindred spirits in other denominations. The conservatives are, for the most part, denominationalists, but the progressives are indifferent to denominational difference. The progressives have broken through the barriers and are removing the obstructions with greater diligence and more rapidly than the conservatives can restore them.[20]

Historical criticism arraigned divided Christendom for its failure to evangelize effectively the "slaves of modern materialism" both at home and abroad, and found it wanting. Not only had Christ's divided followers failed to heed the Great Commission; it was "clear that denominationalism is very much to blame for the evil." But the time for hand-wringing, Briggs announced, had already passed; progressive Christians in all quarters of Christendom had already come to realize that "denominationalism is doomed."[21]

The immediate task of all earnest Christians, Briggs declared, was to enter into the battle against the obstructionists, a battle in which Christian scholars had a special place. Scholars inspired by the evangelical vision and armed with the best of modern scholarship could help to create an "organism that will be the ripe expression of all the historic movements of the past." Briggs in fact offered himself as a prototype of such a Christian scholar, a scholar whose critical researches provided "energy for the vast work of these last days of the age of grace."[22]

The Alienation of Church and People

Briggs's fate at the hands of denominational confessionalists in 1893 undoubtedly contributed to his growing sense that the last days of their graced age would be considerably more contentious than he had originally thought. His fate likewise contributed to a growing sense that his usefulness to the cause of church unity within the Presbyterian fold was becoming increasingly problematic. Even before the outcome of the trial, however, Briggs had begun to wear his Presbyterian mantle rather lightly. When the New York Presbytery had initially dismissed the case against him in November 1891, and Henry Codman Potter, the irenic Episcopal bishop of New York, had penned a warm congratulatory note, Briggs had responded that

> I gladly recognize you as my bishop, although your hands have not been put upon me. I would not hesitate to ask that also, were it not plain that, for the present, I can do more for the unity of Christ's church by working among the Presbyterians. But would that this city were under your episcopal guidance.[23]

Briggs's denominational affiliation "for the present" was, of course, dramatically altered by the events of 1893, and in July of that year Briggs published two articles that presented a clearer if less sanguine view of his prospects as a Presbyterian ecumenical advocate. "The Alienation of Church and People" denounced the evils of denominationalism in general, and of the northern Presbyterian church in particular, arguing that the official teaching of the denominations was so distant from the actual concerns of ordinary men and women that the real wonder was that anyone attended church at all. The spirit of the age had conclusively shown that "denominationalism is the great sin and curse of the church."[24]

But it was "The Future of Presbyterianism in the United States," published in the July number of the *North American Review*, that caused considerably more disquiet, particularly among Briggs's colleagues at Union Seminary. The latter article, in fact, raised constitutional questions about the retention of Briggs on a faculty committed to educating students for the Presbyterian ministry.

An ultraconservative cabal had seized control of the northern church, Briggs declared at the very outset of the latter article, so that it was probable that there would be a "series of heresy trials for several years until [they] exhaust themselves and tire the patience of the church." But the predicted trials would only serve to publicize and vindicate the critical world view, for

> all American churches are in the stream of that tendency which is rushing on towards the unity of Christ's church. The hedges which separate the denominations are traditional theories and practices [which] are no longer realities to thinking men and women. The problem in the near future is this: can the liberals remain in comfort in their several denominations, and so become the bridges of Church

Unity, or will they be forced to unite in a comprehensive frame of Church Unity outside the existing denominations.[25]

At some point during the painful summer of 1893, Briggs seems to have reached a new understanding of his own ability to "remain in comfort" within his own denomination, for in the fall Briggs wrote to Newman Smyth of his growing attraction to the Episcopal fold. But Newman Smyth was considerably exercised, both personally and professionally, about Briggs's proposed Anglican affiliation.[26]

Smyth himself was a major light in the "new theology" firmament, having set forth most of the major themes of the modernist agenda in works like *The Religious Feeling* and *The Orthodox Theology of Today*. These works, published like Briggs's in the early days of the modernist campaign, had established the New Haven theologian as one of the chief priests of the early progressive evangelical cause. But Smyth was likewise becoming obsessed with a crisis that he discerned at the heart of battles of the age — the "passing of the Protestant era of history." Protestantism was losing (or had already lost) cultural authority and control of family life. The "coming Catholicism" — that form of Christianity that would displace the discredited and divided forces of Protestantism — demanded that progressive thinkers should commit themselves in a special way to the cause of organic church union. Like Briggs, Smyth had arrived at his conclusions about the truth of organic ecumenism through his application of historical criticism. Indeed, Smyth had come to see Briggs as his most important fellow theoretician in the cause of organic reunion, and thus sought to place the question of Briggs's denominational status within a larger context of political strategy. Smyth wrote to Briggs that the Episcopal church would "hardly afford you, in my judgment, the best point of leverage for the work laid upon you." That work demanded a platform well within the evangelical mainstream, and equally well above any suspicion of "Romanizing" tendencies. Both demands thus appeared to make the Episcopal church an especially unfortunate tactical choice.[27]

But Smyth's tactical recommendations as to denominational affiliation notwithstanding, Briggs was increasingly drawn to the Episcopal stream of ecumenical activity, a stream directed from

William Reed Huntington's fashionable Grace Church "down the street" from Union Seminary on New York's East Side. Indeed, in the spring of 1895 Briggs became one of the founding members of Huntington's "League for Catholic Unity," a group of Episcopalians, Congregationalists, and Presbyterians who sought organic church unity on the basis of the Lambeth Quadrilateral.

The League for Catholic Unity represented at once one of the most concrete and one of the least successful institutional attempts to realize the ideal of organic church reunion in America. While Huntington himself provided the league's intellectual ammunition, its practical organizer was Charles W. Shields, a Presbyterian from Princeton University.

Charles Shields experienced something like a conversion on reading the Lambeth Quadrilateral, and immediately wrote to Huntington asking his advice as to the best means of implementing the ecumenical vision of the 1888 pastoral letter. The result was *The Historic Episcopate*, published by Shields in 1894, which offered a plan of campaign to American Protestants concerned about church unity. Shields's book, the more impressive because offered by a non-Anglican, argued that American Christians should accept the Lambeth Quadrilateral as the likeliest stepping-stone towards the unification of American Christianity. Episcopal government incorporated within itself the congregational and presbyterian polities, Shields argued, by fusing them into a higher unity while retaining distinct congregational and synodical rights. The quadrilateral, moreover, based church unity on *polity* rather than on the more problematic (and dimmer) prospects of doctrinal consensus.[28]

Shields's book provoked considerable discussion among non-Episcopal Protestants, and in March 1894, the *Magazine of Christian Literature and Review of the Churches*, a joint Anglo-American periodical that reflected trans-Atlantic evangelical concerns, devoted an entire issue to the discussion and criticism of Shields's book. Huntington himself, Josiah Strong, Lyman Abbott, and other giants in the Anglo-American evangelical pantheon submitted essays offering reactions and reflections on Shields's work. Indeed, save for the strongly critical essay offered by Josiah Strong, the Congregationalists and Presbyterians among the contributors had been especially receptive both to the Lambeth proposals and to

Shields's explication of it. So positive had been the reception, in fact, that Huntington conceived the idea of a league, composed of representatives from the Episcopal, Presbyterian, and Congregational churches, committed to pressing the "historic episcopate" as a "possible bond of organic union among Christian denominations." This historic episcopate would function as an impetus towards union by "completing" the "Congregational, Presbyterian or Episcopal systems, and at length recombining them into one Holy Catholic and Apostolic Church."[29]

In Huntington's mind, the league would be the kernel of a much grander and more comprehensive movement, a movement that would eventually incorporate all American Christians — Protestant, Catholic, and Orthodox — into one organic body. This reunited body would incorporate their various traditions into a catholicity both more diverse and more unified than any body then existing.[30]

The public announcement of the proposed league aroused considerable notice in both the secular and the religious press. Thus, when the league published its constitution in the summer of 1895, the *New York Times* and the *New York World* remarked on its impressive potential for ecumenical good, while the *Providence Journal* editorialized simply that the proposed league would be an organization of "great *practical* significance, that offers encouragement to those who dream of a united church."[31]

Huntington had long kept an interested eye on Briggs's critical efforts on behalf of church unity, so that from the initial discussions of the league, Briggs had appeared as its most obvious scholarly spokesman. Thus, in December 1894, Briggs was formally (albeit secretly) invited to join the proposed league, proudly affixing his name to a constitution that was published with considerable fanfare. That document stated the intention of the ten signers, "without detaching ourselves from the Christian denominations to which we severally belong," to work for the reunion of all Christian churches on the basis of the quadrilateral as articles of agreement

> upon which the unification of the Christian denominations of this country may proceed cautiously and steadily, without any alteration of their existing standards of doctrine, polity and worship, which

might not reasonably be made in a spirit of brotherly love for the sake of unity.[32]

Briggs immediately became an important presence and a much sought-after speaker for the league on the lecture circuit. But Briggs's efforts on behalf of the league subtly but profoundly transformed its ecumenical gospel from Huntington's essentially Anglican, broad church ideal into a historicist crusade. It was, in fact, precisely this transformation effected by Briggs that helps to explain the league's fate — "crossing the sky of American religious history like a comet, causing a great deal of comment when it issued its manifesto in 1895, but then being heard no more."[33]

Briggs's frequent speaking engagements for the league seem to have affected many American Protestants just as his earlier efforts on behalf of creedal revision affected many fellow Presbyterians — with widespread fear and distrust, in about equal proportions. Clearly, a large part of Briggs's lack of success was due to his own bellicose personality, which made him democratically adept at alienating people of widely disparate beliefs.[34]

But a more important source for the league's (and the organic ecumenical vision's) failure to capture the popular imagination was the fear of a "creeping Catholicism" that many discerned in the historicist call for a reunited, monolithic church. Wasn't it *precisely* that kind of "unity" that had led to the abuses against which the Reformers had railed? Indeed, wasn't it just such a monolithic organism that had lately issued the blasphemous pronouncements on papal infallibility?

Thus were Newman Smyth's worst predictions concerning Briggs's chosen "point of leverage" fulfilled. Briggs's redaction of Huntington's irenic call for "catholic unity," in fact, appeared far more menacing than the quadrilateral on which it was ostensibly based, for Briggs purported to base his arguments on the authority of modern science itself. To evangelicals genuinely committed to incorporating the best scientific thought of the age into their religious world view, Briggs's campaign appeared, at best, naive, and possibly even duplicitous.

The wonder then was not that the organic ecumenical gospel so presented by Briggs disappeared after crossing the sky in 1895, but rather that Briggs's campaign lasted as long as a year. It was

likewise little wonder that the World's Student Christian Federation — organized by John Mott during the same year as the
league's appearance and incorporating the federationist approach
to practical interchurch cooperation in missions — proved to
be a far more important training ground for the leadership of
the modern American ecumenical movement than Huntington's
league.[35]

Mott's federation stressed students' loyalty to their own church
traditions while calling for cooperation in working for the evange-
lization of the world in their generation, thus offering a far more
amenable package to Protestant evangelicals than that presented
by Briggs. The cherished denominational boundary markers were
left untouched in the united effort towards world conversion, while
one's privileged (Protestant) mainstream position in an increasingly (immigrant Catholic) pluralistic culture was clearly demar-
cated by the very effort to band together for good works. The true
wonder, then, was that Briggs's (and the league's) unitive voice
was heard at all.

Catholic — The Name and the Thing

Briggs's ecumenical efforts on behalf of the league, however,
aroused more immediate concerns among the beleaguered seminary Board of Directors. The General Assembly of 1895 had already disciplined the seminary for its contumacious retention of
Briggs on its faculty after his suspension from the ministry. It had
instructed the New York Presbytery not to receive under its "watch
and care" any students who "pursued their studies in theological seminaries respecting whose teaching the General Assembly
disavows responsibility." Briggs's escalating antidenominational
rhetoric in the service of the league raised troubling constitutional
questions about Briggs's continued tenure on the already-embattled
faculty.[36]

The disquiet among the seminary directors, in fact, was further
exacerbated by rumors of Briggs's bolting the Presbyterian fold
for the more catholic pastures of the Episcopal church. These rumors were confirmed in January 1898, when Briggs informed the
seminary board of his intention to renounce his Presbyterian affiliation and seek admission and orders in the "widest of bodies

in this country, the one which will eventually absorb all the other Protestant bodies."[37]

The board was not amused, either by the thought of Briggs's denominational change, or by the thought of Briggs's episcopal *re*-ordination, the latter adding insult to injury by casting doubt on the validity of presbyterian ordination. But the long-suffering board, now accustomed to the storms of controversy that seemed to follow Briggs's campaigns, likewise recognized Briggs's usefulness to the seminary as the most famous Protestant scholar in America, and decided that the path of wisdom lay in "letting Dr. B. make his change and taking no official notice of the fact in any way, shape or manner." Thus, the seminary offered no comment at all when besieged by the press on the morning of March 29, 1898. For on the previous afternoon, Briggs had sent a letter to the clerk of the New York Presbytery, announcing that

> after long and careful reflection I have decided to sever my connec-
> tion with the Presbytery of New York and more especially with the
> Presbyterian Church of the United States of America. I withhold the
> reasons for this decision in the interests of peace and quietness. I
> may simply say that I have remained under your jurisdiction as long
> as I could do so with a good conscience.[38]

In the spring of 1899 — a year whose intimations of millennial fulfillment were noted by many fellow evangelicals — Charles Augustus Briggs claimed to have found ecclesiastical peace at last. On May 14, 1899, despite a much-publicized campaign by a small contingent of Anglo-Catholic priests to block the event, Briggs was "ordained into the apostolic succession" at the hands of Bishop Potter.[39]

Briggs's reception into the Episcopal priesthood seems to have unloosed some block in his scholarly life, for two exegetical works which he had labored over for several years suddenly saw the published light of day. *A General Introduction to the Study of Holy Scripture*, an expanded and updated version of his *Biblical Study* that had appeared fifteen years before, was published in the fall by Scribner's. The *General Introduction*'s sheer massiveness and encyclopedic treatment of the various fields of biblical study assured Briggs's reputation as one of the premier scripture scholars well into the twentieth century. But the 1899 edition of the earlier work likewise witnessed to the fact that, by the turn of the century, American biblical scholarship had moved well beyond Briggs in both exegetical skill and interpretation.[40]

In the 1899 *General Introduction*, Briggs himself took a hard line against the dangerous theories of younger evangelical scholars who now used those very critical methods that he himself had championed to question "scientifically" such central doctrines of the evangelical faith as the Virgin Birth and the physical resurrection of Jesus. Briggs thus revealed in the work both his continued allegiance to the older evangelical vision and the fact that the cutting edge of biblical scholarship had long since moved beyond his own work.[41]

Far more important to Briggs's enduring reputation as a biblical scholar was his editorship with S. R. Driver and Francis Brown of the magisterial *A Hebrew and English Lexicon of the Old Testament*. The lexicon represented a revised and expanded edition of the Robinson-Gesenius work issued three decades earlier, and offered a breathtaking compendium of Semitic linguistics. Indeed, the lexicon represented Briggs's biblical critical abilities at their best: a rigorously detailed compendium whose enduring strength lies not in interpretation or exegesis but rather in exhaustive linguistic "close work."[42]

The very "dated" nature of these works published in the early years of the new century, moreover, pointed to Briggs's signal contributions in the early days of the field. Honors began to pour in from various institutions and learned societies that, one suspects, wished to build monuments on the grave of a now safely buried prophet. Thus, in 1901 Briggs learned that he would be awarded the Doctor of Letters by Aberdeen and Oxford Universities, and immediately made plans to travel to Britain in the spring.

The travel and ceremony took their toll, and by midsummer Briggs wrote to the seminary requesting a leave of absence for the fall semester. The leave was quickly granted, but word of the leave found Briggs already in Rome. For Briggs had displayed a deepening interest in a movement gathering strength within the Roman church at the turn of the century, a movement of modernist scholars committed to the same critical agenda as their liberal Protestant brethren. Thus began, in the fall of 1901, one of the more interesting episodes in the history of Protestant-Catholic relations.[43]

Catholic modernism has been described by its most famous chronicler as a temporally circumscribed congeries of movements that emerged suddenly around the year 1890, and disappeared with equal abruptness in 1907. The various biblical, historical, and philosophical efforts that were pursued during those seventeen years represented a spectrum of widely disparate critical crusades; but these disparate crusades were united into something like a movement by the shared desire to reconcile Catholic doctrine with "the scientific outlook characteristic of the modern world." The heart of this scientific outlook was a ubiquitous concern for the historical process itself. "Since Christianity is an historical religion," as one of the leaders of the movement could thus observe,

> claiming that certain alleged historical events are of vital significance for the relations of God and man, a special problem is that of determining the historicity of its original traditions by the light of historical criticism.[44]

It was this consciously historicist emphasis that united the disparate theological interests of Alfred Loisy, Maurice Blondel, and George Tyrrell, and that explains their passionate longing for the intellectual renewal of Catholicism through the recasting of Catholic dogma within a historico-critical framework. And the door to such a recasting had been opened by the Roman pontiff himself. The election of Leo XIII to the papacy in 1878 led progressives throughout the European church to predict a new day for Catholic intellectual life. And progressive encomiums to the new pope appeared justified in 1880 when, for the first time in its history, the doors to the Vatican Library were opened to scholars of all faiths. This action was widely read as proof positive that the new pope not only actively encouraged historical studies, but also

> encouraged their pursuit in the most absolutely candid and critical spirit. He has *meant* what he said — that history is to be pursued by its own methods and independently of its giving such results as are most acceptable to Catholic controversialists.[45]

This atmosphere of promise and progressive optimism that flourished in the early years of Leo's papacy was especially pronounced among French Catholic scholars at the Institut Catholique, so that by 1890 the renowned church historian Louis Duchesne had trained a generation of young scholars firmly committed both to the new critical methods and to Catholic truth. It was, in fact, Duchesne's most brilliant student at the Institut — Alfred Loisy — who pressed to its logical conclusion his mentor's critical program launched in this sunny atmosphere, in the process provoking the great twentieth-century intellectual trauma for European Catholicism.[46]

Duchesne's lectures on the historical method, as well as later critical studies under Ernest Renan at the Collège de France, had brought the young Loisy to the conclusion that Scripture, while a deposit entrusted to the church for its teaching, was also a historical document conditioned by its cultural environment and thus a proper subject for the historical method. Indeed, by 1890, when he was appointed to the chair of biblical studies at the Institut, Loisy had come to believe that "historical criticism necessarily precedes, and thus informs, theology and edification."[47]

Both Briggs and Newman Smyth had begun to take notice of Loisy's critical efforts within the Roman church well before the publication in 1902 of *L'Évangile et l'Église*, Loisy's book that officially launched the modernist controversy in Catholic Europe. Both had recognized, with that special sense granted to kindred spirits, the ecumenical possibilities of such a movement (so similar to their own progressive program) that sought to synthesize the ancient Christian world view with modern thought.[48]

Briggs had thus been seeking an introduction to Catholic modernist scholars generally, and to Loisy in particular, when he arrived in Rome in the fall of 1901. He immediately called on Denis O'Connell, an American prelate of considerable political power and distinct liberal leanings, who as rector of the North American College had himself been a principal participant in the "Americanist Controversy" that had exercised the American Catholic church just two years before. It was thus through this American prelate that Briggs met, on November 19, 1901, the "lay bishop of the modernists," the Baron Friedrich von Huegel.[49]

Von Huegel was an Anglo-Austrian noble who combined devout

Catholic sensibilities with wide learning and almost irresistible social charm. Indeed, von Huegel's social skills have been credited
with engineering the entire Catholic modernist movement. The
baron had consciously sought out scholars whose work had evinced
the critical brilliance he prized so highly, encouraging and stimulating them in their pursuits, and introducing them to one another's
work. Thus, to the Catholic intellectuals who formed the loose band
of modernists who would shortly provoke unparalleled ecclesiastical wrath, von Huegel occupied the status of guide, philosopher,
and friend.[50]

Von Huegel's friendship with Loisy, Tyrrell, and other promising scholars, moreover, rested on their shared concern for the
autonomy of historical science. Insofar as modernism meant complete liberty for theologians to apply the critical approach to the
religious records of the past, von Huegel supported and even sponsored the modernist movement. But the good baron had no desire
for the martyr's crown; if the critical campaign proved to be too
dangerous for overt campaigning, then other, less overt, methods
had to be brought into play to ensure its eventual victory within the
church. And it was precisely here that the baron's famous American
visitor would eventually prove to be of special value.[51]

Briggs's meeting with the "modernist bishop" provided him
with the firsthand confirmation that he and Smyth had sought —
that Catholic scholars committed to critical methods likewise
sought a repristination of the faith through the application of modern scientific methods and insights. Briggs was euphoric after the
meeting: here was the bridge for reuniting Protestant and Catholic Christians into one organism, a bridge resting firmly on the
sure supports of historical criticism! Briggs returned to America
confirmed in his commitment to church union based on the use
of historical criticism, a renewed commitment whose clearest (and
most disastrous) embodiment found expression in an essay entitled
"Catholic — The Name and the Thing."[52]

Briggs's article in the July 1903 number of the *American Journal
of Theology* announced that there was no word in theology more
misused than the term "catholic" and set out to "trace the word
in the lines of its historic meanings." The recent historical studies of scholars like Arthur C. McGiffert, Philip Schaff, and Adolf
Harnack, Briggs announced, had uncovered the fact that the ante-

Nicene church had defined catholicity by insisting on a three-fold bond of unity: historical unity with the apostles ("apostolicity"); geographical unity throughout the world ("catholicity in its narrow sense"); and vital unity linking all believers with the enthroned Christ (the church's "holiness"). It was the combination of these three types of unity that thus defined the historical meaning of the term "catholic."[53]

There could be no doubt, Briggs announced, that by the close of the second century the terms "Roman" and "Catholic"

> were so closely allied that they were practically identical. Thus, the Roman Catholic church of our day is the heir by unbroken descent to the Roman catholic church of the second century, and it is justified in using the name "catholic" as the name of their church.[54]

But Briggs further observed that the Reformers' "wantonness in separating from the jurisdiction of Rome and breaking the unity of the church" was more than justified in their commitment to redeeming the church's essential holiness — a far more important mark of the true church than its catholicity in a narrow geographical sense. In forfeiting geographical unity for ethical integrity, however, the various Reformed churches nonetheless retained apostolic warrant for their disparate polities and orders (apostolicity). It had been precisely this pluralist "evidence of the centuries" as to the apostolicity of the various ecclesiastical forms of modern Christendom that the new criticism offered to the ecumenical movement.[55]

If the problem of apostolicity had been thus resolved by historical criticism, however, the problems of geographic and ethical unity remained. It was precisely in considering these two "marks of the church" that the nexus of Briggs's concerns was revealed. The most important movement of their age was "the catholic reaction," a movement wherein "God's Holy Spirit is breaking the way for the revival, the recatholization, and the reunion of Christendom in holy love."[56]

This "catholic reaction" could be found among both Catholic and Protestant scholars, and would recover the rich three-fold meaning of the ancient term "catholic" through the critical reappropriation of truths lost through the accidents of history. Catholic scholars, Briggs confidently announced, were now willing to allow — as a result of their own critical scholarship — that many of the Reformers' concerns regarding the church's holiness had been justified. The chief problem for the Protestant side, however, was that "most Protestants do not as yet wish to be catholic, but desire simply to be Christians." Such indifference to full catholicity, especially the callous indifference to movements attempting to realize the geographic institutional unity of Christendom, represented a stunted understanding of Christianity itself: "loving, growing Christianity strives for the maximum. Christianity, so soon as it began to grow, grew into catholicity."[57]

The "greatest step in a catholic direction" that had been taken in their age was the 1888 quadrilateral — a prophetic call that justified Anglican claims to a mediatorial role in preparing for the coming catholicism. And although its platform for church reunion was far from perfect, it nonetheless represented the

> best platform for catholic unity thus far proposed. The truest catholicity is brotherly love, and if the Quadrilateral could be used with this vital force beneath it, it would accomplish a great work in the reconciliation, the recatholization and the eventual reunion of the Christian Church.[58]

Briggs's article, for all of its talk of scientific impartiality and critical rigor, nonetheless bore all the usual marks of Briggsian tendentiousness. Indeed, the secular and religious press all but fell over itself in speculating on the "real issue" behind this amazing tribute to Catholicism from one of the premier evangelical scholars in America. The article immediately provoked a public (and published) response not unlike the reaction to his inaugural address over a decade before. The New York *Sun* and the *Catholic News* both asserted that the article witnessed to Briggs's imminent departure "into the arms of the Mother of Churches," while the *Examiner* baldly reported that "Dr. Briggs is now ready to be elevated into the Roman Church." The Episcopal *Churchman*, on the other hand, simply observed that Briggs had made "an honest attempt at scientific impartiality" on a difficult subject. The *Evangelist* likewise asserted that the spirit of the article was "eminently catholic," and thus stood as a guarantee against any such "Roman nonsense" as that predicted in other papers.[59]

It was in this somewhat kinetic atmosphere that the (Episcopal) Church Club of New York in early 1904 invited Briggs to deliver before them an expanded version of the much-controverted article. Briggs's address, now entitled "How May We Become More Truly Catholic?," in fact provoked an even greater furor, forcing Bishop Henry Potter, like the New York Presbytery over a decade before, to "pronounce" on Briggs's orthodoxy.[60]

Briggs's Church Club address, in its revelation of the unitive and divisive impulses preoccupying the American evangelical establishment in the early years of the twentieth century, clearly rivaled in importance his earlier, more famous, January address. The address (giving rise to the "Second Briggs Case" — as the furor following it was quickly labeled) announced that critical scholars of "other traditions" had offered irrefutable scientific evidence to Protestants that they "should frankly recognize the mistakes of the Reformers" for the sake of a larger, higher vision — the vision of the one, holy, catholic church. Rome, Briggs assured his listeners, "can teach us many things we ought to learn" — a fact that he said would become evident to any dispassionate observer of the modernist movement then promising to reform the Roman church from within. Such an internal Roman reform, moreover, would leave the progressive Protestant tradition behind in the ongoing evolution of salvation history. Thus, the necessity of bridging the gulf between Protestantism and Rome had taken on a new urgency. To this now-pressing question, Briggs offered in answer the example of the most impressive technological feat of the modern age:

> How has the East River been bridged? At first two huge towers are built on each side of the river, then a slender wire is stretched from the top of these towers; this wire gives place to cables.... So it will be in the Church. The world has learned many new things. We have new ideas of God's universe; we have new scientific methods. Reconstruction is in progress on the grandest scale. Out of it will spring, in God's own time, a rejuvenated, a reorganized, a truly universal Christianity.[61]

Briggs's elaborate metaphor of the Brooklyn Bridge, of course, confirmed what many in the Church Club audience already suspected — that Briggs had been deeply affected (clearly too much so) by the secular, mechanistic spirit of their age. But the metaphor further intimated a conception of "catholic" that must have raised Protestant hackles and knit evangelical brows throughout the audience, just as Briggs's efforts on behalf of the League for Catholic Unity had nearly a decade before. The coming Christianity would be built equally by Protestant and Catholic scholars using critical methods. Further, the new critical scholarship now made it mandatory, especially for good Anglicans long associated with a *via media* tradition, to recognize that "there were other and in some respects greater Reformers in the sixteenth century than Luther, Zwingli and Cranmer." Briggs offered as examples of such greater reformers the loyal Catholics Thomas More, Staupitz, and Erasmus.

> These three immortals, who did not separate themselves from the Roman Catholic Church, who remained in the Church to patiently carry on the work of reform therein — these three were the irenic spirits, the heroic representatives of all that is truly Catholic, the beacons of the *greater* Reformation which is impending.[62]

The most fruitful thing the English church could contribute to the battle for the coming catholicism, Briggs announced, was an example of a broad spectrum of Catholic and Protestant sensibilities peacefully coexisting within one institution. The Anglican tradition, "broadened by the discipline of history," had learned how to integrate theological and liturgical differences into a higher unity. This unity was a distant but important precursor to the modern, critical catholicism that would define the new Christianity emerging in the present:

> There is greater diversity in the Anglican Church at the present time than in any other body. If we would be truly Catholic, we should stretch forth our hands frankly and cordially to the sister churches of Christendom. We should break down the walls of prejudice and remove all misunderstanding. Let us emphasize the consensus.[63]

"More Briggsian Heresy!" proclaimed the *Mail and Express*, while the New York *Sun* reported that although "no one in the Episcopal diocese from Bishop Potter on down is very keen about putting Dr. Briggs on trial," the very force of the public reaction to Briggs's speech called for decisive action. The *New York Tribune* and the *Brooklyn Times* announced that another trial was unavoidable and even desirable to vindicate Episcopalian honor. The (Anglo-Catholic) *Living Church* gloated over its earlier predictions of doom in allowing Briggs into the church in the first place, while the *Catholic Universe* of Cleveland, Ohio, and New York's *Catholic World* both predicted Briggs's imminent departure from the "schismatic fold" into the true church.[64]

The outcry that followed the Church Club address emerged from a complex web of factors. Briggs had recently been named a canon of Henry Potter's architectural dream (the Cathedral of St. John the Divine) then rising on the east slope of Morningside Heights, so that many Episcopal hackles were understandably raised by headlines that screamed "Briggs a Menace to the Cathedral Fund!"[65]

But Briggs's address also represented, at least among a sizable portion of American Protestants, the realization of the deepest evangelical fears. Only one as quixotic and headstrong as Briggs could have failed to understand the fear and loathing such promises of "catholic union" would instill among American evangelicals still distrustful, for all of their progressivism, of the Beast on the Tiber. Briggs promised that the application of critical methods to the most important institutional question before mainline Protestants — ecumenism — would bring about the dissolution of the boundaries separating Protestants and Catholics. It was as though the ghosts of all the Hodges and Warfields had risen up and stood witness against Briggs and his abominable methods. This, they seemed to say, was the end result of baptizing the godless works of historicism into the evangelical camp; this was the promise held out by historical criticism to a Christian America.

Briggs's application of historical criticism to the cause of Christian unity thus contributed, quite inadvertently, to the victory of the federationist model of ecumenical activity among American Protestants at the beginning of the twentieth century. More specifically, it was the centuries-old evangelical fear of "Roman idolatry" — a fear raised among progressive evangelicals by Briggs's rhetoric in campaigns on behalf of organic ecumenism — that aided the federationist cause. Thus, while neither his name nor his address was mentioned, a little over a year later on November 15, 1905, when the Inter-Church Conference on Federation was organized, one can discern in that first organizational step towards the Federal Council of Churches a widespread desire to effect unified action for apostolic activity while avoiding the disturbing specters raised by Briggs's style of ecumenical thought. The Inter-Church Conference witnessed to the fact that American evangelicals did indeed desire to erect an ecclesiastical bridge over the span that separated them; but both towers that supported the structure were to rest solidly on American evangelical soil, and the flood that flowed between them was recognized as the Hudson, not the Tiber.[66]

The members of the Church Club were shaken as much by the public denunciations of the "un-Protestant sentiments" expressed in the address as by their own outraged sensibilities, so that their president, George M. Miller, felt compelled to report the entire episode to Bishop Potter. Miller in fact sought to vindicate the truly Protestant nature of their fellowship by requesting a formal judgment from the bishop as to Briggs's orthodoxy. But Potter was convinced that a calming influence was now in order, and proceeded to inform both Miller and the press that he had found the address eminently satisfactory, displaying a true irenic spirit as well as loyal Anglican hopes for church reunion.[67]

But fears of ecclesiastical unpleasantness (like that which had so quickly developed a decade before) grew even more distinct throughout 1904. These fears, however, were built on far more solid foundations, for Briggs was indeed involved in the kind of conspiracy with members of the Roman church that appeared to justify the darkest fears of his and his methods' detractors.

6

Mediating Modernism

Reform in the Church Catholic

By 1900, the challenge of historical criticism had produced a pattern of conflict within the American evangelical mainstream that would define the theological battles between conservative and liberal Protestants until well into the twentieth century. While this pattern of conflict was played out with special drama and poignancy throughout the career of Charles Briggs, it was the last decade of his life — more than any other period in his career — that revealed with special vividness the pattern of those divisive impulses. In the years before his death in 1913, Briggs's most cherished theological conviction — that a critically informed modernism would provide Western Christianity with the most effective vehicle for mediating the gospel to a new age — underwent profound assault from both within and without the progressive camp.

The increasingly radical works produced by Briggs's spiritual children within the modernist scholarly camp raised disturbing questions in his own mind about the evangelical integrity of the progressive cause. Briggs's theological heirs produced critical works resting on the foundations he himself had laid, but shorn of the heart-felt piety and doctrinal certainty forged in the fires of personal conversion. To Briggs this modernist "second generation" appeared to have lost the ability to successfully balance scientific rigor with a soul-warming evangelicalism, thereby leaving the duty of "preaching conversion" to the obscurantists. At the same time, Briggs's bitter experience with ecclesiastical reactionaries during the Roman Catholic modernist crisis — a direct result of his ecumenical campaign to reunite divided Christendom — raised equally disquieting questions about the entrenched confessionalism of the churches. How were intelligent and educated persons to be brought to Christ when the ecclesiastical institutions entrusted with the gospel message evinced such hostility to the best thought of the age?

Briggs died without resolving these troubling questions; indeed, the questions remain today. But his story during these years throws a human light on the impulses effecting the dissolution of the mainstream religious tradition into warring factions. Indeed, Briggs's faithful adherence to the gospel of mid–nineteenth-century progressive evangelicalism, despite growing pressures from the theological left and right, offers a stable position from which to chart the widening chasm dividing the American religious establishment.

Briggs's very perseverance in advocating a resolutely evangelical gospel based on the best modern scientific thought, moreover, even in the face of unresolved personal and professional doubts, revealed the true mettle of that modernist vision of Christianity to which he had committed his life — a vision of believers facing an ambiguous universe with open minds and loving hearts, strong in faith.

In the spring of 1904, Charles Briggs was formally transferred from the Robinson Chair of Biblical Studies to the chair of "Theological Encyclopedia and Symbolics," the transfer representing a belated but sincere institutional attempt to establish Briggs in an academic position in which his interests and energies would find freedom for expression. But the chair and the transfer represented as well the realization of Briggs's long-expressed dream (first enunciated in 1895) of a "theological university" — a graduate theological faculty that would be resident at Union Seminary and that would train scholars as well as ministers in the scientific study of religion.[1]

With his new appointment, moreover, Briggs was granted a year's leave of absence from the seminary to prepare for his new professorship, a year that found him in Europe, in the thick of the theological maelstrom exercising the Roman church.[2]

Briggs's involvement in the controversy exercising European Catholic intellectuals derived in part from his own long-held belief that both Catholic and Protestant modernists represented various divisions of the same army. This ecumenical army, moreover, battled for a reformed and purified gospel — freed from the dross of human traditions — to effect a saving encounter between modern Christians and the living Christ. But Briggs's decision to lend a hand to the embattled Catholic progressives was fueled as well by a personal audience with Pope Pius X, an interview that had been arranged by Roman theologian Giovanni Genocchi. Genocchi was a Catholic biblical scholar of decidedly progressive sentiments with whom Briggs had carried on a regular correspondence since his first Roman visit, a Roman insider who would become Briggs's informant on Vatican intrigue in the troubled days ahead.[3]

The interview, as Briggs reported it to his daughter, was a "delightful" one in which he and the pontiff talked "in a most friendly way and in the frankest manner about infallibility, liberty of conscience, Reunion, etc." Briggs left the interview convinced that the pope himself had given him an implicit (but clear) signal as to the latent sympathy that the very highest authorities in the church harbored for the reforms being pressed by the Catholic modernists.[4]

Within a month of the papal interview, Briggs published an article for the London *Expositor* that marked his first active participation in the European modernist controversy. "Loisy and His Critics in the Roman Catholic Church" represented an extended defense of the modernist abbé on four charges lately proffered against him by anonymous critics. But the article, especially its rhetorical strategy, likewise represented a superb display of intellectual shadowboxing — as though both Briggs and the Roman authorities really knew that the furor involved more bluster than substance, and that it had to be played out for the sake of appearances.[5]

Loisy, Briggs argued, had quite correctly observed that there was not sufficient historical evidence to prove definitely that Jesus had taught his own divinity, that he had risen physically from the tomb, or that he had founded the church before his resurrection.

Loisy had based these conclusions, Briggs announced, on critical investigations that were above scholarly reproach. But Loisy professed acceptance of those doctrines — despite the fact that they were clearly not revealed in Scripture — solely on the authority of the church. Protestant scholars around the world, Briggs announced, marveled at such piety and submissiveness, and at the institution that could command them. Further, Briggs intimated that the holy father himself recognized the value of such scholarly submissiveness and piety, despite the efforts of a curial cabal to punish Loisy.[6]

In the *Expositor* article Briggs had scrupulously avoided any implication that the pope himself was involved in the criticism of Loisy's theological program; indeed, believing that his papal interview had given him clear evidence of the opposite, Briggs had gone out of his way to separate the person of the pontiff from the critics of theological reform. This rhetorical distancing of the pope from Loisy's critics was furthered in an article written for the July issue of the *North American Review.* "Reform in the Roman Catholic Church," as Briggs's article was entitled, announced that the "history of the Roman Church since the 16th century has been a history of reforms," a history that would reach culmination in the pontificate of the present pope, who promised to be a "still greater reformer." There could be little doubt, Briggs further stated, that "Pius himself is at the head of the reform movement" that many inside the Roman curia sought to portray as the work of the modernists. Indeed, Briggs argued that American evangelicals must keep a watchful eye on Catholic reform, since

> it is of great importance to understand the fundamental principle of reform in the words of the Pope himself, namely to make Jesus Christ himself the center and mainspring of all reform. This is exactly what the most enlightened Protestants desire for their own churches; what more can they ask from the Church of Rome? If now the Pope can succeed in raising up Catholics through-out the world to reforming everything in Christ, there will be ere long the greatest revival and reformation known to history, and the Protestant Churches will have to bestir themselves to keep pace with it.[7]

Protestants would indeed have to "bestir themselves," Briggs announced, since such reform was all but assured "under a Pope of such spirituality, simplicity and open-mindedness; a man possessed of unusual grasp of mind, insight, and real moral power." Further, this reform-minded, *evangelical* pontiff sought to eradicate those institutional evils that had played the most important role in causing the divisions of the Western church at the time of the Reformation — the bureaucratic curia and the moribund Code of Canon Law. Once these ecclesiastical evils were corrected, Christians "outside the walls" would stand condemned as unreformed schismatics.[8]

The disparity between Briggs's published estimate of Rome's sentiments as to ecclesiastical and theological reform, and the curia's subsequently ruthless (but quite effective) campaign to eradicate the modernists' reformist agenda, constituted a chasm of formidable breadth. Indeed, that chasm was considerably wider than can be easily explained through reference to such factors as Briggs's political naiveté on things *romanità*, or deliberate subterfuge on the part of Vatican officials (and of the pope himself) as to their true feelings on theological reformation.

A more cogent explanation of this disparity takes account of both Roman political posturing and of American ecclesiastical naiveté, but contextualizes it far more satisfactorily within intellectual and institutional impulses then exercising the Western religious world. Two self-contained (indeed mutually exclusive) universes of discourse collided on that fateful afternoon when Briggs and the Roman pontiff discussed "in a most friendly and frank manner" the prospects of Christianity in the modern world. As in the Presbyterian debates over inspiration and creedal revision several decades before, both parties to the discussion honestly presented their views, and both appear to have been genuinely delighted to discover that the other sought a movement to "reform all things in Christ" in order to make the gospel more effective in the modern world. Both thus perceived in the other a truly evangelical, truly catholic, brother Christian.

What neither perceived, however, was the vast ideational expanse that separated them in defining that reformist goal. For Briggs, any reform at all was predicated on the necessity of refracting the received tradition through the lens of criticism. The resulting evangelical message would allow intelligent, scientifically critical men and women to encounter the saving presence of Christ in their world. The pontiff saw precisely that process as the ultimate betrayal of the deposit of faith; the very encounter between Christ and modern believers so passionately sought by Briggs depended, in the eyes of the Roman pontiff, on insulating the gospel from the acids of those critical methods pressed by the modernists.

Moreover, conservative fears among both Protestant and Roman ecclesiastical officials had grown considerably over the previous decades. Vatican bureaucrats (no less than Presbyterian denominational officers) now perceived the organized efforts of the liberals, heretofore dismissed as a good-hearted but misguided crusade of ineffective academics, as a genuine threat to the received tradition. Conservative resolve, like liberal confidence, had grown and solidified since the last decades of the nineteenth century. What was now widely feared as a "plot" by the liberals to gain very real ecclesiastical power grew more threatening as the chances for its success increased, for the theological integrity of the deposit of faith appeared to be at stake. And with such high stakes, curial monsignori — like embattled confessionalists within American denominations — believed that in the modernist camp they contended not against mere men, but against principalities and powers.[9]

The ideational expanse that separated Briggs and Pius, however, was revealed with greater clarity for both parties in June 1906. The Pontifical Biblical Commission formally decreed (in the face of almost universal scholarly opinion to the contrary) that the entire Pentateuch was "genuinely Mosaic" in composition, and that apparent textual difficulties could be attributed to Moses' use of secretaries.[10]

Briggs cried "bad faith," while von Huegel set about organizing what has come to be termed the "last symbolic act of defense for the cause of intellectual freedom in the Church." The baron called in all known personal and professional debts to prevent the commission's decision from becoming a dogmatic proposition. But the baron's plan — to orchestrate a public outcry against the decision by noted scholars from a variety of religious traditions — likewise resembled precisely the kind of plot most feared by curial conservatives, a plot of heretics to undermine the authority of the Roman see. Von Huegel's plan (rumors of which quickly gained circulation in the corridors of the Roman curia) thus served to increase the alarm and distrust of an already frightened pope.[11]

On August 25, 1906, the baron wrote to the noted Anglican biblical scholar S. R. Driver, proposing that Driver write a critique of the commission's decision for either the London *Times* or the *Guardian*. The Oxford scholar declined outright to participate in such dangerous (and potentially disastrous) political goings-on. But in the meantime, on August 28, von Huegel had penned the first of several dozen long letters to Charles Briggs (marked "strictly confidential" across the top) in which he announced that Briggs stood "in quite an exceptional position to help; indeed there is something of a *duty* on you to do in the affair whatever you can."[12]

The baron, in fact, had quite specific ideas as to what the American scholar could do in the effort to answer the "toothless blind apologetic" being imposed upon Catholic intellectuals. *Now* was the time, von Huegel announced, for showing "the emptiness and utter intellectual lightheadedness of this 'solution'"; if they hesitated at all, utter ruin for the cause of evangelical reform would result. Indeed, the baron announced that he had unimpeachable evidence that the "fantastic, quite impossible decision of the Commission" was soon to be cast as the opening proposition of a syllabus that powerful members of the curia were even then pressing the pope to issue. Von Huegel thus proposed that

> if we can get, say by October 1–15, some three or four solid and emphatic non-Roman Catholic denunciations, then two or three Roman Catholic ones, partly in formal criticism, but in substantial endorsement of the "outside" denunciations, and then, say seven strong, resounding oppositions (kept scrupulously respectful to Rome) this will, my friend, save us all from the misfortune of having such impossibilities solemnly tied upon our anyhow much-burthened backs.[13]

Briggs responded from Italy on September 4 offering his wholehearted support and also agreeing to write the letter requested by von Huegel; but Briggs likewise expressed his anger at having publicly portrayed the pope as an evangelical leader "who desired above all the Reform of the Roman Catholic Church and the Reunion of Protestant Churches with Rome." Indeed, Briggs lamented that it would be a "great grief to me if it should appear that I have been misled, and that I have been the means of misleading others."[14]

Von Huegel offered no words of comfort for Briggs's grieved sense of betrayal, focusing instead on practical measures that would neutralize the curial cabal he was convinced lay behind the commission's pronouncement. He reported that Briggs's letter would "suit exactly in the learned part, and in practically all the personal part," but that there was one material change that had to be made.

> I feel that this letter ought to appear as an inquiry from you to me — you are amazed and indignant, etc., at this impossible decision, and you, a life-long student and leading authority on the very subject, and though not a Roman Catholic, yet a man full of respect for and sympathy with Rome at her best, want to know from me, a Roman Catholic Old Testament scholar and friend, what on earth the thing means. But it must *not* look in any way as if I began the discussion: it is *you* who do so. It is *most* important that this should appear non-prompted.[15]

This rather amazing epistolary exchange between the modernist baron and the American scholar, in fact, demands something of a revision in the traditional historiographic line taken by scholars on the Catholic modernist crisis — that the Vatican's fears of "orchestration" among modernist scholars were the result of hysteria or of rhetorical strategy, or possibly of both. The standard accounts of the European theological controversy have overlooked this important *sub rosa* campaign; for the good baron's "plan" resembled precisely the kind of modernist plot feared (and posited) by the Roman curia. Thus, the fears that had led S. R. Driver to decline to participate in the baron's plan proved to be well-founded, for word of von Huegel's planned response to curial suppression quickly gained credence in Rome. The doomed nature of the enterprise, however, failed to dampen liberal spirits in November 1906 when the London publisher Charles Longman printed a sixty-page monograph, a monograph in the form of two extended "letters" exchanged between Briggs and von Huegel.

The Papal Commission and the Pentateuch ostensibly addressed the relationship of critical scholarship and religious authority in general, and the recent decree of the Pontifical Biblical Commission in particular. Briggs's letter — after careful editing by von Huegel — opened the work as a query about the recent decree. Briggs allowed that there were indeed many able scholars on the commission, but it was singularly destitute of biblical critics. Thus its judgment, whatever its importance in ecclesiastical circles, would have "no influence whatsoever in the scholarly world"; such a judgment would make as much of an impact on critical research "as the decisions of the General Assembly of the Free Church of Scotland against William Robertson Smith, and of the American Presbyterian General Assembly against me." Further, the Roman authorities would betray considerable ineptitude if they sought to include such a decision in a syllabus, for

> it would be a stumbling block to scholars; it would rejoice the enemies of the Church; it would reawaken Protestant polemic; it would greatly injure all irenic movements; it would make the present Pontificate a desperate failure, instead of being, as we had hoped, a great reformatory influence in the Church.[16]

Von Huegel's reply, which constituted the great body of the work, answered that he could not materially challenge or add to Briggs's criticism of the commission's decree, outlining instead the "necessary impulses" already working within Catholicism to assure the eventual acceptance of historical criticism by ecclesiastical authorities.[17]

The joint published effort of Briggs and von Huegel made no discernible impact whatsoever on the Vatican's resolve to condemn the shocking redaction of Christianity presented in the works of progressive Catholic scholars. The decision of the Pontifical Biblical Commission as to the Mosaic authorship of the Pentateuch, in fact, was followed in July 1907 by the syllabus *Lamentabili*. The new syllabus raised the ecclesiastical ante considerably, condemning sixty-five "errors concerning the interpretation of Sacred Scripture and the principle mysteries of the Faith" — errors that included the "deluded sophistry" that Moses had not composed the entire Pentateuch. But the syllabus also went considerably beyond specifically condemned propositions to identify the modern critical world view itself as the "synthesis of all heresies." This heretical world view was antithetical to true Christianity in its very essence, since rather than offering mother church as the interpreter of doctrine, it offered an alternative. Catholics, in fact, could only practice "criticism" provided they reached the conclusions already prescribed by the church — the definitive interpreter and critic of doctrine.[18]

The syllabus, in turn, was followed in September with the encyclical *Pascendi Dominici Gregis*, which offered an elaborate "systemization of the so-called doctrines of the modernists." Curial conservatives had decided that the time to act against the heinous theological (and political) campaign of the liberals had arrived. But their very attempt to systematize into a logically coherent whole the disparate modernist agendas of Loisy, Tyrrell, and Blondel underlined the artificial, makeshift character of the encyclical's condemned "system." Indeed, despite repeated Vatican claims of having uncovered a carefully orchestrated cabal "cleverly disguised" as a loosely related congeries of scholars, the relief expressed by Rome sounded hollow and forced to the European academic community.[19]

But the encyclical was more than just a theoretical condemnation of modernism; it ordained practical measures for its suppression. Anyone who openly or secretly "lent countenance to modernism, either by extolling the modernists, or excusing their culpable conduct, or by carping at scholasticism," indeed, anyone who showed a "love of novelty in history," was to be immediately reported to Rome, and was to be "excluded without compunction from teaching or ecclesiastical office."[20]

Within a month of the appearance of *Pascendi* Briggs wrote to von Huegel reporting on a secret Paris meeting held with French Protestant theologian Auguste Sabatier "and a number of liberal Catholics," a meeting in which Briggs and Sabatier "became like brothers." Briggs announced that the consensus of all of those present was that Briggs should attempt a marshalling of support for the European modernists from the heretofore silent American scholarly world. Briggs himself (as one of the foremost liberal scholars in America) was to issue the call in order to arouse the slumbering American academic community. On his return to America, however, Briggs found only one collaborator in his plan, fellow ecumenical theorist Newman Smyth, who contributed several sections of his *Passing Protestantism and Coming Catholicism* to Briggs's American "campaign."[21]

But Briggs was especially disappointed with the lack of enthusiasm among American Catholics for any show of support; indeed, symbolic of the fear debilitating the Catholic side was a letter Briggs received from his long-time friend James Driscoll. Driscoll was a progressive Catholic theologian teaching at New York's Dunwoodie Seminary and, far more perilously, the editor of the soon to be suppressed *New York Review*. The New York priest apologetically declined an invitation from Briggs to speak at Union Seminary. Under "ordinary and normal ecclesiastical circumstances," Driscoll announced, the invitation would have been welcomed by all.

> But in the present acute crisis it is different.... Nothing so violent and drastic as the recent curial document has appeared on the part of Vatican authorities since the days of the Inquisition. I can compare the crisis to nothing but a cyclone during which people must simply make for the cellar.[22]

Briggs reported dispiritedly to von Huegel that the American Catholic bishops desired to remove themselves as far from the center of fire as possible, "seeking to evade [the encyclical] as they did the one against Americanism, although whether with the same success I doubt."[23]

Briggs had come to believe that if there were to be an American outcry on behalf of the European Catholic progressives, it would have to come from Protestant scholars. He therefore published "The Great Obstacle in the Way of a Reunion of Christendom," as a call to battle to American evangelicals. The article argued that since the movement for church unity represented the most important theological movement of their age, the primary concern of all Christians should be reunion with the "Mother of Churches." Recent Protestant scholarship, moreover, provided compelling evidence that only the papacy possessed the necessary authority and experience to form the center of unity around which separated Christians could re-form. But Briggs sought to vindicate the true nature of the papacy in the eyes of fellow Protestants by distinguishing between the papacy itself and the corrupt "Italianate" curial influences that threatened its destruction:

Those who recognize the historic and valid jurisdiction of the Pope, in accordance with the teaching of Jesus Christ our Saviour, and the consent of the ancient Catholic Church, are not thereby compelled to acknowledge an unlimited jurisdiction. The jurisdiction of the Pope is limited by the divine teaching of Holy Scripture, and by the unanimous consent of the Christian Fathers.[24]

A "platform of reconciliation" had to be pressed by Protestants, and especially by Protestant scholars, Briggs announced — a platform that would constitute an ineluctable attraction to Rome, as it would promise the return of Protestant Christians to papal jurisdiction. But the only possibility for the acceptance of such a platform on the Protestant side would be to limit the jurisdiction of the pope to "that which Jesus Christ prescribed in the Gospel, and the primitive Church recognized. The pathway to reunion is to *constitutionalize* the Papacy."[25]

"The Encyclical against Modernism," published in the January 1908 number of the *Review*, attempted to affix the blame for the inquisition then being enforced in the Roman church on the corrupt Roman curia. The curia had proven to be "too strong for Pius, persuading him to oppose the Reform as the most dangerous of errors." Thus, the essentially *curial* condemnations of 1907 represented

not simply an attack upon liberal Catholics, but upon all that is characteristic of the modern age in Philosophy, Science, Biblical Criticism, and History. It is an effort to overcome Modernism by Medievalism, by making the scholastic Philosophy of the Middle Ages the norm for all things in all time.[26]

But it was in June 1909 that Briggs published what was, perhaps, his most cogent and insightful piece on the battle then exercising conservatives and liberals of all churches. "Modernism Mediating the Coming Catholicism" — as the article published in the *Review* was entitled — represented more an extended reflection on the ideological battle in which he found himself than a call to arms. Borrowing much of his argument (and title) from Newman Smyth, whose magisterial *Passing Protestantism and Coming Catholicism* had just been published, Briggs noted that the Protestant scholastics and the Roman Curia see eye to eye in this fight. Progressive Protestants and Catholic modernists are lined up in the same ranks. It is no longer a battle between Protestants and Catholics.... It is evident that Christianity has, in this conflict between Medievalists and Modernists, entirely new lines of cleavage. The old lines have become indistinct, the new lines are rapidly obliterating them.[27]

Like previous generations, Briggs declared, his contemporaries had to fight for the legitimate insights gained from the best scientific methods of their time, just as the theologians of the Middle Ages had to fight against the "methods of antiquity." And the best scientific methods of their time derived from the critical world view, methods that were mediating the "transition from the Middle Age of the World into the Future Age, just as the Middle Age mediated the transition of the Ancient into the Modern."[28]

To the question as to which of the two great Christian traditions, Protestant and Catholic, would prevail in the religion of the future, Briggs answered without hesitation, "Neither." Modern criticism would mediate whatever was best in both traditions into a new synthesis, a synthesis in which the "reformations of the past" would be fulfilled and completed in the now scientifically verified *ethical* basis of Christian truth — truth revealed in "holy, Christlike, self-sacrificing love." The shape of the "Coming Catholicism" would thus retain the best features of all Christian bodies while transcending all of their limitations.[29]

The curial suppression of modernism proceeded apace in the Roman church, largely without reaction from American scholars. Indeed, the deafening silence of the evangelical critical world, despite Briggs's apologetic campaign in the pages of the *Review*, the *Independent*, and other widely read American periodicals, introduced the first real tremors of uncertainty into Briggs's heretofore secure ideological world. Perhaps — just perhaps — the relevance and accessibility of a gospel in tune with the best scientific scholarship held less attraction for the mass of modern believers than the certainty and immutability promised by the confessionalists. The papal condemnations appeared to ride on a wave of popular confessionalism that made the pope (soon to be "Saint Pius X") more beloved than any pontiff in modern times, and that made the modernist program proscribed by the encyclical genuinely feared among masses of faithful Christians. How was the Christian message to survive as an option for the educated people in the modern world, Briggs wrote to his European confreres, if it became associated with such mindless obscurantism?[30]

But during the same decade in which he began to fear for the future of an enlightened gospel in the face of mounting ecclesiastical confessionalism, Briggs likewise came to worry that the very core of the catholic, evangelical faith was being betrayed by critical scholars within his own modernist household.

Criticism and Dogma

By the opening of the new century, younger progressive scholars like Walter Rauschenbusch and William Adams Brown, while laying claim to the older mantle, were constructing a modernist gospel along lines far more radical (and far more unsettling) than anything Briggs or his generation of scholars thought seemly or even orthodox. Both the poignancy and the irony of the resulting story were heightened by the fact that this second generation of modernist scholars so readily and sincerely acknowledged Briggs and his generation as fathers in the faith while moving on to ever more radical (or thorough) applications of the critical method to the evangelical message. Systematic thinkers like William Newton Clarke, theoreticians of Christian socialism like George Herron, and church historians like Arthur Cushman McGiffert applied critical methods to the tradition with increasingly radical results, results that older liberals like Briggs found difficult to accept. In fact, McGiffert — Briggs's colleague and former student at Union Seminary — represented a superb example of this group that considered itself the legitimate inheritor of the progressive evangelical mantle worn for so long by Briggs himself.[31]

With the retirement of Philip Schaff in 1893, Union Seminary had called Arthur McGiffert from Cincinnati's Lane Seminary to fill its prestigious chair of church history. McGiffert was well known to the Union faculty — a promising former student who had gone on to Berlin to study under the church historian Adolf Harnack, whose historical presuppositions and theological outlook the young American had taken over entirely. McGiffert had already demonstrated his scholarly brilliance in 1890, in a remarkable translation of Eusebius's *Church History* published in Schaff's own series on the Nicene and post-Nicene Fathers. McGiffert's brilliant introduction to the work (contextualizing the apostolic author within the late Mediterranean world) and his extensive notes accompanying the text, revealed him to be a scholar of the first rank; but McGiffert's notes offered no indication that the young historian harbored radical theological views.[32]

McGiffert's relatively "neutral" early historical scholarship was followed, in 1897, by *A History of Christianity in the Apostolic Age*, a work whose demythologized portrait of the early church went beyond what Briggs or the older generation of liberals could countenance as evangelically orthodox. From his faithful application of historical criticism to the earliest Christian records, McGiffert questioned the ascription of the Synoptic Gospels to the apostolic names associated with them, and credited the unknown author of the Fourth Gospel with certain high christological passages traditionally assigned to Jesus himself.[33]

But far more disquieting to Briggs and his generation of liberals was McGiffert's fearless explication of the doctrinal implications of his critical scholarship. The doctrine of the Virgin Birth that rested on the Synoptic infancy narratives had to be recognized as a later, mythical interpretation of Jesus' origin, an interpretation cast in premodern language and categories; the sacrament of the Lord's Supper, traditionally dependent on the scriptural account of the last days of Jesus' historical ministry, must rather be seen as the product of the evolving communal life of the primitive church; and even the doctrine of Jesus' physical resurrection — a doctrine, McGiffert averred, that made sense only within the older conception of a two-storied universe — could not be "scientifically" proven by the biblical narratives of the empty tomb.[34]

McGiffert's fellow Presbyterians were as disturbed by these "scientific findings" as they had been earlier in the decade by the pronouncements of Briggs, and in 1898 the Pittsburgh Presbytery (voicing a disquiet widely shared in the northern church) formally overtured the General Assembly to pronounce on McGiffert's work. Thus did the General Assembly of the church stamp "with its emphatic disapproval all utterances in [McGiffert's] book called to its attention." The assembly further declared that while its fractious church desperately needed peace and while it thus deemed it "wise to take no action at present," it earnestly hoped that McGiffert would be led to "make satisfactory explanation of his position in relation to the Standards of our Church, or in default thereof, [would] peaceably...withdraw from the Presbyterian ministry." Further, the assembly of the following year issued a "Deliverance" in which it reaffirmed the "traditional interpretation" of the inerrancy of Scripture, of Christ's miraculous birth, and of the institution of the Lord's Supper by Christ himself during his earthly ministry.[35]

McGiffert's former teacher and elder colleague at Union watched with considerable ambivalence as these events unfolded. Briggs found the thought of yet another ecclesiastical trial over historical criticism abhorrent; and yet he found the results of McGiffert's critical investigations even more abhorrent. Indeed, so upset was Briggs with the very unevangelical scholarship of his younger colleague that he resolved to press the Board of Directors for McGiffert's removal from Union's faculty for (of all things) doctrinal irregularities. Word about Briggs's contemplated action quickly leaked out, however, and Union's president, Francis Brown, met privately with Briggs at the urging of an alarmed faculty. Brown represented to the former heretic how "unfortunate" it would be for the good reputation of both the seminary and of Briggs himself if the latter, whom the seminary had stood by when he was under trial, should now be himself the accuser of a former student and colleague. Briggs was mollified by Brown's emotional appeal, and promised to drop his plan of pressing for McGiffert's removal from the faculty. But Briggs remained profoundly disturbed by some of the latest products of critical scholarship, and he opened a second campaign during the last decade of his life, a campaign against a "faithless generation" within his own household.[36]

Briggs's contemplated protest against a fellow critical scholar and colleague offers a vignette of striking irony and pathos, a vignette that needs explication in light of Briggs's life-long commitment to critical inquiry and academic freedom. Briggs's contemplated presentment against McGiffert indeed represented an emotional and intellectual aberration in Briggs's career, but an aberration built on Briggs's growing personal fears about the evangelical integrity of his intellectual children. Briggs's contemplated action — resting on some of his most deeply held beliefs about the nature of the gospel he sought to save from the acids of modernity — thus represented something of a *cri de coeur* against the betrayal of his evangelical vision from within his own camp.

One of the epistemological certainties of the older progressive camp (carried through four decades by warhorses like Briggs) had been that the central truths of the gospel — like the Virgin Birth and the bodily resurrection of Jesus — lay safely beyond destructive critical fires. It was in order to prove the scientific verifiability of just such doctrines, in fact, that Briggs's generation of liberals had taken up the historicist cause. But in the first years of the twentieth century the McGiffert episode announced the dismantling of this antebellum evangelical tradition of a scientifically respectable gospel. For almost a century, mainstream evangelical Protestantism had held together scientific rigor and heart-warmed piety as necessary concomitants of the true Christian world view. *Both* elements in this tradition, both the rigor and the piety, were necessary in the eyes of evangelicals like Briggs if the gospel was to be mediated successfully to the modern age.

Even in his colloquies with nonevangelical scholars like the Catholic modernists, Briggs had striven to effect a unified and reformed Christian tradition wherein scientific methods could be personally verified through a "heart experience" of the risen Jesus. It was for this reason that Briggs and his generation of critical scholars had sought to use critical methods to eradicate dead human traditions — both Catholic and Protestant — from the central gospel message.

An almost palpable sense of alarm and fury (in about equal proportions) thus characterized "Criticism and Dogma," written by Briggs for the June 1906 number of the *North American Review*. Briggs argued (in tones reminiscent of his former Princeton opponents) that all Christians were obliged to accept ancient doctrines like the Virgin Birth as articles of faith, regardless of the evidence of modern criticism, since such doctrines were

> inextricably involved in the Christological principle that lies at the basis of Christian Dogma and Christian Institutions. [Christians] cannot possibly recognize that the birth of Christ was by ordinary human generation. It would turn back the dial of Christianity nearly

two thousand years; it would break with Historical Christianity and its Apostolic foundation, and imperil Christianity itself.[37]

Such a "break with Historical Christianity" would rend the fabric of the source of all human knowledge (the historical process itself) as well as make personal conversion, traditionally dependent on doctrines like the physical resurrection of Jesus, problematic. As one whose "life work as a professor of theology for thirty-eight years had been to battle and suffer much for the rights of criticism," Briggs declared that he should be able to discern what was, and what was not, truly scientific criticism. The "modern objectors to the Christ of the Church" were neither Christian nor scientific. As for those scholars like McGiffert advancing blasphemous notions about the Lord,

> true modernists reject them, for they prostitute the severe work of scientific criticism, which modern scholarship has so greatly advanced, to their unscientific speculations. Some years ago they said, "Let us go back from the Christologies to the historic Christ." But they have found that the historic Christ of the Gospels corresponds with the Christ of the Church, and now they are seeking a Christ unknown to the Gospels and misunderstood by his apostles.[38]

He had always contended for the revision of theological formulas, Briggs announced, and for the "appropriation of all that has been proven valid in modern science." And much needed doctrinal revision had in fact been accomplished in their time. Moral life had been "christologized," and similar efforts were underway to "christologize the social, economic, and political activities" of the times as well. But the danger, now realized in the works of some younger modernist scholars, was the creation of preposterous interpretations of Christ's earthly ministry for the sake of making the ancient gospel more "relevant." These scholars substituted for Christ's "meek submission to authority a struggle for economic betterments, for sociologic and political rights."[39]

Briggs declared that the church in its "advance in the knowledge of Christ has always been obliged to contend with reactionaries on the one hand and rash speculators on the other." Social gospelers, Jamesian pragmatists, Ritschlian "advocates of experience," and those foolhardy scholars advancing the "shipwreck of Christian dogma to which Harnack would reduce the faith of Christ's Church" — no less than Warfield and Patton — fell far short of the mark of a truly scientific, truly Christian, theology. Those who would truly know Jesus must

> not only study him properly, but have faith in him, love him and adore him. Spiritual things can be understood only by spiritual men. The Christ of the Church can only be known by a Christian who has come into union with him by faith and love.[40]

While thus blasting younger scholars for a loss of "heart piety," however, Briggs attempted to present an apologia for that evangelical modernism that steered clear of both the reactionary Scylla and the radical Charybdis. This apologia found expression in a much larger work, a work that constituted a recapitulation of Briggs's entire career as a progressive evangelical theologian in Gilded Age America. *Church Unity*, as the title proclaimed, sought to address the issue that Briggs still considered the most important of the age while charting a progressive and orthodox *via media*.[41]

The book opened with an extended chapter on "Christian Irenics," a culminating discipline, Briggs announced, "to which all the others contribute their noblest results." The new discipline represented "the apex of Christian theology to which all the lines of Christian scholarship and Christian life tend, and in which they ultimately find their highest end and perfection." The task of this new discipline was to outline the essentials of a truly evangelical, truly catholic, Christianity by means of a critical elimination of all that was "local, temporal and formal from that which is universal." Irenics (as opposed to polemics) would thus enable modern Christians to "rise above all denominational partisanship and sectarian bigotry," to achieve, for the first time since the apostolic age, one holy church. This was possible, of course, because historical criticism — then in the process of "transforming the entire range of theology" — offered a solid scientific foundation for such unity.[42]

But the mediating modernism effecting this dissolution of the sectarian divisions of Christianity also had clearly defined limits to its scientific right of review:

> There are radical Modernists who are impatient of the slow processes of scholarship and jump at conclusions. In their enthusiasm for the

new, they become hostile to the old and so become revolutionary in their notions. Such Modernists discredit the movement, [for] the Modernists are, for the most part, not radicals, but *conservatives*.[43]

The attack of the theological reactionaries on the true (conservative) modernists, in fact, had "strengthened the hands of the radicals, and stayed the hands of those scholars who are mediating the reconciliation of the Church with the modern world." The coming catholicism proclaimed by Briggs and Smyth would recognize the "divine authority of the Bible, the Church and the Reason, reconciling and harmonizing them in a higher and nobler form of Christianity"; but that catholicism would also set definite limits to criticism's reshaping of doctrine.[44]

Church Unity thus represented a kind of theological *inclusio* to Briggs's modernist career, offering a bandaged but unbowed summation of his campaign for the acceptance of historical criticism among American Protestants. Briggs asked modern Christians to accept biblical criticism as enabling believers to "see the Scriptures in their historic origin, and so cast a flood of new light upon the Bible"; to recognize that all dogmatic and creedal symbols must be "reformed in the progress of the Church as she advances under the guidance of the Spirit towards the ultimate Truth"; to appropriate critically the best of the "entire field of history," a field that disclosed "a multitude of facts unknown to the Fathers."[45]

But the book likewise represented an apologia for a progressive but heart-felt evangelicalism that was, just then, becoming deeply problematic as a unified tradition. Even as Briggs wrote, fundamentalism emerging from the right and "realist theology" on the left were making his efforts to hold the two unstable impulses in the tradition together increasingly difficult. Indeed, Briggs appears to have discerned, while writing what he hoped would be his *magnum opus*, the increasingly hostile religious environment.

Church Unity constituted Briggs's last contribution to the intellectual and cultural discussion that had preoccupied him since the end of the Civil War. Briggs's books published after *Church Unity* — *The Fundamental Christian Faith*, which was published in the year of his death, and the two-volume *History of the Study of Theology*, which was published posthumously by his daughter Emilie — although based on his class lecture notes, constituted pedestrian, rather bland efforts, lacking the excitement and passion that readers had come to associate with Briggs's work.[46]

Briggs's retirement from that academic and ecclesiastical discussion that had consumed his professional and personal passions for four decades was due to a complex web of factors: to the fact that, after 1910, Briggs suffered from regular attacks of nervous exhaustion, as well as to the fact that, after his transfer to the chair of symbolics, he was preoccupied with exploring and defining a totally new (and as it turned out, ephemeral) field of theological endeavor. But the personal ambivalence that exacerbated his physical ailments, and that made the exploration of his new field a welcome respite from rejoining the theological fray that was just then building up for the Fundamentalist Controversy, arose from his own personal doubts about the success of the modernist cause itself. The emerging chasm between theological liberals and fundamentalists raised disturbing questions about the heritage of the evangelical gospel that would be passed on to succeeding generations, a heritage that he, as much as any other evangelical scholar, had helped to shape.

There were, thus, elements of poignancy, irony, and Christian hope (in about equal measure) to Briggs's last words — "Peace, peace" — uttered on June 13, 1913. That which had eluded him with such regularity in history was, perhaps, at last glimpsed beyond it.[47]

Charles Briggs and American Religious History

For the student of American religion, the career of Charles Augustus Briggs constitutes a story of singular importance in its own right, quite apart from its having embodied impulses that were representative of the broader intellectual and religious culture. Briggs's famous heresy trials, as well as his central role in the campaigns for biblical criticism, creedal revision, critical historical study, and ecumenism offer ready access to many of the most important episodes marking the history of Gilded Age America.

Further, the range of Briggs's "contacts" within the network of the evangelical establishment provides the historian with rich prosopographical details for evaluating the history of the recent past. From his student relationship with the giants of mid-nineteenth-century evangelical thought — Henry Boynton Smith, Isaac Dorner, Philip Schaff, Edward Robinson — to his professional interaction with the luminaries of modern American religious culture — Arthur Cushman McGiffert, Benjamin Warfield, Newman Smyth — Briggs's career offers important details for understanding the broader cultural story of the period.

But Briggs's career offers as well a microcosm for understanding the more important, if more diffuse, intellectual challenge that defined the entire period, a challenge that underlay and informed the discrete theological battles of the Gilded Age. Briggs's story in fact embodies the story of the American Protestant encounter with the intellectual modernizing impulse par excellence, historical criticism. Indeed, the pattern of Briggs's interaction with that intellectual impulse — from heady discovery to painstaking application to ambivalent defense in the face of disturbing factionalism — faithfully replicates the broader cultural pattern, a pattern that outlined the collapse and fragmentation of the American religious establishment in the early years of our century.

An understanding of the historicist impulse that defined the various causes espoused by Briggs, moreover, offers a unifying framework in which to understand the religious undertaking in which Briggs was only a participant: that of mediating the Christian message to the modern age. The battles that defined what historians have labeled the "spiritual crisis of the Gilded Age" — battles in which Briggs played an important part — were the more bitter precisely because both sides intuited that what divided them went far deeper than questions of biblical authority or denominational polity. What both camps *sensed* (quite correctly) but failed to understand fully or elucidate was that what divided them involved the very presuppositions of what was (and what was not) possible in the "real world."

It was precisely Briggs's central role in purveying the "threats" of higher criticism, creedal reform, and the new history to America that revealed the more profound and disturbing crisis that underlay those challenges. The traditional Christian understanding of revelation, of ecclesiastical authority, and even of the divine redemptive impulses in history itself, all presupposed a model of reality that Briggs recognized as deeply problematic after the onslaught of historicism. The Christian world view that American evangelicalism had inherited, and had spent so much of its history defending, rested on the assumption that the historical arena in which God's dealings with humankind were effected was a stable, circumscribed, and known reality.

Briggs recognized the vulnerability of that world view in light of historicist claims, and sought to incorporate the new criticism into the arsenal of apologetic methods for the older religious vision, just as his forebears had spirited commonsense realism into the evangelical fortress. Little did Briggs or his conservative opponents, both committed to the same evangelical values, guess that their confrontation with the new critical methods would leave their shared vision so fragmented and discredited.

Historicism thus emerges as the main theme in this *fin-de-siècle* tale of internecine betrayal and civil war; but Charles Briggs provides a "human face" for grappling with this tale's very real if very disembodied theme. Briggs's story is the story of the religious mainstream's attempt to appropriate the best scientific thought of the age for its own apologetic purposes. Precisely *because* it was so much of what it claimed to be — the "religion of the culture" — evangelical Protestantism's attempt to incorporate modern critical thought into its arsenal was almost inevitable; almost equally inevitable — especially in light of the pluralism emerging in so many other parts of American culture — was the fragmentation that resulted. Indeed, it was the collapse of the evangelical mainstream in the early years of the twentieth century, faithfully replicating the cultural fragmentation resulting from industrialization, immigration, and urbanization, that precisely witnessed in powerfully ironic fashion to its claims of being "America's religion."

Briggs's career as an evangelical critical scholar offers the student of Gilded Age America an insight into what has often been slighted by religious and cultural historians — that it was the intellectual threat of historicism that informed and united the various religious battles of the period. Briggs's career offers dramatic witness both to the well-founded claims of cultural hegemony made by progressive evangelicals at the close of the nineteenth century, and to the troubled peace that those cultural spokespersons made with the new critical world view.

The attempt to arrive at an accommodation between evangelical values and modern critical presuppositions has largely defined the history of American theology in our century; that history — running from Briggs himself through the "Monkey Trial" to the death-of-God theology and beyond — has been one in which both "liberals" and "conservatives" have played important roles. Briggs's own ambiguous "liberal" position was a product of the progressive evangelical mainstream, and the ambiguity of that position makes his story something like a modern morality tale, a tale that must chasten the claims of both conservatives and liberals in offering definitive models of divine activity within history. Briggs's tale bears witness in contemporary fashion to an ancient doctrine proclaimed by prophets and apostles long before the onslaught of the modern world view — that the "gracious element" in history cannot be circumscribed or exhausted by human categories, no matter how rational or "scientific," and that therein lies redemption.

Notes

Abbreviations used in notes:
> *TLB = Transcribed Ledger Books*
> *CABC = Charles A. Briggs Collection*
> *UTS = Union Theological Seminary*

Introduction

1. On Briggs's evangelical values and conservative nature, see William Adams Brown, *A Teacher and His Times* (New York: Charles Scribner's Sons, 1940), 9; Henry Preserved Smith, "Charles Augustus Briggs," *American Journal of Theology* 17 (1913): 497–508; Arthur Cushman McGiffert, "Charles Augustus Briggs," in *Dictionary of American Biography* (New York: Charles Scribner's Sons, 1958), II:40–41.

Chapter 1: The Problem of History

1. The title for this section is taken from an essay by Scottish biblical critic William Robertson Smith; the essay, "The Question of Prophecy in the Critical Schools of the Continent," is in *Lectures and Essays of William Robertson Smith*, John Sutherland Black and George Chrystal, eds. (London: A. & C. Black, 1912), 163–343. On the crisis of historicism, see Georg G. Iggers, "The Idea of Progress: A Critical Reassessment," *American Historical Review* 71 (October 1965): 1; Grant Wacker, "The Demise

of Biblical Civilization," in *The Bible in America, Essays in Cultural History*, Nathan Hatch and Mark Noll, eds. (New York: Oxford University Press, 1982), 121–138, 123; Gaius Glenn Atkins, *Religion in Our Times* (New York: Round Table Press, 1932).

2. Willis B. Glover, *Evangelical Nonconformists and Higher Criticism in the Nineteenth Century* (London: Independent Press, Ltd., 1954), 12–13. For a more cogent argument against Darwinian evolution as the "chief culprit," see James R. Moore, *The Post-Darwinian Controversies* (Cambridge: Cambridge University Press, 1979), 12; D. H. Meyer, "American Intellectuals and the Victorian Crisis of Faith," *American Quarterly* 27 (1975): 585–602; Paul Carter, *The Spiritual Crisis of the Gilded Age* (DeKalb: Northern Illinois University Press, 1971), 14.

3. Friedrich Meinecke, *Die Enstehung des Historismus*, Zwei Bande (Munich: R. Oldenbourg, 1936), 1; Charles A. Beard and Alfred Vagts, "Currents of Thought in Historiography," *American Historical Review* 42 (April 1937): 460–483, 466; Ernst Cassirer, *The Problem of Knowledge* (New Haven: Yale University Press, 1950), 170. The term *historicism*, used broadly by American scholars in Briggs's time to refer to a historically conditioned, evolutionary understanding of the human past, became a deeply problematic critical concept after World War I. Historical scholars since Briggs's death have fought a long and exceptionally bitter war over von Ranke's perhaps too sanguine view that it was possible to reconstruct past events as they "really happened." Indeed, that very phrase, or rather the philosophical presupposition behind it — that there was an "essence" to past events that could be reconstructed by historical scholarship — has come to be viewed by many (if not most) modern historians as naive, if not disingenuous. This study will prescind entirely from this more recent philosophical debate, taking the term *historicism* to mean what Briggs and his generation of American scholars meant when using it.

4. Carl Becker, *The Heavenly City of the Eighteenth-Century Philosophers* (Cambridge: Harvard University Press, 1932), 18–19; see also R. G. Collingwood, *The Idea of History* (Oxford: The University Press, 1946), 302; Louis Gottschalk, "The Historian and the Historical Document," *Social Science Research Bulletin* 53 (1945): 25.

5. On Herder, see Hans Meyerhoff, *The Philosophy of History in Our Times* (Garden City, N.Y.: Doubleday & Co., Inc., 1959), 10; Georg Iggers, *The German Conception of History* (Middletown, Conn.: Wesleyan University Press, 1968), 30; Frank E. Manuel, *Shapes of Philosophical History*, 2d ed. (Stanford, Calif.: Stanford University Press, 1971), 74–78; Maurice

Mandelbaum, *History, Man and Reason: A Study of Nineteenth-Century Thought* (Baltimore: Johns Hopkins University Press, 1971), 58.

6. Georg Iggers, "Historicism," in *Dictionary of the History of Ideas* (New York: Charles Scribner's Sons, 1973), II:457; Meyerhoff, *Philosophy of History*, 12; Iggers, *German Conception of History*, 6; Ludwig Feuerbach, *Samtliche Werke*, 2 vols. (Leipzig: O. Wigand, 1848–1866), II:143–144.

7. Leopold von Ranke, *The Theory and Practice of History* (Indianapolis: Bobbs-Merrill, 1971), 5–23; Mandelbaum, *History, Man and Reason*, 42–47, 128; Iggers, *German Conception of History*, 30; Manuel, *Shapes of Philosophical History*, 81–87; Meyerhoff, *Philosophy of History*, 143.

8. Karl Marx, "Philosophical Manifesto of the Historical School of Law," in *Writings of the Young Marx on Philosophy and Society*, Loyd D. Easton and Kurt H. Guddut, eds. (Garden City, N.Y.: Doubleday & Co., 1967), 96–105; Georg Hegel, *Lectures on the Philosophy of History*, J. Sibree, trans. (London: George Bell & Sons, 1881).

9. Maurice Mandelbaum, "Historicism," in *The Encyclopedia of Philosophy*, Paul Edwards, ed. (New York: Macmillan Co., 1967), IV:22–24; Dwight E. Lee and Robert N. Beck, "The Meaning of Historicism," *American Historical Review* 59 (1954): 568–577; Meyerhoff, *The Philosophy of History*, 4; Iggers, *German Conception of History*, 3.

10. "Liberals made their peace with modernity in various ways, but in the end they all insisted that God's self-revelation is mediated though the flow of history — Protestant conservatives claimed that the saving knowledge of divine things is given directly, unmediated and uncontaminated by the setting in which it is received" (Grant Wacker, "Augustus H. Strong: A Conservative Confrontation with History," Ph.D. Thesis, Harvard University, 1978, 2).

11. For background on European Protestant liberalism, see Karl Barth, *Protestant Theology in the Nineteenth Century*, 3d ed. (London: SCM Press, 1972); H. R. Mackintosh, *Types of Modern Theology: Schleiermacher to Barth* (London: Nisbet, 1937). On European Catholic liberalism, more often referred to as "modernism," see Alec Vidler, *The Modernist Movement in the Roman Church* (Cambridge: The University Press, 1934); Bernard Reardon, *Roman Catholic Modernism* (London: A. & C. Black, 1970); Gabriel Daly, *Transcendence and Immanence: A Study in Catholic Modernism and Integralism* (Oxford and New York: Oxford University Press, 1980). The best single study of American Protestant modernism is William R. Hutchison's *The Modernist Impulse in American Protestantism* (Cambridge: Harvard University Press, 1976). The present study has taken as axiomatic Hutchison's view that immanentism is the central tenet

of the modernist credo. The conservative confrontation with historicism has been well described by Wacker, "Augustus H. Strong"; for a sympathetic view of the conservative dilemma, see T. J. Jackson Lears, *No Place of Grace: Antimodernism and the Transformation of American Culture, 1880–1920* (New York: Pantheon Books, 1981), 40.

12. Howard M. Teeple, *The Historical Approach to the Bible* (Evanston, Ill.: Religion and Ethics Institute, Inc., 1982), 75; Glover, *Evangelical Nonconformists*, 110; Ira V. Brown, "The Higher Criticism Comes to America, 1880–1900," *Journal of the Presbyterian Historical Society* 38 (December 1960): 193–212; Atkins, *Religion in Our Times*, 39; William A. Beardslee, *Literary Criticism of the New Testament* (Philadelphia: Fortress Press, 1970), 5; Edgar V. McKnight, *What Is Form Criticism?* (Philadelphia: Fortress Press, 1969), 3.

13. In 1753 French Catholic Jean Astruc, building on the two names of God (Yahweh and Elohim) in the creation stories of the book of Genesis, posited that Moses had used two source documents in the writing of Genesis; Johann Eichhorn, basing his theories on linguistic study of the glosses and editorial redactions found in the text, in 1783 dated the appearance of the Pentateuch in its present form at the end of the Mosaic period; Johann Semler, the "founder of the historical study of the New Testament," sought to make New Testament interpretation a science by studying Scripture as a literary product of Judeo-Roman culture. See Teeple, *Historical Approach*, 72–109; Jean Astruc, *Conjectures sur les Memoires originaux dont il parôit que Moyse s'est servi pour composer le Livre de la Genèse* (Paris, 1753); Johann Gottfried Eichhorn, *Einleitung in das Alte Testament* (Leipzig, 1780–83); Johann Semler, *Abhandlung von frier Untersuchung des Canon* (Halle, 1770–75); Wilhelm DeWette's introduction to the Old Testament is generally cited as the most important work of biblical criticism produced in the first half of the nineteenth century, incorporating the insights of earlier scholars while offering fresh insights, especially on the Davidic authorship of the Psalms. Abraham Kuenen published between 1861 and 1865 one of the most original and controversial introductions to the Hebrew Scriptures, applying advanced historico-critical methods to the reconstruction of Israel's history. Julius Wellhausen was perhaps the most famous nineteenth-century compiler and practitioner of source and redaction criticism, made famous today by the "Graf-Wellhausen Theory," positing four main documents (J, E, D, and P) redacted over time to produce the present Pentateuch. On DeWette, Kuenen, and Wellhausen, see T. K. Cheyne, *The*

Founders of Old Testament Criticism (New York: Charles Scribner's Sons, 1893), 195.

14. Glover, *Evangelical Nonconformists*, 12; Atkins, *Religion in Our Times*, 44; Brown, "The Higher Criticism," 194.

15. Jerry Wayne Brown, *The Rise of Biblical Criticism in America, 1800–1870* (Middletown, Conn.: Wesleyan University Press, 1969), 153–170.

16. Owen Chadwick, *The Victorian Church*, 2 vols. (New York: Oxford University Press, 1966), II:44; J. Estlin Carpenter, *The Bible in the Nineteenth Century* (London: Longmans, Green & Co., 1903), 72; Alec R. Vidler, *The Church in an Age of Revolution*, 12th ed. (New York: Penguin Books, 1981), 123; Moore, *Post-Darwinian Controversies*, 102.

17. Chadwick, *The Victorian Church*, II:75; Vidler, *Church in an Age of Revolution*, 125–126.

18. P. B. Hinchcliff, *John W. Colenso, Bishop of Natal* (London: Nelson, 1964), 101; idem, *The Anglican Church in South Africa* (London: S.P.C.K. for the Church Historical Society, 1968), 27–110.

19. John C. Greene, *The Death of Adam* (Ames, Ia.: Iowa State University Press, 1959), 249; Friedrich Max Mueller, *Lectures on the Origin and Growth of Religion as Illustrated by the Religions of India* (London: Longmans, Green & Co., 1878); Charles Darwin, *The Origin of Species by Means of Natural Selection* (London: John Murray, 1859); idem, *The Descent of Man and Selection in Relation to Sex* (New York: D. Appleton & Co., 1872).

20. The lines of the poem most often quoted to illustrate the sense of loss that Tennyson expressed for his generation are from section 54, stanzas 13–20:

> I falter where I firmly trod,
> And falling with my weight of cares
> Upon the great world's altar-stairs
> I call upon the name of God.
> I stretch lame hands of faith, and grope
> I gather dust and chaff, and call
> To what I feel is Lord of all
> And faintly trust the larger hope.

21. Winthrop Hudson, "How American Is Religion in America?," in Jerald Brauer, ed., *The Reinterpretation of American Church History* (Chicago: University of Chicago Press, 1968); Ernest Sandeen, "The Distinctiveness of American Denominationalism: A Case Study of the 1846 Evangelical Alliance," *Church History* 45 (1976): 222–234; Charles I. Foster, *An Errand of Mercy: The Evangelical United Front, 1790–1837* (Chapel Hill: University of North Carolina Press, 1960); Richard Carwardine, *Trans-Atlantic*

Revivalism, Popular Evangelicalism in Britain and America, 1790–1865 (Westport, Conn.: Greenwood Press, 1975); Martin Marty, *The Modern Schism: Three Paths to the Secular* (London: SCM Press, 1969). For *evangelical*, I have taken the definition offered by one of the evangelicals' most important advocates, Robert Baird, who in 1844 described as evangelical "those churches whose religion is the Bible, the whole Bible, and nothing but the Bible — On no one point are all these churches more completely united or more firmly established than on the doctrine of the supremacy of Christ in his Church" (*Religion in America* [1944; reprint, New York: Harper & Row, 1970], 210, 258).

22. Robert Handy, *A Christian America, Protestant Hopes and Historical Realities*, 3d ed. (Oxford and New York: Oxford University Press, 1974), 95; Sydney E. Mead, *The Lively Experiment: The Shaping of Christianity in America*, 2d ed. (New York: Harper & Row, 1976), 134; C. Howard Hopkins, *The Rise of the Social Gospel in American Presbyterianism, 1865–1915* (New Haven: Yale University Press, 1940), 14; William R. Hutchison, *Between the Times: The Travail of the Protestant Establishment in America, 1900–1960* (New York: Cambridge University Press, 1989).

23. H. Richard Niebuhr, *The Kingdom of God in America* (1935; reprint, Hamden, Conn.: Shoe String Press, 1956); Handy, *Christian America*, 95; Mead, *Lively Experiment*, 134.

24. Arthur M. Schlesinger, Sr., "A Critical Period in American Religion, 1875–1900," *Massachusetts Historical Society Proceedings* 64 (1930–1932): 523–536; Carter, *Spiritual Crisis*, 3–42; Atkins, *Religion in Our Times*, 38–51; Lears, *No Place of Grace*, 25; Henry F. May, *The Protestant Churches and Industrial America* (New York: Harper & Brothers, Publishers, 1949), chapters 1 and 2.

25. The denominations considered by this work as providing the "spiritual glue" for the culture, and thus occupying "establishment status" in American culture, are the northern Methodist, Congregationalist, northern Presbyterian, northern Baptist, Disciples of Christ, Episcopal, and Lutheran churches. The concept of this seven-member evangelical establishment is a useful if somewhat fluid one, important for general discussions but not to be pressed too literally. See Handy, *A Christian America*, 52; Robert Baird, *Religion in America*, Books 4 and 6; Perry Miller, *The Life of the Mind in America*, 2d ed. (New York: Harcourt, Brace & World, 1965), 36.

26. Washington Gladden, *Recollections* (Boston: Houghton, Mifflin & Co., 1909), 260; William Jewett Tucker, *My Generation: An Autobiograph-*

ical Interpretation (Boston: Houghton Mifflin & Co., 1919), chapter 7; Daniel Day Williams, *The Andover Liberals: A Study in American Theology* (New York: King's Crown Press, 1941); George Shriver, *American Religious Heretics* (Nashville: Abingdon Press, 1966), 56–58; William W. Manross, *A History of the American Episcopal Church*, 3d ed. (New York: Morehouse-Gorham, 1959), 311; Raymond W. Albright, *Focus on Infinity: A Life of Phillips Brooks* (New York: The Macmillan Co., 1961), 361–373.

27. Lefferts A. Loetscher, *The Broadening Church: A Study of Theological Issues in the Presbyterian Church since 1869* (Philadelphia: University of Pennsylvania Press, 1954), 1–18; George M. Marsden, *The Evangelical Mind and the New School Presbyterian Experience* (New Haven: Yale University Press, 1970), 97.

28. Leonard J. Trinterud, *The Forming of an American Tradition: A Re-examination of Colonial Presbyterianism* (Philadelphia: Westminster Press, 1949), 26; Charles A. Briggs, *American Presbyterianism, Its Origin and Early History* (New York: Charles Scribner's Sons, 1885), 250; Ernest Trice Thompson, *A History of the Presbyterian Churches in the United States* (New York: Christian Literature Publishing Co., 1895), 353.

29. Henry F. May, *The Enlightenment in America*, 3d ed. (New York: Oxford University Press, 1976), 342; Miller, *Life of the Mind*, 321; Daniel Howe, *The Unitarian Conscience: Harvard Moral Philosophers, 1805–1861* (Cambridge: Harvard University Press, 1970), 5; Theodore Bozeman, *Protestants in an Age of Science* (Chapel Hill: University of North Carolina Press, 1977), 3–21, 105.

30. Glover, *Evangelical Nonconformists*, 110; Warner Bailey, "William Robertson Smith and American Biblical Studies," *Journal of Presbyterian History* 51 (1973): 285–303; Ira V. Brown, "The Higher Criticism Comes to America," 196; George Ernest Wright, "The Study of the Old Testament," in *Protestant Thought in America*, Arnold S. Nash, ed. (New York: The Macmillan Co., 1951), 18.

31. Bailey, "Smith and American Biblical Studies," 287; T. O. Beidleman, *William Robertson Smith and the Sociological Study of Religion* (Chicago and London: University of Chicago Press, 1974), 38; William Robertson Smith, "Christianity and the Supernatural," in *Lectures and Essays of William Robertson Smith*, John S. Black and George Chrystal, eds. (London: A. & C. Black, 1912), 123.

32. William Robertson Smith, "The Question of Prophecy," 163–203.

33. Cited in Bailey, "Smith and American Biblical Studies," 287.

34. Cheyne, *Founders of Old Testament Criticism*, 212; Bailey, "Smith and American Biblical Studies," 301. See also *The Libel against Professor W. Robertson Smith; Report of the Proceedings of the Free Church Presbytery of Aberdeen, February 14 to March 14, 1878* (Aberdeen: Murray, 1878). For the list of accusations, see Beidleman, *William Robertson Smith*, 17; W. G. Blackie, *Professor W. Robertson Smith: The Action of the Free Church Commission Ultra Vires* (Glasgow: D. D. Blackie & Son, 1881); *Special Report of the College Committee on Professor Smith's Article "Bible"* (Edinburgh: E. Maclaren & Macnivan, 1877); anon., *The Fallibility of Inspired Scripture, as Maintained by Modern Criticism, Being an Examination of Views Propounded by Prof. W. R. Smith* (Glasgow: D. Bryce, 1877).

35. Cited in Beidleman, *William Robertson Smith*, 18.

36. Smith, "The Question of Prophecy," 164–165.

37. Beidleman, *William Robertson Smith*, 19–22; W. Robertson Smith, "Animal Tribes in the Old Testament," *Journal of Philology* 19 (1881): 75–100; Smith, "Hebrew Language and Literature," in *Encyclopaedia Brittanica*, 9th ed. (Edinburgh and London: A. & C. Black, 1875–1888), II:594–602; the statement of the 1881 General Assembly of the Scottish Free Church is found in George Chrystal and John S. Black, *The Life of William Robertson Smith* (London: A. & C. Black, 1912), 381–382.

38. Among the *Independent* articles, see the April 19, 1877, issue for Smith's arguments before the Aberdeen Presbytery; the March 7 and 21, 1878, issues reported his successful defense; the June 19 and 26, 1879, issues reported the General Assembly's decision to try Smith again. In *Bibliotheca Sacra*, see A. Duff, "Method of the Typological Use of the Bible, Especially of the Old Testament," 37 (1880): 77–98, 86; Charles F. Thwing, "Professor W. Robertson Smith and His Theories of Old Testament Criticism," 39 (1882): 133–159. In the *Methodist Quarterly Review*, see H. K. Carroll, "Present Aspects of Scotch Theology," 61 (January 1879): 94–114, 107; review of Smith's *The Old Testament in the Jewish Church*, 63 (October 1881): 772–776.

39. For variations on this handling of Smith and Briggs, and of the challenges of the "Critical Period" that they ostensibly represent, see Schlesinger, "Critical Period"; Winthrop Hudson, *Religion in America*, 3d ed. (New York: Charles Scribner's Sons, 1981), 281; Sydney Ahlstrom, *Religious History of the American People*, 4th ed. (New Haven and London: Yale University Press), 777; George Shriver, *American Religious Heretics* (Nashville: Abingdon Press, 1966), 89; Carl Hatch, *The Charles A.*

Briggs Heresy Trial (New York: Exposition Press, 1969), 24; Warner Bailey, "Smith and American Biblical Studies," 287; Max Rogers, "Charles A. Briggs: Conservative Heretic," Ph.D. Thesis, Columbia University, 1964, 46. The description of the Briggs trial as "the most notorious event — " is from Ira Brown, "Higher Criticism Comes to America," 196.

40. Charles Briggs, *Biblical Study: Its Principles, Methods and History* (New York: Charles Scribner's Sons, 1883), 12, 78–135, 196, 355; *General Introduction to the Study of Holy Scripture* (New York: Charles Scribner's Sons, 1899), 117, 247–289, 427; *American Presbyterianism, Its Origin and Early History* (New York: Charles Scribner's Sons, 1885); *The Fundamental Christian Faith* (New York: Charles Scribner's Sons, 1913); *History of the Study of Theology* (New York: Charles Scribner's Sons, 1916); *Whither? A Theological Question for the Times* (New York: Charles Scribner's Sons, 1889); *How Shall We Revise the Westminster Confession of Faith?* (New York: Charles Scribner's Sons, 1890); "The Authority of Holy Scripture," in *Inaugural Address and Defense, 1891–1893* (Reprint, New York: Arno Press, 1972).

Chapter 2: The Evangelical Basis

1. William G. McLoughlin, *Revivals, Awakenings and Reform* (Chicago and London: University of Chicago Press, 1978), 141; idem, *Modern Revivalism, Charles Grandison Finney to Billy Graham* (New York: Ronald Press, 1959); Timothy Smith, *Revivalism and Social Reform in Mid-Nineteenth Century America*, 2d ed. (Baltimore: Johns Hopkins University Press, 1980), 63–84; Philip A. Bruce, *A History of the University of Virginia, 1819–1919* (New York: The Macmillan Co., 1921), 139; Paul Barringer, James Garnett, et al., *The University of Virginia* (New York: Lewis Publishing Co., 1904), 169.

2. Theodore Dwight Bozeman, *Protestants in an Age of Science* (Chapel Hill: University of North Carolina Press, 1977), 3–21. For other works on commonsense realism, see Sydney E. Ahlstrom, "The Scottish Philosophy and American Theology," *Church History* 24 (1955): 257–272; Daniel Walker Howe, *The Unitarian Conscience: Harvard Moral Philosophy, 1805–1861* (Cambridge: Harvard University Press, 1970); S. A. Craven, *The Scottish Philosophy of Common Sense* (Oxford: Oxford University Press, 1960); Henry F. May, *The Enlightenment in America*, 3d ed. (Oxford: Oxford University Press, 1976).

3. Bozeman, *Protestants in an Age of Science*, 4–7.

4. Ibid., 36–56; Richard Hofstadter, *Anti-Intellectualism in American Life* (New York: Random House, 1963), 55; Perry Miller, *The Life of the Mind in America* (New York: Harcourt, Brace & World, Inc., 1965), 30. On the attractiveness of this scientific world view after the onslaughts of "modern" civilization, see T. J. Jackson Lears, *No Place of Grace: Antimodernism and the Transformation of American Culture, 1880–1920* (New York: Pantheon Books, 1981), 25.

5. *Catalogue of the University of Virginia* (Washington, D.C.: Henry Polkinhorn, 1859), 4–5; Emilie Grace Briggs, "Sketch of Dr. Charles A. Briggs," *Alumni Bulletin of the University of Virginia* 5 (1899): 92–100. Briggs's observation is from a letter in *TLB*, III: letter of November 1, 1858, 142; see also *TLB*, III: letter of November 29, 1859, 146, CABC, UTS.

6. *TLB*, III: letter of November 30, 1858, 125–126, CABC, UTS. For background on the Briggs family history, see "Briggs Family Genealogy," box 44, folder 49, CABC, UTS; Max Rogers, "Charles A. Briggs: Conservative Heretic," Ph.D. Thesis, Columbia University, 1964, 1–4. Marvin Briggs's correspondence followed his nephew through the latter's formal education, a peripatetic enterprise that entailed attendance at three different boarding schools in the course of seven years: the school run by his uncle in Rye, New York, from 1849–1854; the Hamilton Collegiate Institution in White Plains, New York, from 1854–1855; and the Reading Ridge Institute in Reading, Conn., from 1855–1857; *TLB*, I: 14, 22, 27–30, 32–40; III: 124–126, 141–143, 145–150.

7. On John Krebs, the Briggses' family pastor at the Rutgers church, see Robert P. Booth, *History of the Rutgers Riverside Church* (New York: Styles & Cash, 1898), 18–19; William B. Sprague, *A Discourse Commemorative of the Late Rev. John M. Krebs* (Albany: Van Benthuysen & Sons, 1867), 23–24, 35ff.; John M. Krebs, "The Purpose and Success of the Gospel," *Presbyterian Preacher* 2 (1834): 322–338; "Backsliding and Apostasy," *The Herald of Truth* 1 (1859): 87–89.

8. Lefferts A. Loetscher, *The Broadening Church: A Study of Theological Issues in the Presbyterian Church in 1869* (Philadelphia: University of Pennsylvania Press, 1954), chapter 1; Timothy Smith, *Revivalism and Social Reform*, 55.

9. *TLB*, III: letter of December 7, 1858, 180–181, CABC, UTS.

10. *TLB*, III: letter of November 30, 1858, 125–126, CABC, UTS.

11. *TLB*, III: letter of May 4, 1861, 281; letter of May 11, 1861, 283–284; letter to Millie Briggs, 44–45, CABC, UTS.

12. George L. Prentiss, *The Union Theological Seminary: The First Fifty Years* (New York: Anson D. F. Randolph, 1889), 254–266; Robert E. Thompson, *A History of the Presbyterian Church in the United States* (New York: n.p., 1895), 114; *Union Theological Seminary in the City of New York: Alumni Catalogue, 1836–1936* (New York: Union Seminary, 1937); Charles A. Briggs, "Notes and Lectures from Union Seminary," box 34, CABC. Robert T. Handy, *A History of Union Theological Seminary in New York* (New York: Columbia University Press, 1987), 1–9.

13. *TLB*, II: "Cogitations," notebook, 189–191, 189.

14. Jerry Wayne Brown, *The Rise of Biblical Criticism in America, 1800–1860* (Middletown, Conn.: Wesleyan University Press, 1969), 45–48, 111–115; Henry Boynton Smith and Roswell Hitchcock, *The Life, Writings and Character of Edward Robinson* (New York: Anson D. F. Randolph, 1863), 5–6, 15; T. K. Cheyne, *The Founders of Old Testament Criticism* (New York: Charles Scribner's Sons, 1893), 229.

15. Brown, *Rise of Biblical Criticism*, 115–120; Claude Welch, *Protestant Thought in the Nineteenth Century* (New Haven and London: Yale University Press, 1972), 194–197.

16. James Hastings Nichols, *Romanticism in American Theology: Nevin and Schaff at Mercersburg* (Chicago: University of Chicago Press, 1961), 3; George Marsden, "The Mediating Theology of Henry Boynton Smith," in *The Evangelical Mind and the New School Presbyterian Experience* (New Haven and London: Yale University Press, 1970), 156; William K. B. Stoever, "Henry Boynton Smith and the German Theology of History," *Union Seminary Quarterly Review* 24 (1968): 69–89.

17. Elizabeth L. Smith, ed., *Henry Boynton Smith, His Life and Work* (New York: A. C. Armstrong & Son, 1881), 12–16; Lewis F. Stearns, *Henry Boynton Smith* (Boston and New York: Houghton, Mifflin & Co., 1892), 31–35; Channing Jeschke, "The Briggs Case: The Focus of a Study in Nineteenth Century Presbyterian History," Ph.D. Thesis, University of Chicago, 1966, 77–83; Stoever, "Henry Boynton Smith," 67.

18. Elizabeth Smith, *Henry Boynton Smith*, 42–63; Stearns, *Henry Boynton Smith*, 60.

19. Stearns, *Henry Boynton Smith*, 60.

20. Henry Boynton Smith, "The Relations of Faith and Philosophy," in *Faith and Philosophy, Discourses and Essays* (New York: Scribner, Armstrong & Co., 1877), 3–43. By the time Smith gave this address, Philip Schaff had already been tried twice for heresy with historicism being the central issue. See Philip Schaff, *The Principle of Protestantism as Related to the Present State of the Church* (Chambersburg, Pa.: Publication Office

of the German Reformed Church, 1845), and *What Is Church History?* (Philadelphia: J. B. Lippincott and Co., 1846). Both works testify to the influence of the "mediating theology" on Schaff's thinking. On Schaff, see George Shriver, *Philip Schaff, Christian Scholar and Ecumenical Prophet* (Macon, Ga.: Mercer University Press, 1987).

21. Smith, "The Relations of Faith and Philosophy," 14–21.

22. Marsden, *The Evangelical Mind*, 162; Stoever, "Henry Boynton Smith," 80–81; Jeschke, "The Briggs Case," 83.

23. Elizabeth Smith, *Henry Boynton Smith*, 166; Henry B. Smith, "Nature and Worth of the Science of Church History, Being His Inaugural Address at Union Theological Seminary, February 12, 1851," 54; "The Idea of Christian Theology as a System, Being His Inaugural Address as Professor of Systematic Theology at Union Theological Seminary, May 6, 1855," 126, both in *Faith and Philosophy*.

24. Henry Boynton Smith, "Dorner's History of the Doctrine of the Person of Christ," *Bibliotheca Sacra* 6 (1849): 175–177; Smith, "The Problem of the Philosophy of History" (Phi Beta Kappa Address, 1854), *Presbyterian Quarterly Review* 3 (1854): 1–111.

25. Stoever, "Henry Boynton Smith," 83–84; Smith, "Nature and Worth," 50; idem, "The Reformed Churches of Europe and America in Relation to General Church History," in *Faith and Philosophy*, 87.

26. William R. Hutchison, *The Modernist Impulse in American Protestantism* (Cambridge: Harvard University Press, 1976), 43; Harold Y. Vanderpool, "The Andover Conservatives: Apologetics, Biblical Criticism and Theological Change at Andover Theological Seminary, 1808–1880," Ph.D. Thesis, Harvard University, 1971; Frank Hugh Foster, *The Modern Movement in Theology* (New York: Fleming H. Revell Co., 1939), 14.

27. Briggs's admiration and respect for H. B. Smith emerges in the regular correspondence exchanged between them; see *TLB*, III: letter of October 17, 1867, 446–447; letter of December 13, 1867, 449–451; letter of April 14, 1868, 460–461; letter of May 6, 1868, 461–465; letter of November 25, 1868, 467–470; *TLB*, V: letter of May 19, 1869, 18–21; letter of June 9, 1869, 22–24, CABC, UTS.

28. "Lectures of Henry Boynton Smith," box 34, folder 5; "Christian Anthropology," box 34, folder 6; "Soteriology," box 34, folder 6; "Notes from Henry Boynton Smith's Classes in Natural Theology, Apologetics and Christian Evidences," *TLB*, I: 19, CABC, UTS.

29. "Lectures by Henry B. Smith, 1861," box 34, folder 5; "Lectures, 1862," box 34, folder 6; "Lectures, 1863," box 34, folder 6, CABC, UTS.

30. The most famous such reference to Smith as mentor occurred in Briggs's reply to A. A. Hodge and B. B. Warfield's article on "Inspiration" in the *Presbyterian Review* 2 (1881): 551. But Briggs's letters to Smith from Germany abound with such reverential references. See *TLB*, III: letter of January 24, 1867, 417; letter of May 6, 1868, 463; *TLB*, V: letter of June 9, 1869, 22, CABC, UTS.

31. *TLB*, I: 21–22, notation by Emilie Grace Briggs, CABC, UTS.

32. *TLB*, III: letter of May 31, 1865, 358–359; see also letters of January 31, 1865, 358–359; February 23, 1865, 354–356; July 12, 1865, 362–354, CABC, UTS.

33. *Certificate of Licensure, TLB*, III: 109; "Trial Lecture before the Presybtery of New York, April 18, 1866," *TLB*, I: 33, CABC, UTS. His exercises before the Old School Presbytery included a "critical exercise" on 1 John 5, a trial lecture on Matthew 4:1–11, and a trial sermon on Isaiah 45:15.

34. "Journal of Berlin," box 33, folder 6; "Diary of Emilie Grace Briggs," entry for June 4, 1895, *TLB*, I: 68; *TLB*, I: letter of November 22, 1867, 27–29; III: letter of December 13, 1867, 449–451, CABC, UTS.

35. *TLB*, I: letter of January 9, 1867, 3. For a detailed account of his studies in Berlin, see "Journal of Berlin, June–October 1866," box 33, folder 6, and "Diary, February–March 1869," *TLB*, II: 212, CABC, UTS. For background on American students studying in Berlin and in Germany generally in the nineteenth century see Jurgen Herbst, *The German Historical School in American Scholarship* (Ithaca, N.Y.: Cornell University Press, 1965), 1–55.

36. *TLB*, I: letter of January 14, 1867, 414, CABC, UTS.

37. *TLB*, III: letter of January 24, 1867, 419, CABC, UTS.

38. Isaac A. Dorner, *Geschichte der Protestantischen Theologie* (Munich: n.p., 1867). For this work Dorner plied Briggs with questions about the theological positions of American theologians, especially Henry B. Smith and Horace Bushnell; see Briggs's "Berlin Journal," CABC, UTS.

39. Karl Barth, *Protestant Theology in the Nineteenth Century* (London: SCM Press, 1959), 577–588; Claude Welch, *Protestant Thought in the Nineteenth Century* (New Haven and London: Yale University Press, 1972), 274–275; Otto Pfleiderer, *The Development of Theology in German since Kant* (London: Sonnenschein & Co., 1893), 157–158; Claude Welch, *God and Incarnation in Mid-Nineteenth-Century Theology* (New York: Oxford University Press, 1965), 5–14.

40. Welch, *Protestant Thought*, 274; Barth, *Protestant Theology*, 580–582; Welch, *God and Incarnation*, 115.

41. Welch, *Protestant Thought*, 275–276.

42. *TLB*, III: letter of May 6, 1868, 462, CABC, UTS.

43. Ibid., 426.

44. Ibid., 463.

45. Welch, *God and Incarnation*, 5; "Journal of Berlin," box 33, folder 5, 14; letters of May 6, 1868, 461, and November 25, 1868, 467, CABC, UTS.

46. *TLB*, I: letter of January 8, 1867, 38, CABC, UTS.

47. On perfectionism as a long-term theme in American religious history, see Timothy Smith, *Revivalism and Social Reform*; Perry Miller, *Life of the Mind in America*, Book 1.

48. *TLB*, IV: sermon of April 23, 1871, 447; Max Rogers, "Briggs," 37; Briggs was ordained in the Presbytery of Elizabeth, New Jersey, on June 30, 1870, and was installed as pastor at Roselle the next morning. Briggs quickly became an important figure in the presbytery, being appointed to the Financial Committee in 1871, and being elected the following year as a delegate to the General Assembly in Detroit. In 1873 he was appointed a representative to the International Conference of the Evangelical Alliance as well as an overseer of the Reformed Seminary in Brunswick, New Jersey.

49. *TLB*, IV: "First Anniversary Sermon," 468; sermon on "Put on the Lord Jesus Christ," 190, CABC, UTS.

50. Briggs, "Biblical Theology with Especial Reference to the New Testament," *American Presbyterian Review* 2 (1870): 105–133, and the following series entitled "Recent German Works," all in the 1870 volume of the *Review:* January 1870, 560–562; April 1870, 364–367; July 1870, 560–562. Karl Moll, *The Psalms*, 9 vols., *Lange's Commentary on Holy Scripture* (New York: Scribner, Armstrong & Co., 1872). Translation was shared by Briggs, John Forsyth, James B. Hammond, and J. Frederick McCurdy. Briggs wrote the introduction and translated Psalms 1 to 41, 51–72; see "Diary of Emilie Grace Briggs," entry for June 4, 1895, 68–69; "Notebook from Roselle," 51, *TLB*, I, CABC, UTS.

51. *TLB*, IV: sermon 89, "For the Memorial Fund of the General Assembly," January 29, 1871, CABC, UTS.

52. Loetscher, *Broadening Church*, 9: Robert Handy, *A Christian America: Protestant Hopes and Historical Realities*, 3d ed. (Oxford and New York: Oxford University Press, 1974), 65.

53. *TLB*, I: 60; *History, Essays, and Other Documents of the Sixth General Conference of the Evangelical Alliance, Held in New York, October 2–12, 1873*, Philip Schaff and S. Irenaeus Prime, eds. (New York: n.p., 1874); George Marsden, *Fundamentalism and American Culture* (New York and Oxford: Oxford University Press, 1980), 11.

54. James Findlay, *Dwight L. Moody, American Evangelist, 1837–1899* (Chicago and London: University of Chicago Press, 1969), 20; Robert T. Handy, "Fundamentalism and Modernism in Perspective," *Religion in Life* 24 (1955): 381–394; Ernest R. Sandeen, "Towards an Historical Interpretation of the Origins of Fundamentalism," *Church History* 36 (1967): 66–83.

55. Ernest R. Sandeen, *The Roots of Fundamentalism, British and American Millenarianism, 1800–1930*, 2d ed. (Grand Rapids: Baker Book House, 1970), 145; on the Niagara Bible Conference, see especially chapter 2. Marsden, *Fundamentalism*, 48; Ernest Lee Tuveson, *Redeemer Nation: The Idea of America's Millennial Role* (Chicago: University of Chicago Press, 1968).

56. Marsden, *Fundamentalism*, 148; Major L. Wilson, "Paradox Lost: Order and Progress in the Evangelical Thought of Mid-Nineteenth Century America," *Church History* 44 (1975): 352–366.

57. Marsden, *Fundamentalism*, 51; Sandeen, *Roots of Fundamentalism*, 148; Nathaniel West, ed., *Premillennial Essays: The Report of the Proceedings of the First American Bible and Prophetic Conference, New York, October 30–November 1, 1878* (Chicago: n.p., 1879). The articles were: Briggs, "Shall the Premillennialist Be Tolerated?," New York *Evangelist*, September 12, 1878, 1; "Premillenarianism and the Standards," October 10, 1878, 4; "Premillenarianism and the Westminster Divines," October 31, 1878, 1; "Testimonies against the Premillenarians from the Westminster Period," November 7, 1878, 1; "Premillenarianism and the Westminster Confession," November 21, 1878, 2; "Various Forms of Premillenarianism," November 28, 1878, 2; "Reformation Testimonies against the Premillenarians," December 5, 1878, 2; "The Ancient Church and Premillenarianism," January 2, 1879, 6; "The Ante-Nicene Church and Premillenarianism," January 9, 1879, 6; "The Premillenarianism Defense," February 20, 1879, 6; "Premillenarianism and the Westminster Standards," February 27, 1879, 6.

58. Briggs, "The Anti-Nicene Church and Premillenarianism," New York *Evangelist*, January 2, 1879, 6.

59. Ernest R. Sandeen, "The Distinctiveness of American Denominationalism: A Case Study of the 1846 Evangelical Alliance," *Church History*

45 (1976): 222–234; John Ewing, *Goodly Fellowship* (London: Marshall, Morgan and Scott, 1946).

60. "Notebook and Journal from May 1878–May 1879," *TLB*, I: 85; TLB, V: 261–262, CABC, UTS.

61. "Diary for 1876," *TLB*, II: 199, CABC, UTS.

62. Briggs, sermon 89, *TLB*, IV: 396, CABC, UTS.

63. Ibid., 398.

64. "Diary and Notebook, 1880–1881," *TLB*, I: 102, CABC, UTS.

65. Jeschke, "The Briggs Case," chapter 1: "The Founding of a Review"; "Letter from Archibald A. Hodge to President William Adams," *TLB*, V: 251, CABC, UTS.

Chapter 3: The Politics of Truth

1. *TLB*, V: letter of September 30, 1879, 321; see also *TLB*, V: letter of October 13, 1879; *TLB*, V: letter of November 16, 1879, 335, CABC, UTS. Both Union and Princeton Seminaries were anxious to ensure that the publication representing the church would remain in the Eastern states, especially after the David Swing affair in Chicago and the growing support for the premillennial movement in the Midwest.

2. Winthrop Hudson, *Religion in America*, 3d ed. (New York: Charles Scribner's Sons, 1981), 279–281; William R. Hutchison, *The Modernist Impulse in American Protestantism* (Cambridge: Harvard University Press, 1976), appendix, sections A–C; Frank Luther Mott, *A History of American Magazines, 1865–1885* (Cambridge: Harvard University Press, Belknap Press, 1957), III:70, 75–79.

3. On the northern Baptist denominational problems, see Grant Wacker, *Augustus H. Strong and the Dilemma of Historical Consciousness* (Macon, Ga.: Mercer University Press, 1985), 110ff.

4. Editorial control of the *Presbyterian Review* would be shared by two managing editors, one of whom would represent the views of the New School/Union faction (Briggs), while the other would represent the Old School/Princeton camp (Hodge). Further, four associate editors would represent the theological faculties of Auburn, Allegheny, Lane, and Western (McCormick) Seminaries. No article would appear in the *Review* unless it had been approved by both managing editors, or, in case of their disagreement, by the majority of associate editors. *TLB*, II, p. 13, CABC, UTS. "The Idea and Aims of the Presbyterian Review," *Presbyterian Review* 1 (1880): 4; see also: George L. Prentiss, *The Union Theological Seminary in the City of New York: Its Design and Another Decade of Its History*

(Asbury Park, N.J.: M., W. & C. Pennypacker, 1899), 329; *TLB*, V: letter of December 11, 1879, 349, CABC, UTS. Briggs remained the "Union" managing editor for all ten volumes of the *Review*. The Princeton editorial position was occupied by Archibald Hodge from 1880 to 1882; by Francis L. Patton from 1883 to 1888; and by Benjamin Warfield from 1888 to 1889. For the first three numbers of 1880, however, Charles Aiken filled Hodge's place while the latter completed a two-volume biography of his father, Charles Hodge. *TLB*, II, 13, CABC, UTS.

5. The first (January 1880) number of the *Presbyterian Review* included: Benjamin B. Warfield, "The Apologetical Value of the *Testament of the Twelve Patriarchs*," 57–89; Henry M. Baird, "Notes on Theological Education in the Reformed Churches of France and French Switzerland," 83–103; Charles A. Briggs, "Documentary History of the Westminster Assembly," 127–163. For background on the founding of the *Review*, see: letters of January 4, 1879, 251; February 19, 1879, 257; July 4, 1879, 285; July 6, 1879, 306; July 18, 1879, 298, CABC, UTS.

6. Briggs, "Documentary History," 128. Briggs followed this historical study with another a year later, meant as a companion piece ("The Provincial Assembly of London, 1647–1660," *Presbyterian Review* 2 [1881]: 54–79); this second article was very important for his monograph on *American Presbyterianism*, although it has been largely forgotten because of the "debate" then raging in the pages of the *Review* over the Robertson Smith affair.

7. *TLB*, I: "Diary/Notebook for 1880–1881," 100ff., CABC, UTS. *TLB*, V: letters of January 19, 1880, 367; January 26, 1880, 371; June 8, 1880, 416; June 19, 1880, 425, CABC, UTS. Letters of May 30, 1880; November 29, 1880, in the Archibald A. Hodge Collection, Hodge Family Papers, Firestone Library, Princeton University.

8. *TLB*, V: letters of June 8, 1880, 416–417; June 9, 1880, 423–424; June 19, 1880, 425; October 28, 1880, 453–454, CABC, UTS.

9. Briggs, "The Robertson Smith Case," *Presbyterian Review* 1 (1880): 737–745, 745.

10. *TLB*, V: letter of July 9, 1880, 423, CABC, UTS.

11. Letters of May 30, 1880; November 29, 1880; December 8, 1880, in Archibald A. Hodge Collection, Princeton University.

12. "We are both of us in between the extremes, and are nearer to one another than you are to the ultraconservatives and I am to the radicals. If the discussion can go on calmly and steadily for a year or two, we may be able to overcome the difficulties without conflict" (Briggs to Hodge,

letter of July 30, 1881, Archibald A. Hodge Collection, Princeton University). The "bounds" of the debate were set by Hodge: "Neither side is to go beyond the positions occupied by you and me, i.e., none shall exceed in conservativism the positions laid down in my article on inspiration, and no relaxation of doctrine shall be admitted beyond the views held and stated by you" (*TLB*, V: letter of February 15, 1881, 491). See also *TLB*, V: letters of November 17, 1880, 459; November 29, 1880, 461–463; December 3, 1880, 468, CABC, UTS. Letters of November 29, 1880; December 8, 1880; December 10, 1880, in Archibald A. Hodge Collection, Princeton University; Lefferts A. Loetscher, *The Broadening Church: A Study of Theological Issues in the Presbyterian Church in 1869* (Philadelphia: University of Pennsylvania Press, 1954), 34.

13. Archibald A. Hodge and Benjamin B. Warfield, "Inspiration," *Presbyterian Review* 2 (1881): 225–260; George Marsden, *Fundamentalism and American Culture* (New York and Oxford: Oxford University Press, 1980), 109–118; Mark A. Noll, ed., *The Princeton Theology, 1812–1921* (Philadelphia: Fortress, 1985), 27ff.; Ernest R. Sandeen, "The Princeton Theology," *Church History* 31 (1962): 307–321. Benjamin Warfield (1851–1921) came to Princeton Seminary in 1887; he became the "most technically brilliant" of the Princeton theologians, a group that included Archibald Alexander, Charles Hodge, and his son, Archibald Alexander Hodge. More than those three, Warfield faced the wholesale intellectual defection from the evangelical Protestantism that had been the "cultural given" in the America of Alexander and the elder Hodge. Thus, Warfield, more than any other theologian of the Princeton school, set as his life's work the exposition of the fallacies of the modern alternatives to his understanding of "historic Christianity"; Warfield thus saw Briggs as a heresiarch attacking an entire civilization, not just an advocate of heterodox biblical theories. See Mark A. Noll, "The Princeton Theology," in *Reformed Theology in America: A History of Its Modern Development*, David F. Wells, ed. (Grand Rapids, Mich.: William B. Eerdmans Publishing Co., 1985), 16ff.

14. Noll, "Princeton Theology," 19–20, 27.

15. Hodge and Warfield, "Inspiration," 225, 226–227.

16. Ibid., 238.

17. Noll, *Princeton Theology*, 36; Marsden, *Fundamentalism*, 111. Perhaps the most quoted passage illustrating the new Princeton commitment to mathematical specificity was made by Charles Hodge: "The Bible is to the theologian what nature is to the man of science. It is his great storehouse of facts" (*Systematic Theology*, 2 vols. [New York: Charles Scribner's

Sons, 1872], 1:10). On Benjamin Warfield's development of the conservative Princeton tradition into the unique position of the late nineteenth century, see Randall Balmer, "The Princetonians and Scripture: A Reconsideration," *Westminster Theological Review* 44 (1982): 352–365, 354ff.; John H. Gerstner, "Warfield's Case for Biblical Inerrancy," in *God's Inerrant Word*, John W. Montgomery, ed. (Minneapolis: Bethany Fellowship, 1974).

18. Hodge and Warfield, "Inspiration," 245; on the "original autograph" theory, see Sandeen, "Princeton," 316ff.

19. Briggs, "The Critical Theories of the Sacred Scriptures in Relation to Their Inspiration," *Presbyterian Review* 2 (1881): 550–579, 551.

20. Ibid., 554.

21. Ibid., 556–557.

22. Ibid., 551ff.

23. Ibid., 573, 579.

24. *TLB*, VI: letters of August 8, 1881, 45; August 2, 1881, 42; September 16, 1881, 56; November 8, 1882, 224; November 24, 1882, 229, CABC, UTS.

25. The four articles between Briggs's first and second articles in the series published in the *Presbyterian Review* were William H. Green, "Professor W. Robertson Smith on the Pentateuch," 3 (1882): 108–156; Henry Preserved Smith, "The Critical Theories of Julius Wellhausen," 3 (1882): 357–388; Samuel Ives Curtiss, "Delitzsch on the Origin and Composition of the Pentateuch," 3 (1882): 553–588; Willis Beecher, "The Logical Methods of Professor Kuenen," 3 (1882): 701–731. Briggs's second article in the exchange was "A Critical Study of the History of the Higher Criticism with Special Reference to the Pentateuch," 4 (1883): 69–130, 84.

26. Briggs, "Critical Study," 70ff., 81ff., 110.

27. Ibid., 130.

28. On Patton's role in the David Swing affair, see Hutchison, *Modernist Impulse*, 48–75; Francis L. Patton, "The Dogmatic Aspect of Pentateuchal Criticism," *Presbyterian Review* 4 (1883): 341–410, 343ff. For contemporary scholarly defense of Patton's biblical theories as legitimate restatements of the ancient Protestant tradition, see Randall Balmer, "The Princetonians and Scripture: A Reconsideration," *Westminster Theological Journal* 44 (1982): 352–365, 354ff.

29. Patton, "Dogmatic Aspect," 344ff.

30. Briggs, *Biblical Study: Its Principles, Methods and History* (New York: Charles Scribner's Sons, 1883), ix. In the preface to the work Briggs

acknowledged the previous articles and address from which much of the book was derived; preface, vii–viii, 16.

31. Ibid., 78–79, 80–84, 101ff.

32. Ibid., 365ff. Briggs's process of exegesis, outlined in the first chapter of the book, began with "grammatical exegesis," in which the student of Scripture analyzed the form and etymology of biblical language; next came "rhetorical exegesis," in which the words of Scripture were analyzed in terms of the author's purpose; one then applied "historical exegesis," utilizing both archaeological and geological tools; this was followed by "comparative exegesis," studying similar passages written by the same author in other parts of Scripture. "Literary exegesis" came next, in which the interpretations of biblical passages by commentators through the ages were studied, followed by "doctrinal exegesis," in which the exegete reconstructed the systems of theology advanced in the text; finally, the task of "practical exegesis" required that the pastoral and catechetical implications of Scripture be expounded for God's people (Briggs, *Biblical Study*, 29–35).

33. George F. Moore, "Review of *Biblical Study*," *Andover Review* 1 (1884): 101–103. For other sympathetic reviews of *Biblical Study*, see *Bibliotheca Sacra* 41 (1884): 414–417; *Old Testament Student* 3 (1884): 213–216; *Unitarian Review* 20 (1883): 479–480. T. W. Chambers, "Review of *Biblical Study*," *Presbyterian Review* 5 (1884): 154–157, 154. See also the *Lutheran Church Review* 3 (1884): 73; *Presbyterian Quarterly and Princeton Review* 5 (1884): 154–157; *Reformed Quarterly Review* 31 (1884): 149–150.

34. *TLB*, I: "Diary for 1887," 163ff.; quote from Prentiss, *Union Theological Seminary*, 333. This revisionist basis of the later trials was clearly recognized at the time, both by Briggs and his fellow laborers for creedal revision. See Briggs, "The Future of Presbyterianism in the United States," *North American Review* 440 (July 1893): 2–10, 5–7; "Dr. Briggs and His Friends," *New York Times*, May 14, 1892; *Scrapbook of the Briggs Case*, 4: 38, CABC, UTS.

35. Robert Ellis Thompson, *A History of the Presbyterian Churches in the United States* (New York: Christian Literature Co., 1895), 245ff.; A. Taylor Innes, "The Creed Question in Scotland," *Andover Review* 12 (1889): 1–15, 2.

36. Briggs, "Second General Council of Reformed Churches," *Presbyterian Review* 2 (1881): 169–174; Briggs, "Third General Council of the Alliance of Reformed Churches," *Presbyterian Review* 5 (1884): 330–337;

T. W. Chambers, "The Alliance of Reformed Churches," *Presbyterian Review* 9 (1888): 122–124; *TLB*, I: "Briggs Diary for 1887," entries for January 2, 163; April 10, 164; April 11, 164, CABC, UTS; Loetscher, *Broadening Church*, 41ff.

37. Thompson, *History of the Presbyterian Churches*, 245.

38. Briggs, "Second General Council," 169–171; Philip Schaff, *Creed Revision in the Presbyterian Churches* (New York: Charles Scribner's Sons, 1890), 12ff.

39. Archibald A. Hodge, *Commentary on the Confession of Faith, With Questions for Theological Students* (Philadelphia: Presbyterian Board of Publication and Sabbath School Work, 1869).

40. Briggs, "Second General Council," 169ff.; idem, "Third General Council."

41. Briggs, "Third General Council," 333.

42. The historical articles in the *New York Evangelist* during 1884 were "The Earliest American Presbyterianism," January 31; "The Origin of the First American Presbytery," February 14; "The Character of the First American Presbytery," February 21; "Origin and Character of the Synod of Philadelphia," February 28; "Origin of the Adopting Act," March 6; "Nature of the Adopting Act," March 13; "The First Heresy Trial in Our Church," March 20; *TLB*, II: 41. The five biographical sketches for the third volume of the 1884 edition of the *Schaff-Herzog Encyclopedia* were on Herbert Palmer, William Perkins, Matthew Poole, Anthony Tuckney, and Richard Vines; *TLB*, II: 39. Briggs, "The Principles of Puritanism," *Presbyterian Review* 5 (1884): 656–675.

43. Archibald A. Hodge, "The Consensus of the Reformed Confessions," *Presbyterian Review* 5 (1884): 266–304, 269. See also his *Commentary on the Confession*, 5ff.

44. Hodge, "Consensus," 276–277.

45. Francis L. Patton, "The General Assembly of 1884," *Presbyterian Review* 5 (1884): 497–500, 500.

46. My own understanding of the importance of the revision issue in the battles of the northern Presbyterian church derives from Loetscher, *Broadening Church*, 42ff., being confirmed by primary evidence in the Briggs collection. See note 37, chap. 2, above.

47. Briggs, *American Presbyterianism, Its Origin and Early History* (New York: Charles Scribner's Sons, 1885), xii, 27.

48. Ibid., 218ff.

49. Ibid., 208–221.

50. Ibid., 249.

51. Noll, *Princeton Theology*, 28ff.; Loetscher, *Broadening Church*, 37–38; Charles Starbuck, "Review of *American Presbyterian*," *Andover Review* 4 (1885): 385–389.

52. *Minutes of the General Assembly of the Presbyterian Church in the U.S.A.* (Philadelphia: McCalla & Co., Printers, 1888), 115; Loetscher, *Broadening Church*, 39–48.

53. *Minutes of the General Assembly* (1888), 115.

54. *Minutes of the General Assembly of the Presbyterian Church in the U.S.A.* (Philadelphia: McCalla & Co., Printers, 1889), 79; John W. Worral, "The Northern General Assembly of 1889," *Presbyterian Quarterly* 3 (1889): 436–445.

55. *Confessional Revision, Being a Collection of 395 Articles Appearing in the Religious Press Prepared for the Committee of Revision, General Assembly, 1890*, Thomas S. Hastings Collection, Burke Library, Union Theological Seminary, New York. My discussion of the revision controversy in 1887–1888 is based on that collection, especially on the following articles that appeared in the *New York Evangelist*. All entry listings noted are those in that collection: S. Brewer, "The Confession of Faith," November 3, 1887, entry A.; "Another View of the Confession: How It Reads to a Ruling Elder," September 29, 1887, entry B.; Herrick Johnson, "Defense of the Confession," September 29, 1887, entry C.; "Wishing a Revised Confession of Faith, by a Pastor," October 13, 1887, entry F.; Rev. John Waugh, "The Functions of a Creed," October 20, 1887, entry G.; Herrick Johnson, "The Confession in Its Entirety," October 1887, entry H. In the *Presbyterian Review*, the most heated revision discussion during 1887 (volume 8) was that exchanged between E. R. Craven and Francis Patton: Craven, "The Constitution of the Presbyterian Church in the U.S.A. — What It Is, and the Mode of Amending It," 85–101; Patton, "The Pending Overtures," 122–126, and "The Constitution of the Presbyterian Church: A Reply to Dr. Craven," 282–296.

56. Loetscher, *Broadening Church*, 42ff. *TLB*, VII: letters of November 8, 1886, 233; May 30, 1889, 466; June 7, 1889, 470, CABC, UTS.

57. Briggs, *Whither? A Theological Question for the Times* (New York: Charles Scribner's Sons, 1889), ix–x.

58. Ibid., 7–8.

59. Ibid., 7, 9.

60. Ibid., 160.

61. W. W. Moore, "Review of *Whither?*," *Presbyterian Quarterly* 4 (1890): 124–132, 124–125, 126. For other reviews, see George Harris,

"Review of *Whither?*," *Andover Review* 12 (1889): 552–555; G. Frederick Wright, "Dr. Briggs's Whither?," *Bibliotheca Sacra* 47 (1890): 136–153. Jack B. Rogers views *Whither?* as Briggs's most overt attack on the Princeton theology, and the most important hostile force that contributed to its emergence; see *Scripture in the Westminster Confession: A Problem of Historical Interpretation for American Presbyterianism* (Grand Rapids: William B. Eerdmans Publ. Co., 1967), 29–36.

62. *TLB*, VII: letter of June 11, 1888, 419, CABC, UTS. On Warfield's opinion of the revision issue and of *Whither?*, see the following published articles by Warfield: "The Presbyterians and Revision," 4; "The Revision of the Confession," 20; "What Is the Confession?," 27; "The Meaning of the Revision of the Confession," 60, all in the Thomas Hastings Scrapbook, Thomas Hastings Collection, Union Theological Seminary, New York.

63. For the published debate between Briggs and Warfield in the *Independent*, see Briggs, "The Westminster Standards," July 4, 1889, 1; Warfield, "The Presbyterians and the Confession of Faith," July 18, 1889, 4; Briggs, "The Westminster Standards the Difficulty," July 25, 1889, 5; Warfield, "Reply to Dr. Briggs," July 31, 1889, 6, all in the Thomas Hastings Scrapbook, Thomas Hastings Collection, UTS. For the debate as carried on in other publications, see Hastings Scrapbook, 60ff.; *TLB*, VII: letter of May 30, 1889, 466, CABC, UTS.

64. Briggs, "The General Assembly of the Presbyterian Church in the U.S.A.," *Presbyterian Review* 10 (1889): 465–470, 466.

65. Philip Schaff, "The Revision of the Westminster Confession of Faith," 529–552; John DeWitt, "Revision of the Confession of Faith," 553–589; Benjamin B. Warfield, "The Presbyterian Churches and the Westminster Confession," 646–657, all in *Presbyterian Review* 10 (1889). *TLB*, VII: letters of September 22, 1889, 492; October 4, 1889, 500, CABC, UTS.

66. "The Articles of Faith: Presbyterians Discuss Their Revisions," *New York Times*, December 3, 1889, 74, Hastings Scrapbook. The addresses of both Briggs and Patton were printed in the *Independent*, December 3, 1889. Briggs's address was likewise published as "The Revision of the Westminster Confession," in the *Andover Review* 13 (1890): 45–68, 45.

67. Prentiss, *Union Theological Seminary*, 331.

68. *TLB*, VIII: letter from James McCosh to Briggs, October 30, 1889, 21, CABC, UTS. James McCosh, *Whither? O Whither? Tell Me Where* (New York: Charles Scribner's Sons, 1889); W. G. T. Shedd, *The Proposed Revision of the Westminster Standards* (New York: Charles Scribner's Sons,

1890); Max Rogers, "Charles A. Briggs: Conservative Heretic," Ph.D. Thesis, Columbia University, 1964, 112ff.; Briggs, "The Advance Towards Revision," in *How Shall We Revise the Westminster Confession of Faith?* (New York: Charles Scribner's Sons, 1890), 1–33.

69. Briggs, "The Advance Towards Revision," 28ff.

70. *Minutes of the General Assembly of the Presbyterian Church in the U.S.A.* (Philadelphia: McCalla & Co., Printers, 1890), 19, 85, 122–123; Thomas A. Hoyt, "The Northern General Assembly of 1890," *Presbyterian Quarterly* 4 (1890): 456–469, 458ff.

71. For the fears of the conservatives after the 1890 General Assembly, see "Dr. Duffield on Revision," *New York Evangelist*, July 18, 1889, 15; Thomas Nichols, "Revision of the Confession of Faith: How Far Shall It Go?," *New York Evangelist*, August 1, 1889, 19; John Fox, "Concerning Revision," *Presbyterian Banner,* August 28, 1889, 25; B. B. Warfield, "What Is the Confession of Faith and Does It Need Revision?," *Presbyterian Banner*, September 4, 1889, 27; W. G. T. Shedd, "Revision of the Westminster Confession," *New York Evangelist*, September 5, 1889, 30; "Dr. Shedd's Seven Reasons against Revision of the Confession of Faith," *New York Evangelist*, September 26, 1889, 31; "Subscription to the Standards, An Editorial," *Northwestern Presbyterian*, September 14, 1889, 34; B. B. Warfield, "The Meaning of Revision," *Presbyterian Journal*, November 14, 1889, 60, all in the Thomas Hastings Scrapbook, Thomas Hastings Collection, UTS. *The Edward Robinson Chair of Biblical Theology in the Union Theological Seminary* (New York: Union Theological Seminary, 1891), 1–2.

Chapter 4: The Theological Crisis

1. On the traditional historiographic interpretation of the inaugural address and the subsequent Briggs trial, see note 39, chap. 1. See also Gaius Glenn Atkins, *Religion in Our Times* (New York: Round Table Press, 1932), 96ff.; George Shriver, *American Religious Heretics* (Nashville: Abingdon, 1966), 93ff. The typescript original of the inaugural address from which Briggs read on January 20, 1891, is in box 16, folder 6, of the Briggs Collections, UTS. The published version of the address most easily available (with an unchanged text) is in Briggs, *The Authority of Holy Scripture, An Inaugural Address, With Preface and Appendix*, 2d ed. (New York: Charles Scribner's Sons, 1891). This second edition is the text quoted in this chapter.

2. The continued "unified" self-identity of future modernists and fundamentalists has been superbly described by George Marsden, *Fundamentalism and American Culture* (New York: Oxford University Press, 1980), 11–39; see also James Findlay, *Dwight L. Moody, American Evangelist, 1837–1899* (Chicago: University of Chicago Press), 5–21.

3. *Minutes of the Board of Directors of the Union Theological Seminary in the City of New York, 1884–1904* (handwritten ledger), Burke Library, UTS, 122–123. *The Edward Robinson Chair of Biblical Theology in the Union Theological Seminary, in the City of New York* (New York: Union Theological Seminary, 1891), 1–4, 7. *TLB*, VIII: letter of January 7, 1891, 108, CABC, UTS.

4. Briggs, *Authority of Holy Scripture*, 24; George L. Prentiss, *The Union Theological Seminary in the City of New York: Its Design and Another Decade of Its History* (Asbury Park, N.J.: M., W. & C. Pennypacker, 1899), 333; "Dr. Briggs and His Friends," *New York Times*, May 14, 1892, *Scrapbook of the Briggs Case*, 1: 38.

5. Briggs, *Authority of Holy Scripture*, 24.

6. Ibid., 25.

7. Ibid., 26–27.

8. Ibid., 28.

9. Ibid., 28.

10. Ibid., 67.

11. Briggs may have borrowed both the term and the concept of the "middle state" from his German mentor, Isaac Dorner; see Claude Welch, *Protestant Thought in the Nineteenth Century* (New Haven: Yale University Press), 273ff. He likewise undoubtedly discussed this concept with Philip Schaff, who had an informal heresy trial in 1846 due to his published views on the "middle state." On christology, Briggs said that "it was the merit of my beloved teacher, Henry B. Smith, that he made 'Incarnation in order to redemption' the structural principle of his theology" (*Authority of Holy Scripture*, 62).

12. Briggs himself perceived the address under this broader rubric as an assault on the entire older *Weltanschauung*. See Briggs, "The Theological Crisis," *North American Review* 153 (July 1891): 99–114. See also *Scrapbook of the Briggs Case*, 1: "Dr. Briggs and His Friends," *New York Evening Post*, May 14, 1892, 38, CABC, UTS.

13. *New York Tribune*, January 21, 1891, 1. *Scrapbook of the Briggs Case*, 4: "Briggsdoxy," *Mail and Express*, July 11, 1891, 42. "Is Professor Briggs a Heretic?" *New York Sun*, April 12, 1891, 8. For various other evaluations of the ceremony in the *Evangelist, Observer, Herald and*

Presbyter, and *Independent*, see Francis R. Beattie, "The Inauguration of Dr. Charles A. Briggs at Union Seminary, New York," *Presbyterian Quarterly* 5 (1891): 270–283. See also "A Very Important Question," *New York Sun*, February 12, 1891, and "Religious Breastworks," *Independent*, February 19, 1891, 1–2.

14. Briggs, "The Theological Crisis," 101, 103; for background on this article, see *TLB*, VIII: letters of April 20, 1891, 147; April 27, 1891, 160–161, CABC, UTS.

15. Briggs, "The Theological Crisis," 101, 104.

16. Ibid., 104–105.

17. Ibid., 112.

18. Ibid., 114.

19. *The Case against Professor Briggs* (New York: Charles Scribner's Sons, 1892); Max Rogers, "Charles A. Briggs: Conservative Heretic," Ph.D. Thesis, Columbia University, 1964, 144ff. *TLB*, VIII: letters of April 15, 1891, 147; April 22, 1891, 152; April 23, 1891, 153, CABC, UTS.

20. *TLB*, VIII: letter of May 12, 1891, 163ff., CABC, UTS; *Case against Professor Briggs*, 2–7.

21. *Case against Professor Briggs*, 164ff.; John J. McCook, *The Appeal in the Briggs Heresy Case before the General Assembly of the Presbyterian Church* (New York: John C. Rankin, Co., 1893), 12ff.

22. *Case against Professor Briggs*, 2ff.; McCook, *The Appeal*, 11ff. *TLB*, VIII: letter of May 20, 1891, 178–179. Minutes for the meeting of May 19, 1891, in *Minutes of the Board of Directors of the Union Theological Seminary, 1884–1904* (handwritten ledger), 155–156, Burke Library, UTS.

23. *Scrapbook of the Briggs Case*, 1: "What Dr. Briggs's Case Implies," *New York Times*, May 17, 1891, 40; "The Case of Dr. Briggs," *New York Tribune*, May 17, 1891, 39. *TLB*, VIII: letters of May 20, 1891, 179–181; June 24, 1891, 205, CABC, UTS.

24. *Scrapbook of the Briggs Case*, 1: "Defenders of Professor Briggs," *New York Sun*, May 21, 1891, 14, CABC, UTS. *Minutes of the General Assembly of the Presbyterian Church in the United States of America* (Philadelphia: McCalla & Sons, 1891), 23–26.

25. *Minutes of the General Assembly* (1891), 50ff. The committee appointed at the 1891 General Assembly to consider the question of creedal revision recommended that, before acting on the overwhelmingly positive response of the presbyteries to the revision overture from the previous assembly, specific recommendations be gathered from the presbyteries and "compiled," thus safely burying the issue for another year.

26. *Minutes of the General Assembly* (1891), 94ff.; Prentiss, *Union Theological Seminary*, 96ff; Lefferts A. Loetscher, *The Broadening Church: A Study of Theological Issues in the Presbyterian Church since 1869* (Philadelphia: Westminster Press, 1949), 53–57; Rogers, "Briggs," 160–172. The technical point of contention between Union Seminary and the General Assembly was whether the transfer of a faculty member from one chair to another within the same institution constituted an "election" in the same sense as the original appointment. The General Assembly at Detroit argued that a transfer did not essentially differ from an election. The real point of the legal battle, however, was the attempt by the antirevisionists to block Briggs's transfer and possibly even effect his removal from the seminary. Union Seminary perceived this from the beginning, and argued that, technically, the original election of Briggs to the Davenport Chair in 1876 had not been vetoed, and that thus this earlier appointment had fixed Briggs's status on the Union faculty permanently. The Union Board of Directors informed Patton's committee that the transfer of 1890 constituted a simple reassignment of duties, and rested solely within the jurisdiction of the seminary's directors. See Prentiss, *Union Theological Seminary*, 50ff.

27. Minutes for the meetings of May 19, 1891, and of June 4, 1891, in *Minutes of the Board of Directors of the Union Theological Seminary, 1884–1904*, 155–156, 158–162. For a detailed defense of Union's position on the "veto right" of the General Assembly and of Briggs's transfer, see Prentiss, *Union Theological Seminary*, 63–74, 92–104, 122–136, 158ff.

28. *TLB*, VIII: letter of July 6, 1891, 213, CABC, UTS. On the place of higher criticism itself in the fears of the General Assembly, George Prentiss later wrote that "I doubt if one in twenty of the commissioners in Detroit would have dared to stand up and state what the higher criticism is. Their one impression seemed to be that it was a frightful doctrinal disease of some kind, and that Dr. Briggs had it in its most malignant form" (*Union Theological Seminary*, 94).

29. *Minutes of the Board of Directors of the Union Theological Seminary, 1884–1904*, 158; *TLB*, VIII: letters of June 6, 1891, 195; June 24, 1891, 205; July 6, 1891, 212–213. *Scrapbook of the Briggs Case*, 1: "Professor Briggs Sustained," *New York Sun*, June 6, 1891, 19; "Briggs's Triumph," *New York World*, June 6, 1891, 22, CABC, UTS. Philip Schaff, "Other Heresy Trials and the Briggs Case," *Forum* 12 (January 1892); Schaff names Briggs as "orthodox and conservative" by German standards, and emphasizes the important role played by Briggs's aggressive personality.

30. *Scrapbook of the Briggs Case*, 1: "The Presbyterian Schism," *New York Times*, June 7, 1891, 6, CABC, UTS.

31. *The Presbyterian Church in the United States of America against the Reverend Charles A. Briggs: The Report of the Committee of Prosecution with the Charges and Specifications Submitted to the New York Presbytery, October 5, 1891* (New York: John C. Rankin, 1891); *The Presbyterian Church in the U.S.A. against the Reverend Charles A. Briggs: Charges and Specifications as Delivered to Dr. Briggs by the Moderator in the Presbytery, October 6, 1891* (New York: Douglas Taylor, 1891), 3ff., 40ff.; McCook, *The Appeal*, 14.

32. At the end of January 1891, it was reported to the Board of Directors of Union Seminary that when a special committee was sent to interview Briggs he had affirmed by oath the following positions: that he did *not* believe the church and the reason to be coordinate sources of divine authority with the Bible; that he held the Old and New Testaments to be the only infallible rule of faith and practice; that he believed the "reason" to include the conscience and the "religious feeling"; that he held "inspiration" to mean divine direction to insure an infallible record of revelation; that he believed the Bible was inerrant on all matters pertaining to salvation; that he believed that the miracles recorded in Scripture were due to an extraordinary exercise of divine power; that he believed the eschatological choices made in this life were final and decisive; and that by "middle state" he did not mean purgatory or "second probation." *Minutes of the Board of Directors of the Union Theological Seminary*, 155; Prentiss, *Union Theological Seminary*, 544.

33. *Response to the Charges and Specifications Submitted to the Presbytery of New York by Professor Charles A. Briggs, November 4, 1891* (New York: Charles Briggs, 1891), 6–18, 28ff.

34. Ibid., 6–18, 28ff.

35. *The Case against Professor Briggs* (New York: Charles Scribner's Sons, 1892), 49.

36. McCook, *The Appeal*, 15; Rogers, "Briggs," 183–185.

37. Letters to Briggs following the dismissal of the case by the New York Presbytery on November 4, 1891, included those from: Washington Gladden (259); Arthur C. McGiffert (260); George Foote Moore (261); Crawford Toy (261); Frances Willard (262); William Rainey Harper (266); Newman Smyth (268); and Henry Codman Potter (264–265), all in *TLB*, VIII, CABC, UTS.

38. "Appeal to the General Assembly by the Prosecuting Committee, November 13, 1891," in *The Case against Professor Briggs*, 55–76. George

Birch, leader of the prosecuting committee, also contended that the proceedings of November 4 had been irregular according to the Book of Discipline because: Briggs had been permitted to read his response to the charges before pleading either guilty or innocent; Briggs had submitted his evidence *without* submitting to an oath and without cross-examination by the prosecuting committee, thus invalidating all evidence he submitted in his address before the presbytery; the presbytery had peremptorily dismissed the case before evidence could be submitted by the prosecuting committee (68). Even before Birch's committee filed its formal appeal to the General Assembly, however, Briggs had filed a complaint to the Synod of New York, contending (on the basis of section 10 of the Book of Discipline) that with the dismissal of charges against him by the presbytery, the prosecuting committee had ceased to be an "original party" in the case, and thus had no constitutional right to appeal to the General Assembly as it was no longer a legal body in the eyes of the Presbyterian church. See *Complaint to the Synod of New York from the Presbytery of New York, From Its Decision of the Question of the Original Party, November 4, 1891* (New York: John C. Rankin, Co., 1891), 3ff. Shedd's statement is in Loetscher, *Broadening Church,* 56.

39. *Scrapbook of the Briggs Case,* 4: "Anti-Briggs Men Chosen," *New York Tribune,* April 12, 1892, 7; "Anti-Briggs Men Win a Great Victory," *New York Herald,* April 12, 1892, 8; "Sharp Talk by Both Sides," *New York Times,* April 13, 1892, 11, CABC, UTS.

40. *TLB,* VIII: letter of April 29, 1892, 342, CABC, UTS. Briggs, *The Bible, The Church and the Reason* (New York: Charles Scribner's Sons, 1892), vii, viii–ix, 50. The seven lectures that constituted the work were: "The Bible and the Church," 2–28; "The Reason as a Great Fountain of Divine Authority," 29–56; "The Three Fountains of Divine Authority," 57–90; "Is Holy Scripture Inerrant?," 91–117; "The Higher Criticism," 118–151; "Biblical History," 152–176; "The Messianic Ideal," 177–201.

41. *Scrapbook of the Briggs Case,* 4: "Professor Briggs and the Revision," *Presbyterian Journal,* May 12, 1892, 64; "Dr. Briggs and His Friends," *New York Evening Post,* May 14, 1892, 38. *Scrapbook of the Briggs Case,* 5: "How It Seems in Glasgow," *The Occident,* July 28, 1892, 19, CABC, UTS.

42. *The Case against Professor Briggs,* 77–78; *Minutes of the General Assembly, 1892,* 128–130. The only successful such appeal over a synod directly to the General Assembly had been brought by the defendant in the

case of Bourne Versus the Presbytery of Lexington; see Rogers, "Briggs," 200ff.

43. *Case against Professor Briggs, Part II* (New York: Charles Scribner's Sons, 1893), 4; Rogers, "Briggs," 209.

44. McCook, *The Appeal*, 18–19.

45. *Scrapbook of the Briggs Case*, 4: "The Inerrancy Deliverance," *Presbyterian Journal*, June 23, 1892, 59; Loetscher, *Broadening Church*, 56. See "Papers in the Briggs Case," 84–89, *TLB*, III, CABC, UTS.

46. For Briggs's understanding of the Portland Deliverance, see Prentiss, *Union Theological Seminary*, 333ff. Briggs's supporters, both at the time and later, agreed on his reading of it; see Henry Van Dyke, *The Bible as It Is, A Sermon, January 22, 1893* (New York: n.p., 1893), 18; William Adams Brown, *A Teacher and His Times* (New York: Charles Scribner's Sons, 1940), 96–102, 125ff.; Henry Preserved Smith, "Charles Augustus Briggs," *American Journal of Theology* 17 (1913): 487–508, 500ff. For similar press interpretations, see *Scrapbook of the Briggs Case*, 4: "The Inerrancy Deliverance," 59; "The Assembly: A Summary," *The Interior*, June 2, 1892, 52; "Dr. Briggs and His Friends," *New York Evening Post*, May 19, 1892, 38, CABC, UTS.

47. *Minutes of the General Assembly, 1892*, 128–30. The official decision of the Committee on Revision was that it was "not practicable to take up and act on the 35 requests for a new creed at this time" (129).

48. Prentiss, *Union Theological Seminary*, 222–283. *Scrapbook of the Briggs Case*, 5: "Declaration of Independence," *New York Evangelist*, October 20, 1892, 45; "Free from the Assembly: Union Seminary Declares Its Independence," *New York Times*, November 17, 1892, 47, CABC, UTS. George Prentiss — at the request of Charles Butler, Union's president — prepared a working paper published under the title *The Veto Power and How to Solve It*; in that paper Prentiss recommended four reasons why the formal bond between the seminary and the General Assembly — a bond which gave the latter veto right over professorial appointments — should be annulled: that such a veto power granted to the assembly was inconsistent with the chartered obligations of the board to run an autonomous institution; that the veto power allowed by the compact was inconsistent with the plan and constitution of an *educational* institution whose only commitment could be to truth, and not to any denominational creed; that the veto power had proven "highly injurious" to the very object for which the original agreement had been drawn up — "the peace and unity for the church"; that the interests of Christian scholarship in America would

be furthered by an institution free of direct denominational control. See Prentiss, *Union Theological Seminary*, 222–224.

49. *Scrapbook of the Briggs Case*, 5: "The Briggs Case Again," *New York Tribune*, November 9, 1892, 60; "Dr. Briggs on Trial Now," *New York Tribune*, November 10, 1892, 61; Rogers, "Briggs," 219–221.

50. The eight charges presented against Briggs on November 9, 1892, were that he taught that: (1) reason can savingly enlighten those who reject biblical revelation; (2) the church is a fountain of divine authority apart from Scripture; (3) the original texts of Scripture contained errors; (4) many of the prophecies of the Old Testament had been reversed by history; (5) Moses was not the author of the Pentateuch; (6) Isaiah was not the author of half of the book named after him; (7) the process of redemption is extended into the next world; (8) the sanctification of believers is not complete at death, but is extended into the "middle state." See *The Presbyterian Church in the United States of America, Amended Charges and Specifications as Delivered, November 9, 1892* (New York: Douglas Taylor, 1893), 3–31; *The Case against Professor Briggs, Part II*, 51–52; *Defense of Professor Briggs*, 30ff.; McCook, *The Appeal*, 82.

51. *Defense of Professor Briggs*, 40, 100–106, 189. On December 5, Briggs submitted as evidence his books *Biblical Study, American Presbyterianism*, and *Whither?*; Philip Schaff's *Creeds of Christendom* and *German Reformation*; the *Minutes of the Sessions of the Westminster Assembly*; the *Minutes of the Synod of New York and Philadelphia* (of 1765); the letters exchanged between Antony Tuckney and Benjamen Whichcote; John Ball's *Treatise of Faith*; and John Wallis's *Sermon* (1791). See McCook, *The Appeal*, 97ff.; *The Case against Professor Briggs, Part II*, 61–67.

52. On the press coverage of the presbytery's decision, see *Scrapbook of the Briggs Case*, 6: "Professor Briggs Acquitted," *New York Sun*, December 31, 1892, 24; "Briggs Not Guilty of Heresy," *New York Herald*, December 31, 1892, 27; "Briggs and McGlynn," *New York Times*, January 1, 1893, 29, CABC, UTS. In the January 1 article of the *Times*, Briggs's fate was compared with that of the famous Roman Catholic social activist, James McGlynn: "The restoration of Dr. McGlynn to the Roman Catholic priesthood, and the acquittal of Dr. Briggs from the charge of heresy, are two events that show with great clearness the modernization or Americanization of the church." For other press coverage, see W. G. T. Shedd, "The Work before the Next General Assembly," *The Presbyterian*, May 11, 1893, 36; "The Presbyterian Crisis," *New York Times*, February 13, 1893, 9.

53. In February of 1893, a "ministerial memorial" entitled "A Plea for Peace and Work" was circulated throughout the New York Presbytery, calling for an end to hostilities, or at least for an end to judicial proceedings. Birch and his committee viewed the plea as just another tactic from the Briggs camp, and continued their work to have Briggs condemned at the General Assembly. On the plea, which appeared on February 17, 1893, and eventually gathered 235 names, see Rogers, "Briggs," 265ff.; *Scrapbook of the Briggs Case*, 7: "The Appeal in the Case of Professor Briggs," *New York Evangelist*, March 30, 1893, 51, CABC, UTS. *Minutes of the General Assembly of the Presbyterian Church in the United States of America, 1893* (Philadelphia: McCalla & Co., Printers, 1893), 70, 84–93.

54. *Minutes of the General Assembly, 1893*, 84–93, 150–154; McCook, *The Appeal*, 179. See also *Scrapbook of the Briggs Case*, 8: John J. Duffield, "The Crisis in the Presbyterian Church," *The Independent*, April 20, 1893, 21, CABC, UTS.

55. *Case against Professor Briggs*, 116–177; Rogers, "Briggs," 305. McCook offered five "special reasons" why the assembly should hear the appeal, although Briggs was technically correct in stating that the appeal should go to the Synod of New York: (1) that the appeal involved doctrines fundamental to the Presbyterian system; (2) that the case was "ripe" for a final judgment by the General Assembly; (3) that the purity and peace of the church demanded a decision; (4) that the case involved the legal construction of the ordination vow taken by church officers; (5) that unless the General Assembly itself decided the issue, the faith of ministerial students would be shaken, thus aiding in the spread of false doctrines. See Rogers, "Briggs," 311–317; *Minutes of the General Assembly, 1893*, 1500ff.

56. Briggs argued against the assembly's accepting the appeal on a number of technical points that authorities on Presbyterian history agree were probably legitimate and that, under other circumstances, would probably have led to the dismissal of the overture from the prosecuting committee: that the prosecuting committee from the New York Presbytery could not appeal to the General Assembly since it was not an "original party" in the case, but only a legal body appointed by the presbytery whose constitutional identity was dissolved when the presbytery found Briggs innocent; that the appeal to the assembly over the Synod of New York, which should have received the appeal, was without precedent and unconstitutional, since the Book of Discipline allowed appeals over intermediate courts *only* by the defendant and never by the prosecution; that he had already appealed a complaint against the prosecuting committee (as without legal existence) to the Synod of New York, thus making any other trial prej-

udicial in a case outstanding. *The Case against Professor Briggs*, 111ff.; Rogers, "Briggs," 289–299.

57. *TLB*, IX: letter of May 26, 1893, 9, CABC, UTS.

58. *Minutes of the General Assembly, 1893*, 93–95, 153ff.

59. *TLB*, IX: letter of May 27, 1893, 12, CABC, UTS.

60. Rogers, "Briggs," 347–352; *Scrapbook of the Briggs Case*, 7: "Will Dr. Briggs Secede?" *New York Times*, May 30, 1893, CABC, UTS.

61. *Proceedings of the General Assembly of 1893 against Charles Augustus Briggs, 105th Annual Meeting* (Washington, D.C., May 1893), 775–776.

62. *Minutes of the General Assembly, 1893*, 163–165.

Chapter 5: The Advance towards Church Unity

1. Winthrop Hudson, *Religion in America*, 3d ed. (New York: Charles Scribner's Sons, 1981), 357.

2. Ibid., 358.

3. On the "federationist" strain of Protestant ecumenism, see Charles S. MacFarland, *The Progress of Church Federation* (New York: Fleming H. Revell, 1917), 26ff.; idem, *Christian Unity in the Making* (New York: Federal Council of the Churches of Christ in America, 1948), 18ff.; Samuel M. Cavert, *Church Cooperation and Unity in America: A Historical Review, 1900–1870* (New York: Association Press, 1970), 13–19, 34ff.; R. Pierce Beaver, *Ecumenical Beginnings in Protestant World Mission* (New York: Thomas Nelson & Sons, 1962), 18–28, 66–90; Kenneth Scott Latourette, "The Ecumenical Bearings of the Missionary Movement and the International Missionary Council," in Ruth Rouse and Stephen Neill, eds., *History of the Ecumenical Movement, 1517–1948* (Philadelphia: Westminster Press, 1967), 353ff.

4. Cavert, *Church Cooperation*, 15ff.; William Adams Brown, *Toward a United Church* (New York: Charles Scribner's Sons, 1946), 23ff., 41–47.

5. Don H. Yoder, "Christian Unity in Nineteenth-Century America," in Rouse and Neill, *History of the Ecumenical Movement*, 249ff.; John F. Woolverton, "William Reed Huntington and Church Unity: The Historical and Theological Background of the Chicago-Lambeth Quadrilateral," Ph.D. Dissertation, Columbia University, 1963, 38, 77–81; Charles D. Kean, *The Road to Reunion* (Greenwich, Conn.: Seabury Press, 1958), 32–36; Ruth Rouse, "Voluntary Movements and the Changing Ecumenical Climate," in Rouse and Neill, *History of the Ecumenical Movement*, chapter 7. Philip Schaff brought the idea of "evangelical catholicism" to

America and it can be argued that this formed the motif around which his career nucleated.

6. William R. Hutchison, *The Modernist Impulse in American Protestantism* (Cambridge: Harvard University Press, 1976), 177ff.; Peter G. Gowing, "Newman Smyth: New England Ecumenist," Th.D. Dissertation, Boston University, 1960, 24–28, 114ff.; Newman Smyth, *Passing Protestantism and Coming Catholicism* (New York: Charles Scribner's Sons, 1908), 68ff.; John J. Feeney, Jr., "Charles A. Briggs and the Organic Reunion of Christendom," *Historical Magazine of the Protestant Episcopal Church* 47 (1978): 93–112.

7. *TLB*, III: letter of December 7, 1858, 180–181; Max Rogers, "Charles A. Briggs: Conservative Heretic," Ph.D. Thesis, Columbia University, 1964, 7ff.; Feeney, "Charles A. Briggs," 95ff.

8. Briggs, "Theological and Literary Intelligence: Germany," *American Presbyterian Review*, n.s., 1 (1870): 420–421.

9. Briggs, "Biblical Theology with Especial Reference to the New Testament," *American Presbyterian Review*, n.s., 2 (1870): 111.

10. Briggs, *Biblical Study, Its Principles, Methods and History* (New York: Charles Scribner's Sons, 1883), 306.

11. Briggs, *American Presbyterianism, Its Origin and Early History* (New York: Charles Scribner's Sons, 1885), xii–xiii; Feeney, "Charles A. Briggs," 98–99.

12. Briggs, "Rupertus Meldenius and His Word of Peace," *Presbyterian Review* 8 (1887): 743–746; "The Work of John Durie in Behalf of Christian Union in the Seventeenth Century," *Presbyterian Review* 8 (1887): 297–309; "Terms of Christian Union," *Christian Union* 35 (1887): 8–9; "A Plea for an American Alliance of the Reformed Churches," *Presbyterian Review* 9 (1888): 306–308.

13. Briggs, "Plea for an American Alliance," 306.

14. Ibid., 307–308.

15. Joseph R. Jeter, Jr., "The Christian Unity Foundation," *Historical Magazine of the Protestant Episcopal Church* 44 (1975): 451–461; John F. Woolverton, "Huntington's Quadrilateral — A Critical Study," *Church History* 39 (1970): 198–211; William Reed Huntington, *The Church Idea: An Essay toward Unity* (New York: E. P. Dutton & Co., 1870).

16. Kean, *Road to Reunion*, 35–36.

17. Briggs, "The Lambeth Conference of Bishops of the Anglican Communion," *Presbyterian Review* 9 (1888): 657–659; "The Historic Episcopate as a Basis of Reunion," in *Church Reunion Discussed on the Basis*

of the Lambeth Propositions (New York: The Church Review Co., 1890), 48–49.

18. Box 55, CABC, UTS: "Christian Unity," *New York Times*, May 12, 1890; "Unity in Christ," *Brooklyn Daily Eagle*, February 5, 1890. See also "Professor Briggs on Christian Unity," *Christian Union*, May 1, 1890; "Church Reunion and Christian Unity," *Independent*, December 11, 1890.

19. Briggs, "The Advance towards Church Unity," *The Independent*, January 1, 1891, 1.

20. Ibid., 2.

21. Ibid., 3.

22. Ibid., 4.

23. *TLB*, IX: letter of November 11, 1891, 268, CABC, UTS.

24. Briggs, "The Alienation of Church and People," *The Forum* 16 (1893): 366–378, 367.

25. Briggs, "The Future of Presbyterianism in the United States," *North American Review* 157 (July 1893): 1–10, 9.

26. *TLB*, IX: letters of March 29, 1894, 153; September 11, 1894, 178, CABC, UTS. Rogers, "Briggs," 393–397. For a hostile conservative Presbyterian appraisal of Union's "refusal" to deal with the recalcitrant Briggs, see Thomas McDougall, *The Moral Quality of the Conduct of the Directors of Union Seminary* (Cincinnati: Robert Clarke Co., 1893).

27. *TLB*, IX: letters of September 16, 1893, 100; December 5, 1893, 119, CABC, UTS.

28. Woolverton, "Huntington," 78; Charles W. Shields, *The Historic Episcopate* (New York: Charles Scribner's Sons, 1894), 26–27; Jeter, "The Church Unity Foundation," 451–461.

29. "Many Voices Concerning Dr. Shields' Book," *Christian Literature and Review of the Churches* 10 (March 1, 1894): 133–156. The strongest criticism offered of Shield's book was penned by Josiah Strong, 139–140; the warmest support was from Huntington, 133–134. "Constitution of the League of Catholic Unity," original draft in box 44, folder 26, CABC, UTS. *TLB*, IX: letters of July 29, 1893, 87; August 8, 1893, 91; December 29, 1894, 206, CABC, UTS.

30. Woolverton, "Huntington," 77ff.

31. *New York Times*, June 21, 1895; *New York World*, June 17, 1895; *Providence Journal*, June 20, 1895; quoted in Woolverton, "Huntington," 81–82.

32. *TLB*, IX: letter of December 29, 1894, 206, CABC, UTS. "Declaration of the League of Catholic Unity," second draft in box 44, folder 26, CABC, UTS.

33. *TLB*, IX: letters of April 11, 1895, 226; April 16, 1895, 227; November 1, 1895, 279; November 9, 1895, 280; September 18, 1896, 311; September 26, 1896, 312, CABC, UTS.

34. Feeney, "Charles A. Briggs," 104ff. *TLB*, IX: letters of November 1, 1895, 279; November 6, 1895, 279; November 9, 1895, 280, CABC, UTS.

35. On the World's Student Christian Federation, see Samuel M. Cavert, *The American Churches in the Ecumenical Movement, 1900–1968* (New York: Association Press, 1968), 27ff.

36. *TLB*, IX: letters of March 29, 1894, 153; September 11, 1894, 178, CABC, UTS. Rogers, "Briggs," 389ff. See also McDougall, *Moral Quality*.

37. *TLB*, IX: letters of January 25, 1898, 386; February 16, 1898, 389; February 20, 1898, 391, CABC, UTS. Rogers, "Briggs," 403ff.

38. *TLB*, IX: letters of March 28, 1898, 408; April 5, 1898, 410, CABC, UTS.

39. Briggs's priestly ordination had been originally scheduled to be held in St. Peter's Church in Westchester, New York, a church outside New York City chosen to avoid as much of the expected publicity surrounding the ceremony as possible. But the rector of the parish, Frank M. Clendenin — an Anglo-Catholic with pronounced anticritical sensibilities — issued a public letter in the press addressed to Bishop Potter, pronouncing Briggs's scholarly efforts as "fundamentally heretical from first to last" and calling on the bishop to cancel the ordination. Briggs's teaching, "if true, would undermine not only the whole Catholic Church, Greek, Roman and Anglican, but it would destroy even the faith of Protestantism." Clendenin was soon joined in his attack by Benjamin DeCosta, a fellow Anglo-Catholic priest who publicly threatened to prosecute heresy proceedings himself. Potter ignored both the protest and the publicity surrounding it, and moved the ordination site from Westchester to the Pro-Cathedral in the city (his own cathedral, St. John the Divine, still being built). Further, Potter declared in the *New York Herald* that both Clendenin and DeCosta represented a numerically small and untypical position within his diocese on the question of Briggs's ordination, and that he was considering canonical action against both as priests who showed disloyal and scandalous behavior towards their bishop, a violation of their ordination oaths. Briggs himself wrote Clendenin after his ordination, stating that both the earlier (Presbyterian) charges against him and Clendenin's own were unfounded and uncatholic: "Catholic doctrine was condemned when I was condemned on these questions." Rogers, "Briggs," 406–409; Frank M. Clendenin, *Remarks Concerning the Proposed Ordination of the Rev. Charles A. Briggs* (New York: n.p., 1899); *TLB*, X: letters of April 27,

1899, 480; April 28, 1899, 481; May 3, 1899, 486. *TLB*, IX: June 7, 1899, 5–8, CABC, UTS.

40. Briggs, *General Introduction to the Study of Holy Scripture. The Principles, Methods, History and Results of Its Several Departments and of the Whole* (New York: Charles Scribner's Sons, 1899).

41. Ibid., 42, 158–159, 289ff., 471ff., 508ff., 585–591.

42. Francis Brown, Charles A. Briggs, and S. R. Driver, *A Hebrew and English Lexicon of the Old Testament, With an Appendix Containing the Biblical Aramaic, Based on the Lexicon of William Gesenius, as Translated by Edward Robinson* (Boston: Houghton, Mifflin & Co., 1906).

43. *TLB*, X: letters of May 27, 1901, 103; July 15, 1901, 123; August 20, 1901, 123; September 2, 1901, 124, CABC, UTS.

44. See Alec R. Vidler, *The Modernist Movement in the Roman Church. Its Origins and Outcome* (New York: University Press, 1932), xii; John Ratté, *Three Modernists: Loisy, Tyrrell and Sullivan* (Cambridge: Harvard University Press, 1968), 3ff.; Bernard Reardon, *Roman Catholic Modernism* (Stanford, Calif.: Stanford University Press, 1970).

45. Wilfred Ward, *William George Ward and the Catholic Revival*, as reported in Vidler, *Modernist Movement*, 65.

46. Vidler, *Modernist Movement*, 17–18; Alec Vidler, *A Variety of Catholic Modernists* (Cambridge: The University Press, 1970), 65.

47. Reardon, *Roman Catholic Modernism*, 16–21; Vidler, *Modernist Movement*, 89–94.

48. Smyth, *Passing Protestantism*, 40–45, 108–135. *TLB*, X: letters of April 11, 1898, 415–416; January 29, 1899, 462. *TLB*, IX: May 17, 1898, 423; January 29, 1899, 462, CABC, UTS. Feeney, "Charles A. Briggs," 107; Briggs, "Reform in the Roman Catholic Church," *North American Review* 181 (1905): 80.

49. James J. Kelly, *Baron Friedrich von Huegel's Philosophy of Religion* (Leuven: University Press, 1983), 72; Michael de la Bedoyere, *Life of Baron von Huegel* (London: J. M. Dent & Sons, Ltd., 1951), 366ff.

50. Vidler, *Variety of Catholic Modernists*, 109–126; J. J. Heaney, *The Modernist Crisis: Von Huegel* (Washington, D.C.: Corpus Books, 1969), 21ff.

51. Vidler, *Variety of Catholic Modernists*, 113; Heaney, *Modernist Crisis*, 28–35.

52. Rogers, "Briggs," 414–415; Bedoyere, *Life of von Huegel*, 366ff.; Briggs, "Catholic — The Name and the Thing," *American Journal of Theology* 7 (1903): 417–442.

53. Briggs, "Catholic — The Name and the Thing," 417, 420ff.

54. Ibid., 427.

55. Ibid., 427–428, 430.

56. Ibid., 441.

57. Ibid., 441–442.

58. Ibid., 439.

59. *Scrapbook of the Briggs Case*, 5: "Will Dr. Briggs Wind Up in the Catholic Church?," *New York Sun*, August 9, 1903; "Dr. Briggs's Article," *The Catholic News*, August 29, 1903; "Professor Briggs and Roman Catholicism," *New York Evangelist*, October 10, 1903; "Dr. Briggs's Remarkable Tribute to Catholicism," *Literary Digest*, September 19, 1903; "Current Thought on Catholicity," *The Churchman*, September 12, 1903, CABC, UTS.

60. Briggs, "How May We Become More Truly Catholic?," *The Independent* 56 (January 28, 1904): 177–184.

61. On the response of the press to Briggs's address and on its dubbing the affair the "Second Briggs Case," see "Another Controversy," *New York Tribune*, January 18, 1904; "Dr. Briggs Will Not Go to Rome," *New York Herald*, January 18, 1904; "Bishop Potter Says Dr. Briggs Is No Heretic," *New York Sun*, January 19, 1904; "Professor Briggs's Address," *The Independent*, January 28, 1904; "More Briggsian Heresy," *The Mail and Express*, January 28, 1904, all in *Briggs Scrapbook*, CABC, UTS. Briggs, "How May We Become More Truly Catholic?," 182.

62. Briggs, "How May We Become More Truly Catholic?," 184.

63. Ibid., 181.

64. "More Briggsian Heresy," *Mail and Express*, January 28, 1904; "Church Stirred by Dr. Briggs," *New York Sun*, January 18, 1904; "Another Controversy," *New York Tribune*, January 18, 1904; "Briggs Again," *Brooklyn Times*, January 18, 1904; "Inquiry as to Dr. Briggs's Positions," *The Living Church*, January 19, 1904. See also "Dr. Briggs Stirs Up More Trouble," *New York Daily News*, January 18, 1904; "Will Not Join Roman Church," *Columbus* (Ohio) *State Journal*, January 19, 1904; "Briggs Yet Again," *Indianapolis Journal*, January 24, 1904; "Dr. Briggs and Heresy," *Wheeling* (W. Va.) *Telegraph*, January 21, 1904; "Dr. Briggs's Position," *Living Church*, January 23, 1904; "The Position of Dr. Briggs," *New York Sun*, January 31, 1904; "Dr. Briggs's Paper on Catholicity," *Brooklyn Eagle*, January 27, 1904; "Dr. Briggs's Views Stir Churchmen," *New York Herald*, January 28, 1904; "Catholic or Sectarian," *The Churchman*, January 30, 1904, all in *Scrapbook of the Briggs Case*, CABC, UTS.

65. "Briggs a Menace to the Cathedral Fund," *New York American*, January 19, 1904; "Stirred by Briggs," *New York Evening Sun*, January 18, 1904, in *Scrapbook of the Briggs Case*, CABC, UTS.

66. On the Inter-Church Conference on Federation, see Cavert, *Church Cooperation and Unity*, 16ff.

67. "Bishop Potter Says Briggs Is No Heretic," *New York Sun*, January 19, 1904; "Regard for Bishop Averts Briggs Trial," *New York Herald*, January 20, 1904; "Not To Leave Church," *New York Tribune*, January 19, 1904, all in *Scrapbook of the Briggs Case*, CABC, UTS.

Chapter 6: Mediating Modernism

1. *TLB*, X: letter of November 10, 1903, 213, CABC, UTS. *Briggs Scrapbook*, 15: "Briggs Transferred," *New York Herald*, May 10, 1904, 9, 15, CABC, UTS. Briggs's inaugural address at his induction into the new chair was published in the *American Journal of Theology* under the title "A Plea for the Higher Study of Theology," 8 (July 1904): 433–451. Briggs lamented in the address that the Christian minister was "no longer what he used to be and ought to be, the best educated man in the community." But Briggs laid the blame for this at feet of obscurantists who were making Christianity the refuge of the intellectually timid. He hoped that Union's new department would become an important force to counteract this (437). That same spring, Union Seminary finally resolved the constitutional question of its identity that had been hanging since Briggs's suspension from the ministry: its constitution was amended to omit the vow of loyalty to the Presbyterian church, thus formally making Union Seminary a nondenominational institution. See Henry Sloane Coffin, *A Half Century at Union Theological Seminary, 1896–1945* (New York: Charles Scribner's Sons, 1954), v, 58–59, 261.

2. Max Rogers, "Charles A. Briggs: Conservative Heretic," Ph.D. Thesis, Columbia University, 1964, 420.

3. *TLB*, X: letter of March 3, 1904, 301, CABC, UTS. "Dr. Briggs Sees Pope," *New York Times*, May 13, 1905; "Dr. Briggs and the Pope," *The Churchman*, May 20, 1905; "Dr. Briggs and the Roman Catholic Church," *Current Literature*, July 1905, all in the *Scrapbook of the Briggs Case*, CABC, UTS. For the correspondence between Briggs and Giovanni Genocchi, see *TLB*, XII: letters of December 30, 1904, 279; August 2, 1905, 327; December 20, 1905, 354; July 4, 1906, 380; May 20, 1907, 466; June 8, 1907, 471; July 14, 1907, 487. *TLB*, X: September 19, 1907,

6; December 15, 1907, 28; January 24, 1908, 42; November 1, 1908, 36, CABC, UTS.

4. *TLB*, X: letter of March 3, 1904, 301, CABC, UTS.

5. Briggs, "Loisy and His Critics in the Roman Catholic Church," *The Expositor*, Sixth Series, 9 (April 1905): 241–256, 243–244.

6. Ibid., 247, 248, 252.

7. Briggs, "Reform in the Roman Catholic Church," *North American Review* 181 (July 1905): 80–89, 81–82.

8. Ibid., 83, 89.

9. On the "hardening" of American Protestant opposition to the modernist program, see William R. Hutchison, *The Modernist Impulse in American Protestantism* (Cambridge: Harvard University Press, 1976), 105–110, 185ff.

10. "The Pontifical Commission on Biblical Matters," as the biblical commission was formally entitled, was organized by Leo XIII on October 30, 1902, its function being defined in the apostolic letter *Vigilantiae* as one of striving "with all possible care that God's word will *both* be given, everywhere among us, that thorough study that our times demand, *and* will be shielded not only from every breath of error and every rash opinion." The obligatory force of its decrees was elucidated by Pius X in 1907 in the motu proprio letter *Praestantia Scripturae*: "All are bound in conscience to submit to the decrees of the Commission; nor can they avoid the stigma both of disobedience and temerity, or be free from grave sin, who by any spoken or written words impugn these decisions." The concern of both von Huegel and of Briggs was that the original secretary of the commission, the well-trained, theologically moderate F. G. Vigouroux, was replaced by the reactionary Benedictine Laurence Janssens, whom both had met and come to fear as an implacable opponent of progressive scholarship. See "Pontifical Biblical Commission," *New Catholic Encyclopedia* (New York: McGraw-Hill Book Co., 1967), 11:551–554, 551, 552–553. Bedoyere, *von Huegel*, 185; Paul Sabatier, *Modernism* (New York: Charles Scribner's Sons, 1908), 42ff.

11. Michael de la Bedoyere, *Life of Baron von Huegel* (London: J. M. Dent & Sons, Ltd., 1951), 185; Lawrence F. Barman, *Baron Friedrich von Huegel and the Modernist Crisis in England* (Cambridge: University Press, 1972), 132–135; Alec R. Vidler, *A Variety of Catholic Modernists* (Cambridge: The University Press, 1970), 123; Bernard Reardon, *Roman Catholic Modernism* (Stanford, Calif.: Stanford University Press, 1970), 50, 174ff. *TLB*, X: letter of August 28, 1906, 384–387, CABC, UTS.

12. Bedoyere, *Von Huegel*, 185; *TLB*, X: letter of August 28, 1906, 385, CABC, UTS.

13. *TLB*, X: letter of August 28, 1906, 385–386.

14. *TLB*, X: letter of September 4, 1906, 392, CABC, UTS.

15. *TLB*, X: letter of September 14, 1906, 394–395, CABC, UTS.

16. Von Huegel originally sent their "letters" to Sir James Knowles, editor of the periodical *Nineteenth Century*, who informed the baron that their letters could not appear in the next issue, thus thwarting the baron's desire to get the work out as soon as possible. Von Huegel then sent it to Charles Longman, who readily accepted it for publication. Briggs wrote to von Huegel on November 22 that "all you say of my friendliness to the Catholic Church and my earnest desire for reunion is true. The main thing is to get a hearing with the authorities of the Church. I want nothing for my work. I wrote to help the liberal Catholics as a labor of love." *TLB*, X: letters of November 6, 1906, 407; November 22, 1906, 420, CABC, UTS. Friedrich von Huegel and Charles A. Briggs, *The Papal Commission and the Pentateuch* (London: Longmans, Green & Co., 1906), 7, 9.

17. Von Huegel, *The Papal Commission and the Pentateuch*, 36ff.; von Huegel outlined four "necessary impulses" that showed that Catholicism — a religion "intrinsically historical" — would eventually come to accept the new criticism: that Catholicism was an assimilationist religion, incorporating the best thought of the various cultures in which it found itself; that Catholicism had always rejected the "Bible only" approach to religious certainty; that it had always appealed to "tradition," thereby taking the historical process itself seriously as a revelatory mode of God's presence; that it had come to think of itself, especially after John Henry Newman, as "an organism growing in all aspects" (45–49).

18. Vidler, *The Modernist Movement in the Roman Church. Its Origins and Outcome* (Cambridge: The University Press, 1934), 217ff.

19. Ibid., 218, 219; Paul Sabatier, *Modernism* (New York: Charles Scribner's Sons, 1908), 65ff.

20. Vidler, *The Modernist Movement*, 219.

21. *TLB*, XII: letter of October 2, 1907, 11–13, CABC, UTS. On July 14, 1907, Giovanni Genocchi wrote to Briggs of a depressing conversation he had had with the pope that day: "I heard the Pope saying that a scholar has to keep his own opinion about the Pentateuch, even if opposite to the decree of the Biblical Commission, but such a man cannot be a Professor in our ecclesiastical schools. We answered freely that in such a condition of things we would see only hypocrites or ignorant men in the Scripture

keeping peace in our biblical chairs. The Pope was struck by that assertion and sighed." *TLB*, X: letter of July 14, 1907, 487–488, CABC, UTS.

22. *TLB*, XII: letter of December 8, 1907, 25–26, CABC, UTS.

23. *TLB*, XII: letter of November 15, 1907, 20, CABC, UTS.

24. Briggs, "The Great Obstacle in the Way of a Reunion of Christendom," *North American Review* 186 (September 1907): 72–82, 73.

25. Ibid., 77.

26. Briggs, "The Encyclical against Modernism," *North American Review* 187 (January 1908): 199–212, 206–217.

27. Briggs, "Modernism Mediating the Coming Catholicism," *North American Review* 189 (June 1909): 877–899, 877, 879–880.

28. Ibid., 881, 882.

29. Ibid., 888.

30. *TLB*, X: letters of February 25, 1907, 452–453; July 21, 1907, 493. *TLB*, XII: September 20, 1907, 7; October 2, 1907, 13; November 15, 1907, 20, CABC, UTS.

31. For a lively if biased narrative of the "generational wars" between American Protestant modernists, see Frank Hugh Foster, *The Modern Movement in American Theology* (New York: Fleming H. Revell Co., 1939). Among the best "representative works" of this second, more radical, generation are William Newton Clarke's *An Outline of Christian Theology* (New York: Charles Scribner's Sons, 1898); William Adams Brown, *Christian Theology in Outline* (New York: Charles Scribner's Sons, 1906); Henry Churchill King, *Reconstruction in Theology* (New York: The Macmillan Co., 1901); George Herron, *The Larger Christ* (Chicago: Fleming H. Revell Co., 1891).

32. Henry Sloane Coffin, *A Half Century at Union Theological Seminary, 1896–1945* (New York: Charles Scribner's Sons, 1954), 34–40; Rogers, "Briggs," 457–458; Arthur Cushman McGiffert, *A History of Christianity in the Apostolic Age* (New York: Charles Scribner's Sons, 1897), 68n., 487ff., 577–578.

33. Arthur Cushman McGiffert, *Eusebius*, in A Select Library of Nicene and Post-Nicene Fathers of the Christian Church, Philip Schaff and Henry Wace, eds. (New York: Christian Literature Co., 1890). Coffin, *Half Century*, 40; letter of July 15, 1901, Brown letters, in John C. Brown Collection, UTS.

34. Henry Warner Bowden, *Church History in the Age of Science* (Chapel Hill: University of North Carolina Press, 1971), 136–169, 139ff.

35. Coffin, *Half Century*, 36–37.

36. Rogers, "Briggs," 458–459.

37. Briggs, "Criticism and Dogma," *North American Review* 182 (June 1906): 861–874, 861.

38. Ibid., 862, 867.

39. Ibid., 874.

40. Briggs, "The Christ of the Church," *American Journal of Theology* 16 (April 1912): 196–217, 199, 200.

41. Briggs, *Church Unity* (New York: Charles Scribner's Sons, 1909). At least half of the work had already been published in article form, including chapter 3 ("Catholic — The Name and the Thing"); chapter 4 ("The Historic Episcopate"); chapter 7 ("The Real and the Ideal in the Papacy"); chapter 9 ("The Theological Crisis"); chapter 13 ("The Encyclical against Modernism"); and chapter 14 ("The Great Obstacle in the Way of a Reunion of Christendom"). The work thus presented an inclusive view of Briggs's work of the previous two decades.

42. Ibid., 4, 12, 13.

43. Ibid., 426–427, 440–441.

44. Ibid., 440–441.

45. Ibid., 13, 439–440.

46. Briggs, *The Fundamental Christian Faith* (New York: Charles Scribner's Sons, 1913); *History of the Study of Theology*, 2 vols. (New York: Charles Scribner's Sons, 1916). Prepared for publication by Emilie Grace Briggs.

47. Briggs died quietly on June 8 in his residence at the seminary. While the official cause of death was listed as pulmonary pneumonia, Briggs's physical condition had been deteriorating for some time as a result of stress and overwork. See Rogers, "Briggs," 482.

Bibliography

Primary Sources

Baird, Robert. *Religion in America*. 1844. Reprint. New York: Harper & Row, 1970.

Blackie, W. G. *Professor W. Robertson Smith: The Action of the Free Commission Ultra Vires*. Glasgow: D. D. Blackie & Sons, 1881.

Briggs, Charles Augustus. *American Presbyterianism, Its Origin and Early History*. New York: Charles Scribner's Sons, 1885.

———. *The Authority of Holy Scripture, An Inaugural Address, with Preface and Appendix*. New York: Charles Scribner's Sons, 1891.

———. "The Authority of Holy Scripture." In *Inaugural Address and Defense, 1891–1893*. Reprint. New York: Arno Press, 1972.

———. *The Bible, the Church and the Reason*. New York: Charles Scribner's Sons, 1892.

———. *Biblical Study, Its Principles, Methods and History*. New York: Charles Scribner's Sons, 1883.

———. "Catholic — The Name and the Thing." *American Journal of Theology* 7 (1903): 417–442.

———. "The Christ of the Church." *American Journal of Theology* 16 (1912): 196–217.

———. *Church Unity*. New York: Charles Scribner's Sons, 1909.

———. "Criticism and Dogma." *North American Review* 182 (1906): 861–874.

———. "The Encyclical against Modernism." *North American Review* 18 (1908): 204–212.

———. *The Fundamental Christian Faith.* New York: Charles Scribner' Sons, 1913.

———. "The Future of Presbyterianism in the United States." *Nort American Review* 440 (1893): 2–10.

———. *General Introduction to the Study of Holy Scripture.* New York Charles Scribner's Sons, 1899.

———. "The Great Obstacle in the Way of a Reunion of Christendom." *North American Review* 186 (1907): 72–82.

———. *History of the Study of Theology.* 2 vols. New York: Charles Scrib ner's Sons, 1916.

———. *How Shall We Revise the Westminster Confession?* New York Charles Scribner's Sons, 1890.

———. "Modernism Mediating the Coming Catholicism." *North Ameri can Review* 189 (1909): 877–889.

———. "A Plea for the Higher Study of Theology." *American Journal c Theology* 8 (1904): 433–451.

———. "Reform in the Roman Catholic Church." *North American Reviev* 181 (1905): 80–90.

———. "The Revision of the Westminster Confession." *Andover Reviev* 13 (1890): 45–68.

———. "The Theological Crisis." *North American Review* 153 (1891): 99– 114.

———. *Whither? A Theological Question for the Times.* New York: Charle Scribner's Sons, 1889.

Briggs, Charles A., Francis Brown, and S. R. Driver. *A Hebrew and Eng lish Lexicon of the Old Testament, with an Appendix Containing th Biblical Aramaic.* Boston: Houghton, Mifflin & Co., 1906.

Briggs, Emilie Grace. "Sketch of Dr. Charles A. Briggs." *Alumni Bulleti of the University of Virginia* 5 (1899): 92–100.

Brown, William Adams. *Christian Theology in Outline.* New York: Charle Scribner's Sons, 1906.

The Case against Professor Briggs. New York: Charles Scribner's Sons 1892.

Catalogue of the University of Virginia. Washington, D.C.: Henry Polkin horn, 1859.

Church Reunion Discussed on the Basis of the Lambeth Propositions. Nev York: The Church Review Co., 1890.

Clarke, William Newton. *An Outline of Christian Theology.* New York Charles Scribner's Sons, 1898.

Darwin, Charles. *The Descent of Man and Selection in Relation to Sex* New York: D. Appleton & Co., 1872.

———. *The Origin of Species by Means of Natural Selection*. London: John Murray, 1859.

Dorner, Isaac A. *Geschichte der Protestantischen Theologie*. Munich, n.p., 1867.

The Edward Robinson Chair of Biblical Theology in the Union Theological Seminary. New York: Union Seminary, 1891.

The Fallibility of Inspired Scripture, as Maintained by Modern Criticism, Being an Examination of the Views Propounded by Professor W. R. Smith. Glasgow: D. Bryce, 1877.

Feuerbach, Ludwig. *Samtliche Werke*. 2 vols. Leipzig: O. Wigand, 1848–1866.

Gladden, Washington. *Recollections*. Boston: Houghton, Mifflin & Co., 1909.

Hegel, Georg. *Lectures on the Philosophy of History*. Translated by J. Sibree. London: George Bell & Sons, 1881.

Herron, George. *The Larger Christ*. Chicago: Fleming H. Revell Co., 1891.

History, Essays and Other Documents of the Sixth General Conference of the Evangelical Alliance, Held in New York, October 2–12, 1873, edited by Philip Schaff and S. Irenaeus Prime. New York, n.p., 1874.

Hodge, Archibald Alexander. *Commentary on the Confession of Faith, with Questions for Theological Students*. Philadelphia: Presbyterian Board of Publication and Sabbath School Work, 1869.

Huegel, Friedrich von, and Charles A. Briggs. *The Papal Commission and the Pentateuch*. London: Longmans, Green & Co., 1906.

Huntington, William Reed. *The Church Idea: An Essay Toward Unity*. New York: E. P. Dutton & Co., 1870.

Innes, A. Taylor. "The Creed Question in Scotland." *Andover Review* 12 (1889): 1–15.

King, Henry Churchill. *Reconstruction in Theology*. New York: Macmillan, 1901.

Krebs, John M. "Backsliding and Apostasy." *The Herald of Truth* 1 (1859): 87–89.

———. "The Purpose and Success of the Gospel." *Presbyterian Preacher* 2 (1834): 322–338.

The Libel against Professor W. Robertson Smith; Report of the Proceedings of the Free Church Presbytery of Aberdeen, February 14 to March 14, 1978. Aberdeen: Murray, 1878.

McCook, John J. *The Appeal in the Briggs Heresy Case before the General Assembly of the Presbyterian Church*. New York: John C. Rankin, Co., 1893.

McCosh, James. *Whither? O Whither? Tell me Where*. New York: Charles Scribner's Sons, 1889.

McDougall, Thomas. *The Moral Quality of the Conduct of the Directors of Union Seminary*. Cincinnati: Robert Clarke Co., 1893.

McGiffert, Arthur Cushman. *Eusebius*. New York: Christian Literature Co., 1890.

―――. *A History of Christianity in the Apostolic Age*. New York: Charles Scribner's Sons, 1897.

Marx, Karl. "Philosophical Manifesto of the Historical School of Law." In *Writings of the Young Marx on Philosophy and Society*, edited by Loyd D. Easton and Kurt H. Guddut, 96–105. Garden City, N.Y.: Doubleday & Co., 1967.

Minutes of the General Assemblies of the Presbyterian Church in the U.S.A., 1889–1893. 5 vols. Philadelphia: McCalla & Co., 1889–1893.

Moll, Karl. *The Psalms*. Lange's Commentary on Holy Scripture. Translated by Charles A. Briggs. New York: Scribner, Armstrong & Co., 1872.

Mueller, Friedrich Max. *Lectures on the Origin and Growth of Religion as Illustrated by the Religions of India*. London: Longmans, Green & Co., 1878.

Premillennial Essays: The Report of the Proceedings of the First American Bible and Prophetic Conference, New York, October 30–November 1, 1878. Chicago, n.p., 1879.

The Presbyterian Church in the U.S.A. against the Reverend Charles A. Briggs. *Amended Charges and Specifications as Delivered, November 9, 1892*. New York: Douglas Taylor, 1893.

―――. *Charges and Specifications as Delivered to Dr. Briggs by the Moderator of the Presbytery, October 6, 1891*. New York: Douglas Taylor, 1891.

―――. *Complaint to the Synod of New York from the Presbytery of New York, From Its Decision of the Question of the Original Party, November 4, 1891*. New York: John C. Rankin, Co., 1891.

―――. *Proceedings of the General Assembly of 1893 against Charles Augustus Briggs, 105th Annual Meeting*. Washington, D.C.: Presbyterian Board of Publications, 1893.

―――. *The Report of the Committee of Prosecution with the Charges and Specifications Submitted to the New York Presbytery, October 5, 1891*. New York: John C. Rankin, Co., 1891.

―――. *Response to the Charges and Specifications Submitted to the Presbytery of New York by Professor Charles A. Briggs, November 4, 1891*. New York: Briggs, 1891.

Ranke, Leopold von. *The Theory and Practice of History*. Indianapolis: Bobbs-Merrill, 1971.

Sabatier, Paul. *Modernism*. New York: Charles Scribner's Sons, 1908.

Schaff, Philip. *Creed Revision in the Presbyterian Churches.* New York: Charles Scribner's Sons, 1890.

———. *The Principle of Protestantism as Related to the Present State of the Church.* Chambersburg, Pa.: Publication Office of the German Reformed Church, 1845.

Shedd, William G. T. *The Proposed Revision of the Westminster Standards.* New York: Charles Scribner's Sons, 1890.

Shields, Charles W. *The Historic Episcopate.* New York: Charles Scribner's Sons, 1894.

Smith, Elizabeth L., ed. *Henry Boynton Smith, His Life and Work.* New York: A. C. Armstrong & Son, 1881.

Smith, Henry Boynton. *Faith and Philosophy, Discourses and Essays.* New York: Scribner, Armstrong & Co., 1877.

Smith, Henry Boynton, and Roswell Hitchcock. *The Life, Writings and Character of Edward Robinson.* New York: Anson D. F. Randolph, 1863.

Smith, William Robertson. "Animal Tribes in the Old Testament." *Journal of Philology* 19 (1881): 75–100.

———. "Christianity and the Supernatural." In *Lectures and Essays of William Robertson Smith*, edited by John Sutherland Black and George Chrystal. London: A. & C. Black, 1912.

———. "Hebrew Language and Literature." *Encyclopaedia Britannica*, 9th ed. (1875–1888). II:594–602.

———. "The Question of Prophecy in the Critical Schools of the Continent." In *Lectures and Essays of William Robertson Smith*. 163–343.

Smyth, Newman. *Passing Protestantism and Coming Catholicism.* New York: Charles Scribner's Sons, 1908.

Special Report of the College Committee on Professor Smith's Article "Bible." Edinburgh: E. Maclaren & Macnivan, 1877.

Sprague, William B. *A Discourse Commemorative of the Late Rev. John M. Krebs.* Albany, N.Y.: Van Benthuysen & Sons, 1867.

Tucker, William Jewett. *My Generation: An Autobiographical Interpretation.* Boston: Houghton, Mifflin & Co., 1919.

Manuscript Collections

Briggs, Charles Augustus. Collection. Burke Library, Union Theological Seminary, New York.

Briggs, Emilie Grace. Collection. Burke Library, Union Theological Seminary, New York.

Brown, John C. Letters. Burke Library, Union Theological Seminary, New York.

Hastings, Thomas S. Collection: *Confessional Revision, Being a Collection of 395 Articles Appearing in the Religious Press Prepared for the Committee of Revision, General Assembly, 1890.* Burke Library, Union Theological Seminary, New York.

Hodge, Archibald A. Papers. Hodge Family Papers. Firestone Library, Princeton University, Princeton, New Jersey.

Potter, Henry Codman. Papers. Archive of the Episcopal Diocese of New York, General Theological Seminary, New York.

Smyth, Newman. Papers. Sterling Library, Yale University, New Haven, Connecticut.

Union Theological Seminary Board of Directors. Minutes, 1884–1904. Burke Library, Union Theological Seminary, New York.

Secondary Works

Ahlstrom, Sydney. *A Religious History of the American People.* 4th ed. New Haven: Yale University Press, 1970.

————. "The Scottish Philosophy and American Theology." *Church History* 24 (1955): 257–272.

Atkins, Gaius Glenn. *Religion in Our Times.* New York: Round Table Press, 1932.

Bailey, Warner. "William Robertson Smith and American Biblical Studies." *Journal of Presbyterian History* 51 (1973): 285–303.

Balmer, Randall. "The Princetonians and Scripture: A Reconsideration." *Westminster Theological Review* 44 (1982): 352–365.

Barman, Lawrence F. *Baron Friedrich von Huegel and the Modernist Crisis in England.* Cambridge: The University Press, 1972.

Barringer, Paul, and James Garnett. *The University of Virginia.* New York: Lewis Publishing Co., 1904.

Barth, Karl. *Protestant Theology in the Nineteenth Century.* 3d ed. London: SCM Press, 1972.

Beard, Charles A., and Alfred Vagts. "Currents of Thought in Historiography." *American Historical Review* 42 (April 1937): 460–483.

Beardslee, William A. *Literary Criticism of the New Testament.* Philadelphia: Fortress Press, 1970.

Becker, Carl. *The Heavenly City of the Eighteenth-Century Philosophers.* Cambridge: Harvard University Press, 1932.

Bedoyere, Michael de la. *Life of Baron von Huegel.* London: J. M. Dent & Sons, Ltd., 1951.

Beidleman, T. O. *William Robertson Smith and the Sociological Study of Religion.* Chicago: University of Chicago Press, 1974.

Booth, Robert P. *History of the Rutgers Riverside Church.* New York: Styles & Cash, 1898.

Bowden, Henry Warner. *Church History in the Age of Science.* Chapel Hill, N.C.: University of North Carolina Press, 1971.

Bozeman, Theodore Dwight. *Protestants in an Age of Science.* Chapel Hill, N.C.: University of North Carolina Press, 1977.

Brown, Ira V. "The Higher Criticism Comes to America, 1880–1900." *Journal of the Presbyterian Historical Society* 38 (1960): 193–212.

Brown, Jerry Wayne. *The Rise of Biblical Criticism in America, 1800–1870.* Middletown, Conn.: Wesleyan University Press, 1969.

Brown, William Adams. *A Teacher and His Times.* New York: Scribner's Sons, 1940.

———. *Toward a United Church.* New York: Charles Scribner's Sons, 1946.

Bruce, Philip A. *A History of the University of Virginia, 1819–1919.* New York: Macmillan, 1920.

Carpenter, J. Estlin. *The Bible in the Nineteenth Century.* London: Longmans, Green & Co., 1903.

Carter, Paul. *The Spiritual Crisis of the Gilded Age.* DeKalb, Ill.: Northern Illinois University Press, 1971.

Carwardine, Richard. *Trans-Atlantic Revivalism: Popular Evangelicalism in Britain and America, 1790–1865.* Westport, Conn.: Greenwood Press, 1975.

Cassirer, Ernst. *The Problem of Knowledge.* New Haven: Yale University Press, 1950.

Cavert, Samuel M. *The American Churches in the Ecumenical Movement, 1900–1968.* New York: Association Press, 1968.

———. *Church Cooperation and Unity in America, An Historical Review, 1900–1970.* New York: Association Press, 1970.

Chadwick, Owen. *The Victorian Church.* 2 vols. New York: Oxford University Press, 1966.

Cheyne, T. K. *The Founders of Old Testament Criticism.* New York: Charles Scribner's Sons, 1893.

Coffin, Henry Sloane. *A Half Century at Union Theological Seminary, 1896–1945.* New York: Charles Scribner's Sons, 1954.

Collingwood, R. G. *The Idea of History.* Oxford: The University Press, 1946.

Daly, Gabriel. *Transcendence and Immanence: A Study in Catholic Modernism and Integralism.* Oxford: Oxford University Press, 1980.

Feeney, John J. "Charles A. Briggs and the Organic Reunion of Christendom." *Historical Magazine of the Protestant Episcopal Church* 47 (1978): 93–112.

Findlay, James. *Dwight L. Moody, American Evangelist, 1837–1899.* Chicago: University of Chicago Press, 1969.

Foster, Charles I. *An Errand of Mercy: The Evangelical United Front, 1790–1837.* Chapel Hill, N.C.: University of North Carolina Press, 1960.

Foster, Frank Hugh. *The Modern Movement in Theology.* New York: Fleming H. Revell Co., 1939.

Gerstner, John H. "Warfield's Case for Biblical Inerrancy." In *God's Inerrant Word*, edited by John W. Montgomery. Minneapolis: Bethany Fellowship, 1974.

Glover, Willis B. *Evangelical Nonconformists and Higher Criticism in the Nineteenth Century.* London: Independent Press, Ltd., 1954.

Gottschalk, Louis. "The Historian and the Historical Document." *Social Science Research Bulletin* 53 (1945): 23–37.

Gowing, Peter D. "Newman Smyth: New England Ecumenist." Ph.D. Thesis, Boston University, 1960.

Greene, John C. *The Death of Adam.* Ames, Ia.: Iowa State University Press, 1959.

Handy, Robert. *A Christian America, Protestant Hopes and Historical Realities.* 3d ed. Oxford: Oxford University Press, 1974.

———. "Fundamentalism and Modernism in Perspective." *Religion in Life* 24 (1955): 381–394

———. *A History of Union Theological Seminary in New York.* New York: Columbia University Press, 1987.

Hatch, Carl. *The Charles A. Briggs Heresy Trial.* New York: Exposition Press, 1969.

Herbst, Jurgen. *The German Historical School in American Scholarship.* Ithaca, N.Y.: Cornell University Press, 1965.

Hinchcliff, P. B. *The Anglican Church in South Africa.* London: S.P.C.K. for the Church Historical Society, 1968.

———. *John W. Colenso, Bishop of Natal.* London: Nelson, 1964.

Hofstadter, Richard. *Anti-Intellectualism in American Life.* New York: Random House, 1963.

Hopkins, C. Howard. *The Rise of the Social Gospel in American Protestantism, 1865–1915.* New Haven: Yale University Press, 1940.

Howe, Daniel. *The Unitarian Conscience: Harvard Moral Philosophers, 1805–1861.* Cambridge: Harvard University Press, 1970.

Hudson, Winthrop. "How American Is Religion in America?" In *The Reinterpretation of American Church History*, edited by Jerald Brauer. Chicago: University of Chicago Press, 1968.

———. *Religion in America.* 3d ed. New York: Charles Scribner's Sons, 1981.

Hutchison, William R. *The Modernist Impulse in American Protestantism.* Cambridge: Harvard University Press, 1976.

Iggers, Georg G. *The German Conception of History.* Middletown, Conn.: Wesleyan University Press, 1968.

―――. "Historicism." *Dictionary of the History of Ideas.* II:457–458.

―――. "The Idea of Progress: A Critical Reassessment." *American Historical Review* 71 (October 1965): 1–17.

Jeschke, Channing. "The Briggs Case: The Focus of a Study in Nineteenth-Century Presbyterian History." Ph.D. Thesis, University of Chicago, 1966.

Jeter, Joseph R. "The Christian Unity Foundation." *Historical Magazine of the Protestant Episcopal Church* 44 (1975): 451–461.

Kean, Charles D. *The Road to Reunion.* Greenwich, Conn.: Seabury Press, 1958.

Kelly, James J. *Baron Friedrich von Huegel's Philosophy of Religion.* Leuven: The University Press, 1983.

Latourette, Kenneth Scott. "The Ecumenical Bearings of the Missionary Movement and the International Missionary Council." In *History of the Ecumenical Movement, 1517–1948,* edited by Ruth Rouse and Stephen Neill. Philadelphia: Westminster Press, 1967.

Lears, T. J. Jackson. *No Place of Grace: Antimodernism and the Transformation of American Culture, 1880–1920.* New York: Pantheon Books, 1981.

Lee, Dwight E., and Robert N. Beck. "The Meaning of Historicism." *American Historical Review* 59 (1954): 568–577.

Loetscher, Lefferts A. *The Broadening Church: A Study of Theological Issues in the Presbyterian Church since 1869.* Philadelphia: University of Pennsylvania, 1954.

MacFarland, Charles S. *Christian Unity in the Making.* New York: Federal Council of the Churches of Christ in America, 1948.

―――. *The Progress of Church Federation.* New York: Fleming H. Revell, 1917.

McGiffert, Arthur Cushman. "Charles Augustus Briggs." *Dictionary of American Biography.* II:40–41.

Mackintosh, H. R. *Types of Modern Theology: Schleiermacher to Barth.* London: Nisbet, 1937.

McKnight, Edgar V. *What Is Form Criticism?* Philadelphia: Fortress Press, 1969.

McLoughlin, William G. *Modern Revivalism, Charles Grandison Finney to Billy Graham.* New York: Ronald Press, 1959.

―――. *Revivals, Awakenings and Reform.* Chicago: University of Chicago Press, 1978.

Mandelbaum, Maurice. *History, Man and Reason: A Study of Nineteenth-Century Thought.* Baltimore: Johns Hopkins University Press, 1971.

Manross, William W. *A History of the American Episcopal Church.* 3d ed. New York: Morehouse-Gorham, 1959.

Manuel, Frank E. *Shapes of Philosophical History.* 2d ed. Stanford, Calif.: Stanford University Press, 1971.

Marsden, George M. *The Evangelical Mind and the New School Presbyterian Experience.* New Haven: Yale University Press, 1970.

———. *Fundamentalism and American Culture.* New York: Oxford University Press, 1980.

Marty, Martin. *The Modern Schism, Three Paths to the Secular.* London: SCM Press, 1969.

May, Henry F. *The Enlightenment in America.* 3d ed. New York: Oxford University Press, 1976.

———. *The Protestant Churches and Industrial America.* New York: Harper & Brothers, Publishers, 1949.

Mead, Sydney E. *The Lively Experiment: The Shaping of Christianity in America.* 2d ed. New York: Harper & Row, 1976.

Meinecke, Friedrich. *Die Enstehung des Historismus.* Zwei Bande. Munich: R. Oldenbourg, 1936.

Meyer, Donald H. "American Intellectuals and the Victorian Crisis of Faith." *American Quarterly* 27 (1975): 585–602.

Meyerhoff, Hans. *The Philosophy of History in Our Times.* Garden City, N.Y.: Doubleday & Co., 1959.

Miller, Perry. *The Life of the Mind in America.* 2d ed. New York: Harcourt, Brace & World, 1965.

Moore, James R. *The Post-Darwinian Controversies.* Cambridge: Cambridge University Press, 1979.

Nichols, James Hastings. *Romanticism in American Theology: Nevin and Schaff at Mercersburg.* Chicago: University of Chicago Press, 1961.

Niebuhr, H. Richard. *The Kingdom of God in America.* Reprint. Hamden, Conn.: Shoe String Press, 1956.

Noll, Mark A. "The Princeton Theology." In *Reformed Theology in America: A History of Its Modern Development,* edited by David F. Wells. Grand Rapids, Mich.: William B. Eerdmans Publishing Co., 1985.

Noll, Mark A., ed. *The Princeton Theology, 1812–1921.* Philadelphia: Fortress Press, 1985.

Pfleiderer, Otto. *The Development of Theology in Germany since Kant.* London: Sonnenschein & Co., 1893.

Prentiss, George L. *The Union Theological Seminary: The First Fifty Years.* New York: Anson D. F. Randolph, 1889.

———. *The Union Theological Seminary in the City of New York: Its Design and Another Decade of Its History.* Asbury Park, N.J.: M., W. & C. Pennypacker, 1899.

Ratte, John. *Three Modernists: Loisy, Tyrrell and Sullivan.* Cambridge: Harvard University Press, 1968.

Reardon, Bernard. *Roman Catholic Modernism.* London: A. & C. Black, 1970.

Rogers, Jack B. *Scripture in the Westminster Confession: A Problem of Historical Interpretation for American Presbyterianism.* Grand Rapids, Mich.: William B. Eerdmans Publishing Co., 1967.

Rogers, Max. "Charles A. Briggs: Conservative Heretic." Ph.D. Thesis, Columbia University, 1964.

Sandeen, Ernest. "The Distinctiveness of American Denominationalism: A Case Study of the 1846 Evangelical Alliance." *Church History* 45 (1976): 222–234.

———. "The Princeton Theology." *Church History* 31 (1962): 307–321.

———. "Towards an Historical Interpretation of the Origins of Fundamentalism." *Church History* 36 (1967): 66–83.

Schlesinger, Arthur M., Sr. "A Critical Period in American Religion, 1875–1900." *Massachusetts Historical Society Proceedings* 64 (1930–32): 523–536.

Shriver, George. *American Religious Heretics.* Nashville, Tenn.: Abingdon Press, 1966.

———. *Philip Schaff, Christian Scholar and Ecumenical Prophet.* Macon, Ga.: Mercer University Press, 1987.

Smith, Henry Preserved. "Charles Augustus Briggs." *American Journal of Theology* 17 (1913): 497–508.

Smith, Timothy. *Revivalism and Social Reform in Mid-Nineteenth-Century America.* 2d ed. Baltimore: Johns Hopkins University Press, 1980.

Stoever, William K. "Henry Boynton Smith and the German Theology of History." *Union Seminary Quarterly Review* 24 (1968): 67–89.

Teeple, Howard M. *The Historical Approach to the Bible.* Evanston, Ill.: Religion and Ethics Institute, Inc., 1982.

Thompson, Ernest Trice. *A History of the Presbyterian Churches in the United States.* New York: Christian Literature Publishing Co., 1895.

Thompson, Robert E. *A History of the Presbyterian Churches in the United States.* New York, n.p., 1895.

Trinterud, Leonard J. *The Forming of an American Tradition: A Reexamination of Colonial Presbyterianism.* Philadelphia: Westminster Press, 1949.

Tuveson, Ernest Lee. *Redeemer Nation: The Idea of America's Millennial Role.* Chicago: University of Chicago Press, 1968.

Vanderpool, Harold Y. "The Andover Conservatives: Apologetics, Biblical Criticism and Theological Change at Andover Theological Seminary, 1808–1880." Ph.D. Thesis, Harvard University, 1971.

Vidler, Alec R. *The Church in an Age of Revolution.* 12th ed. New York: Penguin Books, 1981.

——. *The Modernist Movement in the Roman Church. Its Origins and Outcome.* Cambridge: The University Press, 1934.

Wacker, Grant. "Augustus H. Strong: A Conservative Confrontation with History." Ph.D. Thesis, Harvard University, 1978.

——. *Augustus H. Strong and the Dilemma of Historical Consciousness.* Macon, Ga.: Mercer University Press, 1985.

——. "The Demise of Biblical Civilization." In *The Bible in America, Essays in Cultural History*, edited by Nathan Hatch and Mark Noll. New York: Oxford University Press, 1982.

Welch, Claude. *God and Incarnation in Mid-Nineteenth-Century Theology.* New York: Oxford University Press, 1965.

——. *Protestant Thought in the Nineteenth Century.* New Haven: Yale University Press, 1972.

Williams, Daniel Day. *The Andover Liberals: A Study in American Theology.* New York: King's Crown Press, 1941.

Wilson, Major L. "Paradox Lost: Order and Progress in the Evangelical Thought of Mid-Nineteenth-Century America." *Church History* 44 (1975): 352–366.

Woolverton, John F. "Huntington's Quadrilateral — A Critical Study." *Church History* 39 (1970): 198–211.

——. "William Reed Huntington and Church Unity: The Historical and Theological Background of the Chicago-Lambeth Quadrilateral." Ph.D. Thesis, Columbia University, 1963.

Wright, George Ernest. "The Study of the Old Testament." In *Protestant Thought in America*, edited by Arnold Nash. New York: Macmillan, 1951.

Index